The gardener plucks fruits and flowers, but does not harm the trees; the bee sucks the honey but does not damage the flowers. In the same way the king should collect his taxes but should not cause any suffering to his subjects. One who kills the goat at best gets one meal; one who feeds it well can get milk for several years—**Kautilya in *Arthashastra***

Just as the sun extracts water from the reservoirs and gives it back in the form of showers, so does the ruler extract tax from his subjects and gives it back to them in the form of prosperity—**Kalidasa in *Raghuvansa***

Goods and Services Tax (GST) in India

Background, Present Structure and Future Challenges

(As applicable from July 1, 2017)

By

M.M. Sury

New Century Publications
New Delhi, India

New Century Publications
4800/24, Bharat Ram Road,
Ansari Road, Daryaganj,
New Delhi – 110 002 (India)
Tel.: 011-2324 7798, 4358 7398, 4101 7798
E-mail: indiatax@vsnl.com • info@newcenturypublications.com
www.newcenturypublications.com

Editorial office:
LG–7, Aakarshan Bhawan
4754-57/23, Ansari Road, Daryaganj,
New Delhi – 110 002

Tel.: 011-4356 0919

First Published: **2024**

ISBN: **978-81-7708-457-3**

Published by New Century Publications and printed at Milan Enterprises, New Delhi

Designs: Patch Creative Unit, New Delhi

PRINTED IN INDIA

About the Book

The recently introduced Goods and Services Tax (GST) is undoubtedly the biggest tax reform in the fiscal history of India. After missing several deadlines and overcoming almost a decade of political differences—on how to replace a multi-layered set of Central and State taxes and levies with a uniform nationwide tax—GST finally saw the light of day on July 1, 2017.

Implementation of GST leaves behind an inefficient, complicated and fragmented indirect tax system. GST has subsumed a profusion of Central and State indirect taxes to create a single unified market. It is slated to make India a seamless national market, boosting trade and industry and, in turn, growth rate.

GST is expected to represent a leap forward in creating a much cleaner dual VAT. Common base and common rates—across goods and services and across States and between Centre and States—will facilitate administration and improve compliance while also rendering manageable the collection of taxes on inter-State sales.

By amalgamating a large number of Central and State taxes into a single tax and allowing set-off of prior-stage taxes, it would mitigate the ill effects of *cascading* or *pyramiding* and pave the way for a common national market. Introduction of GST would also make India's products competitive in the domestic and international markets. It will help improve governance, strengthen tax institutions, facilitate *Make-in-India by Making-One-India*, and impart buoyancy to the tax base. GST is not merely a tax reform. It is also a reform that will revolutionize the way business is conducted in India.

Signifying the spirit of co-operative federalism, GST is a historic and game-changing tax reform. It is 21st century's global standard for VAT in large federal systems.

Switching over to GST is fraught with many problems—administrative and technical. However, such problems are endemic to any change of revolutionary proportions. The euphoria created by GST is understandable. It is a new tax shrouded in mystery. Stakeholders—State Governments, tax officials, manufacturers, traders, third parties and consumers—are apprehensive, anxious and uncertain about its implications. GST is like an elephant amidst blind men, each holding a part of it and wondering what it is!

It is human nature to resist change because change involves problems, readjustments and additional efforts. Every horse resists the placing of a saddle on its back, but once it is there it prepares itself to run for the rider. Status quo is always cosy but it has deleterious effects in the long-run, particularly in the context of societies.

This book explains and examines various aspects of GST, in simple, lucid and non-technical language, for the benefit of a cross-section of readers including teachers and students of economics, commerce, law, public administration, business management, and chartered accountancy. It will also serve the needs of legislators, business executives, entrepreneurs and investors, and others interested in understanding the basics of GST.

The book is organized into two Parts.

Part I, consisting of five chapters, provides conceptual clarities as regards taxation of goods and services and describes pre-GST indirect tax system of India.

Chapter 1 is focused on the conceptual framework. Chapter 2 explains the erstwhile system of Union excise duties/CENVAT levied by the Central Government. Chapter 3 is devoted to the taxation of services by the Central Government during pre-GST period. Likewise, chapter 4 describes the now-abolished sales tax/VAT system of State Governments. Chapter 5 recalls the problems created by multiple taxation of goods by the Centre and the States.

Part II, comprising thirteen chapters, records the circumstances leading to the introduction of GST, its present structure and future challenges.

Chapter 6 explains the current constitutional provisions pertaining to taxes in India. Chapter 7 traces the various stages of evolution of GST before being finally rolled out on July 1, 2017. Chapter 8 is devoted to GST Council, its various meetings, discussions and decisions. Chapter 9 explains the meaning, justification and components of GST. Chapter 10 sets forth the salient features of GST. Chapter 11 explains the working mechanism of GST with suitable numerical examples. Chapter 12 explains the exemptions, thresholds and rate structure under GST.

Chapter 13 deals with the administrative aspects of GST. Chapter 14 focuses on the technological infrastructure and institutional arrangements for the successful implementation of GST. Chapter 15 examines the implications of GST for various sectors of the Indian economy. Chapter 16 views GST from the angle of India's federal polity. Chapter 17 delves into future challenges facing GST. Chapter 18 gives a brief account of GST in select countries of the world.

There are also 4 appendices to the book. Appendix 1 reproduces Constitution (One Hundred and First Amendment) Act, 2016. Appendix 2 lists main provisions of the Model GST Law (MGL) prepared by the GST Council and released in November 2016. Appendix 3 contains GST rates for services. Appendix 4 gives a brief description of services exempted from GST.

Select bibliography, subject index and name index also form part of the book.

Author's Profile

M.M. Sury received his B.A. (Hons.), M.A., and Ph.D. degrees in economics from the University of Delhi. He taught economics in the same University for 42 years. Specialising in fiscal economics, he has published extensively on the Indian fiscal system in recognised national and international journals, including *Small Industry Bulletin for Asia and the Pacific* (United Nations, Bangkok), *Bulletin for International Fiscal Documentation* (International Fiscal Association, Amsterdam), *Asian-Pacific Tax and Investment Bulletin* (Singapore), *Journal of the Indian School of Political Economy* (Pune), *Indian Economic Journal* (Bombay), and *Margin* (New Delhi). He was a Visiting Fellow at the International Bureau of Fiscal Documentation, Amsterdam (May 1989), a Fellow at the Indian Institute of Advanced Study, Shimla (1991-92) and a Visiting Fellow in the Department of Law and Management, University of Mauritius, Mauritius (September-October, 2000). He was Economic Adviser, First Delhi State Finance Commission (1996-97).

Contents

Preface

Taxes are as old as civilizations. Taxes are imposed so that a government may perform its traditional functions (defence, and maintenance of law and order), undertake welfare and developmental activities, and make provision for public goods to satisfy collective needs of the people. It has also to pay for its own administration. It needs financial resources for these purposes and taxation is one method of transferring money from private to public hands. Taxation is necessary because what the government gives it must first take away.

The Indian tax system has undergone major structural changes since Independence in 1947. It has become comprehensive and complicated over the years. It has successfully mobilised resources to finance developmental, welfare and administrative activities of public authorities. Besides being the main source of revenue, both for the Central and State Governments, it is an effective instrument to realise various socio-economic objectives of national policies.

Restructuring of the tax system constituted a major component of economic reforms initiated in early 1990s. The main focus of the tax reforms was on simplification and rationalisation of both direct and indirect taxes with the objective of augmenting revenues and removing anomalies in the tax structure.

The post-1991 period has witnessed a sharp decline in the rates of income tax, excise duties (now subsumed under GST) and customs tariff. The theory that high rates of duty lead to higher revenue collection has been discarded in favour of lower rates with fewer exemptions and concessions. Tax reforms in recent years have brought the Indian tax system much closer to international tax practices. GST is the latest addition in the fiscal armoury of Central and State Governments.

After an arduous journey of 12 years—beginning with the mention of Goods and Services Tax (GST) by the then Finance Minister Shri P. Chidambaram in his Budget Speech for 2005-06 on February 28, 2005—GST finally became operative on July 1, 2017. The historic tax reform saw various ups and downs during this period.

The basic objective of tax reforms in any country should be to establish a tax system that is economically efficient, distributionally acceptable, and simple to administer. GST is India's most ambitious and remarkable indirect tax reform. Its objective is to levy a single uniform tax across India on all goods and services. Implementing a new tax, encompassing both goods and services, by the Centre and the States in a large and complex federal system, is perhaps unprecedented in modern global tax history.

Signifying the spirit of co-operative federalism, GST is a historic and game-changing tax reform. Domestically, it will help improve governance, strengthen tax institutions, facilitate *Make-in-India by making-one-India*, and impart buoyancy to the tax base. The Indian GST is 21st century's global standard for VAT in large federal systems.

As the world economy slows, and increasing financial volatility and turbulence become the *newest normal*, only a few economies have the resilience to be a refuge of stability and the potential to be an outpost of opportunity. India is one of those few. As oil and commodity prices continue to be soft, macroeconomic stability seems reasonably assured for India. This bedrock of stability coupled with reforms can propel the economy to a high growth trajectory. Key amongst these reforms is the national level GST.

Prior to the introduction of GST, the indirect tax system of India suffered from various disabilities. There was a burden of *tax-on-tax* in the pre-GST system of Central excise duty and the sales tax system of the States. The introduction of Central VAT (CENVAT) did remove the cascading burden of taxes to a good extent by providing a mechanism of set-offs for tax paid on inputs and services up to the stage of production, and was an improvement over the pre-CENVAT Central excise duty. Similarly, the introduction of VAT by the States removed the cascading effect by giving set-off for tax paid on inputs as well as tax paid on previous purchases and again was an improvement over the previous sales tax regime.

However, both the CENVAT and the State VAT had certain deficiencies. CENVAT was deficient because it did not extend to include chain of value additions in the distributive trade below the stage of production. Further, it did not include several Central taxes (such as additional excise duties, additional customs duties, surcharges etc.) in its overall framework. Hence, the benefits of a comprehensive input tax set-offs was not available to manufacturers/dealers under CENVAT.

Likewise, in the State-level VAT scheme, CENVAT load on the goods was not removed and the cascading effect of that part of tax burden had remained unrelieved. Moreover, there were several taxes in the States (such as luxury tax, entertainment tax, etc.) which had not been subsumed under the VAT. In addition, although the burden of Central sales tax (CST) on inter-State movement of goods had been lessened with reduction of CST rate from 4 percent to 2 percent, this burden had also not been fully phased out.

Implementation of GST leaves behind an inefficient, complicated and fragmented indirect tax system. Switch over to GST is fraught with many problems—administrative and technical. However, such problems are endemic of any change of revolutionary proportions. Many of the problems will be transitory in nature. No one should expect a foolproof GST from day one. GST Council has successfully sorted out political, administrative and implementation differences among the stakeholders and it is competent enough to grapple with any future challenges and rectifications.

GST requires a very high level of compliance. The age of hand-written ledgers, account books, balance sheets and manual record-keeping is gone. Everything will now be online and need to be updated regularly.

Since major Central and State indirect taxes have got subsumed under GST, the multiplicity of taxes has been substantially reduced which, in turn, would decrease the operating costs of the country's tax system. With GST in place, the burden of Central sales tax (CST) has also been removed. The uniformity in tax rates and procedures across the country will go a long way in reducing compliance costs.

The introduction of GST has marked a clear departure from the scheme of distribution of fiscal powers envisaged in the Constitution. The dual GST imposes tax on the same taxable event—supply of goods and services—simultaneously by both the Centre and the States. Both the Centre and the States are empowered to levy GST across the value chain from the stage of manufacture to consumption. The credit of GST paid on inputs at every stage of value addition is available for the discharge of GST liability on the output, thereby ensuring GST is charged only on the component of value addition at each stage. This would ensure that there is no *tax-on-tax* in the country.

The Government of Prime Minister Shri Narendra Modi has placed a great deal of emphasis on controlling black money. This has been reflected in a series of measures taken recently. These measures can be significantly complemented by GST which can be less intrusive, more self-policing, and hence more effective way of reducing corruption and rent-seeking. The complementary role of GST in curbing black money has, at least, two aspects. The first relates to the self-policing incentive inherent in GST. To claim input tax credit, each dealer has an incentive to request documentation from the dealer behind him in the value-added/tax chain. Provided the chain is not broken through wide ranging exemptions, especially on intermediate goods, this self-policing feature of GST can work very powerfully. Second, the GST will in effect have a dual monitoring structure—one by the States and one by the Centre. Hence, there will be a greater probability that evasion will be detected. Even if one tax authority overlooks and/or fails to detect evasion, there is the possibility that the other overseeing authority may not.

GST has been an initiative that has commanded broad consensus across the political spectrum. It has also been a model of co-operative federalism in practice with the Centre and States coming together as partners in embracing growth and employment-enhancing reforms. It was a long-awaited reform and its implementation has validated expectations of important government actions and effective political will to modernize the economy. Given the historic opportunity afforded by the GST, the aim should be to clean up the Indian tax system that has effectively become an *exemptions raj* with serious consequences for revenues and governance.

In short, GST is a comprehensive indirect tax levy on manufacture, sale and consumption of goods as well as services at the national level. GST is an indirect tax for the whole of India to make it one unified common market. GST is designed to give India a world class tax system and improve tax collections. It would end the long-standing distortions of differential treatment of manufacturing sector and services sector. GST will facilitate seamless credit across the entire supply chain and across all States under a common tax base.

New Delhi **M.M. Sury**
2017

Explanation of Select GST-related Terms

***Ad valorem* duty:** An *ad valorem* (according to value) duty is imposed as a fixed percentage of the price of the product taxed. This form of duty is preferred when a commodity has many classifications and sub-classifications, e.g. textiles.

Anti-profiteering provision: As per Section 171 of the CGST Act, 2017 any reduction in rate of tax on any supply of goods or services or the benefit of input tax credit shall be passed on to the recipient by way of *commensurate* reduction in prices.

Compliance costs: Compliance costs refer to costs incurred by taxpayers and/or third parties in complying with a tax, over and above the tax payment made to public authorities. The third party compliance costs are those incurred by firms in discharging their legal responsibility as tax deductors and tax collectors.

Composition scheme: Composition scheme is an important feature of GST to protect the interests of small traders and small-scale industries. A composition option (i.e. to pay tax at a flat rate without credits) is available to small taxpayers below a certain threshold. It is a kind of presumptive tax. The objective of composition scheme is to bring simplicity and to reduce the compliance cost for the small taxpayers. Moreover, it is optional and the eligible person opting to pay tax under this scheme can pay tax at a prescribed percentage of his turnover every quarter, instead of paying tax at normal rate. The scheme is available to small taxpayers whose aggregate turnover in the preceding financial year did not cross ₹ 75 lakh. In the case of certain specified States, the limit of turnover is ₹ 50 lakh.

Co-operative federalism: The essence of a co-operative federalism is that the Centre and the State Governments should be guided by the broader national concerns of using the available resources for the benefit of the people.

Countervailing duties: These are duties in addition to the normal import duties levied on goods imported into a country. The rate of countervailing duty is generally equal to the excise duty imposed on like items produced domestically. The argument is that normal import duty represents the desirable degree of protection to internally produced goods which are not subject to excise duty. When excise duty is levied or the rate of an existing one is increased, a corresponding enhancement in import duty is required to preserve the accepted degree of protection.

Demerit goods: Some luxury items (cars, aerated drinks, cigarettes) are often dubbed as demerit goods.

Destination-based consumption tax: GST is a destination-based consumption tax as against the erstwhile origin-based tax system. This implies that all SGST collected will ordinarily accrue to the State where the consumer of the goods and/or services sold resides. In other words, the tax would accrue to the taxing authority which has jurisdiction over the place of consumption which is also termed as place of supply.

Direct tax: A direct tax is one the ultimate burden of which falls on the person on whom it is levied. In other words, it is a tax that cannot be shifted from the original payer to someone else. It is contrasted with indirect tax which can readily be shifted to ultimate consumers of the commodity or service taxed.

Dual GST model: It means the Centre and the States simultaneously levy GST on a common base. This dual GST model is implemented through multiple statutes (one for CGST and one each SGST statute for every State).

Electronic Commerce: Section 2(41) of the MGL defines electronic commerce to mean the supply of goods and/or services including digital products over digital or electronic network. According to Section 2(42), electronic commerce operator means any person who owns, operates or manages digital or electronic facility or platform for electronic commerce.

Empowered Committee of State Finance Ministers (EC): EC was originally set up to monitor the phasing out of the sales-tax based incentive schemes, to decide milestones and methods of States to switch over to VAT and to monitor reforms in the Central sales tax system existing in the country. On August 12, 2004, the Government of India decided to reconstitute the Empowered Committee with State Finance/Taxation Ministers of all States as its members.

Goods: According to clause 12 of Article 366 of the Constitution, *goods* include all materials, commodities, and articles.

Goods and Services Tax: According to clause 12A of Article 366 of the Constitution, *goods and services tax* means any tax on supply of goods, or services or both except taxes on the supply of the alcoholic liquor for human consumption.

Goods and Services Tax Network (GSTN): GSTN is a common portal for the Centre and States that enables electronic processing of the key business processes of registration, returns, and payments related to GST.

GST Council: GST Council was created under the Constitution. GST Council is a joint forum of the Centre and the States. The recommendations made by the Council act as benchmark or guidance to Union as well as State Governments.

GST threshold limits: Threshold exemption is built into a tax regime to keep small traders out of tax net. Presently, a common threshold exemption applies to both CGST and SGST. Taxpayers with a turnover below it are exempt from GST. Thus, businesses with an annual turnover of less than ₹ 20 lakh are exempted from GST. The threshold is ₹ 10 lakh in the case of businesses in 11 North-Eastern and hill states.

Harmonized System of Nomenclature (HSN): HSN is a multi-purpose international product nomenclature developed by the World Customs Organization (WCO). It comprises about 5,000 commodity groups, each identified by a six digit code, arranged in a legal and logical structure and is supported by well-defined rules to achieve uniform classification.

Indirect tax: An indirect tax is one which can be shifted from the original payer to the ultimate consumer of the commodity or service taxed. Import duties, excise levies, and sales taxes are generally regarded as indirect taxes. Thus, an excise duty on cigarettes, levied on producers, is usually passed on to the consumers in the form of higher prices. GST is an indirect tax.

Job work: Section 2(61) of the MGL provides that *job work* means undertaking any treatment or process by a person on goods belonging to another registered taxable person and the expression *job worker* shall be construed accordingly.

Model GST Law (MGL): MGL provides a common draft of Central GST (CGST) Act and State GST (SGST) Act. MGL also includes the draft of Integrated GST (IGST) Act as well as draft GST Valuation Rules.

Presumptive tax: It relates to the use of appropriate indicators of income, wealth, sales etc. instead of the actual records of these tax bases. The chief advantage of presumptive taxation is its simplicity, both for the tax collectors and the taxpayers. It is, therefore, cost-effective for the administration. The simplicity attribute may also encourage tax compliance.

Services: According to clause 26A of Article 366 of the Constitution, *services* means anything other than goods.

Special economic zones (SEZs): SEZs are geographical regions in a country subject to economic laws which are liberal than typical economic laws of that country. The word *special* mainly means special economic system and policies. A SEZ can be deemed as a *foreign territory* for the purposes of trade operations, duties and tariffs. Units in SEZs enjoy lot of fiscal pampering. SEZs are self-contained islands providing high-quality infrastructural facilities. SEZs offer industrial, residential and commercial areas with developed plots/pre-built factories, power, telecommunications, water supply, sewerage and drainage, and educational and medical facilities.

Specific duty: A specific or volumetric duty represents a fixed amount of tax on a unit of the physical quantity of the product. Specific duty is generally preferred for commodities the classifications and sub-classifications of which are not numerous, i.e. the commodity is a standardised one, e.g. sugar.

Specific-cum-*ad valorem duty*: Sometimes, both specific and *ad valorem* duties are levied on a single item. This pattern is called specific-cum-*ad valorem* duty or compound duty. Thus, GST rate on cigarettes is 28 percent plus 5 percent compensation cess plus 79 paise per stick (or ₹ 792 per thousand sticks).

State: According to clause 26B of Article 366 of the Constitution, *State* with reference to Articles 246A, 268, 269, 269A and Article 279A includes a Union Territory with legislature.

Valuation of Supply: The value of taxable supply of goods and services shall ordinarily be *the transaction value* which is actually the price paid or payable, when the parties are not related and price is the sole consideration. It includes any amount which the supplier is liable to pay but which has been incurred by the recipient of the supply.

VAT: VAT is a multi-point tax with set off for tax paid on purchases. It is collected in instalments at each transaction in the production-distribution system. It does not have cascading effect due to the system of deduction or credit mechanism.

Zero-rated goods/services: It means rate of GST on certain goods/services is nil. They can also be called exempted goods/services.

Abbreviations/Acronyms Related to GST

APY	Atal Pension Yojana
B2B	Business-to-business
B2C	Business-to-consumer
CBEC	Central Board of Excise and Customs
CCI	Competition Commission of India
CCPC	Central Consumer Protection Council
CEIB	Central Economic Intelligence Bureau
CENVAT	Central Value Added Tax
CGST	Central Goods and Services Tax
CST	Central Sales Tax
CVD	Countervailing Duty
DTA	Domestic Tariff Area
EC	Empowered Committee
EIC	Economic Intelligence Council
FDI	Foreign Direct Investment
FDP	First Discussion Paper
FIU	Financial Intelligence Unit
FRBM Act	Fiscal Responsibility and Budget Management Act
GST	Goods and Services Tax
GST Council	Goods and Services Tax Council
GSTN	Goods and Services Tax Network
HSN	Harmonised System Nomenclature
IGST	Integrated Goods and Services Tax
IP	Intellectual Property
IRDA	Insurance Regulatory and Development Authority
ITC	Input Tax Credit
MGL	Model GST Law
MIS	Management Information System
MODVAT	Modified Value Added Tax
MOT	Merchant Overtime Charges
MSP	Managed Service Provider
NACEN	National Academy of Customs, Excise and Narcotics
NCAER	National Council of Applied Economic Research
NEFT	National Electronic Funds Transfer
NSDL	National Securities Depository Limited
NSTEDB	National Science and Technology Entrepreneurship Development Board
PMAY	*Pradhan Mantri Awas Yojana*
RBI	Reserve Bank of India
RTGS	Real Time Gross Settlement
SAD	Special Additional Duty

SDI	Skill Development Initiative
SEBI	Securities and Exchange Board of India
SEZs	Special Economic Zones
SFIO	Serious Frauds Investigation Office
SGST	State Goods and Services Tax
TCS	Tax Collection at Source
TDS	Tax Deduction at Source
UT-GST	Union Territory Goods and Services Tax
VAS	Value Added Services
VAT	Value Added Tax
VGF	viability gap funding
WCO	World Customs Organization
WTO	World Trade Organization

Unit and Currency Conversion Table

Unit Conversion

1 lakh	= 0.1 million
10 lakh	= 1.0 million
1 crore	= 10.0 million
100 crore	= 1.0 billion

Currency Conversion

The unit of currency in India is Indian Rupee, symbolized as ₹. As per reference rate of Reserve Bank of India (RBI) for **July 27, 2017**:

US$ 1	= 64.12
UK£ 1	= 84.21
Euro (€) 1	= 75.20
Japanese Yen (¥) 100	= 57.74

Fiscal Year

Fiscal year in India runs from April 1 to March 31 of the following year

Pre- and Post-metric Systems of Currency and Measures in India

Metric system of currency in India was introduced from April l, 1957

In the Pre-metric system, one Rupee was = 16 annas and one anna was = 4 paise

In the Post-metric system,

One Rupee = 100 paise

One mile = 1.6 kilometres

One yard = 0.9144 metre

One acre = 0.4046 hectare

Part I
Taxation of Goods and Services in India Prior to the Introduction of GST

1

Taxation of Goods and Services: Conceptual Framework

Taxes are as old as civilizations. Taxes are imposed so that a government may perform its traditional functions (defence, and maintenance of law and order), undertake welfare and developmental activities, and make provision for public goods to satisfy collective needs of the people. It has also to pay for its own administration. It needs financial resources for these purposes and taxation is one method of transferring money from private to public hands. Taxation is necessary because what the government gives it must first take away.

1.1 Tax Policy and Tax Bases

A tax is a compulsory payment made to general government without any direct *quid pro quo*. General government includes central, state, and local governments. Tax payments are compulsory and the benefits provided by government to taxpayers are neither direct nor proportional to such payments. Every tax is made up of two elements: a base, i.e. the object to be taxed and a rate structure, indicating how the base is to be taxed.

Ultimately, all taxes are imposed by politicians helped by bureaucrats. Tax policy pertains to: (a) level of taxation, i.e. tax-GDP ratio, (b) composition of tax revenue, and (c) use of tax incentives.

Tax policy is an important determinant of the investment climate in a country. Rates of direct taxes determine the incentives to work, save and invest, while the level and structure of indirect taxes influence the aggregate demand and thus the scale of operations on the one hand and relative prices of different goods and services on the other.

The base of a tax is the legal description of the object which is taxed. Tax bases, or what eminent fiscal expert Richard Musgrave calls *tax handles*, are numerous but the common ones are listed in Table 1.1. Broadening the tax base means application of a tax to a larger portion of the object already being taxed. Erosion of the tax base means narrowing of the tax base through special exemptions and concessions. A good tax base is one which can easily be measured and monitored. Thus, a realized capital gain is a good base for taxation as compared to an accrued capital gain.

It is the availability of tax bases that determines the nature of tax system in a country. Furthermore, it is the nature of the tax base that determines the final resting place of the burden of a tax. To quote Richard Musgrave, "Apart from the level and distribution of income, the availability of *tax handles* is related to the economic structure of the country. Thus, the administration of an income tax is much more difficult where employment is in small establishments. Profits taxation is not feasible until accounting practices attain minimal standards, and it is difficult if firms are small and unstable. Product taxes cannot be imposed at the retail level if retail establishments are small and impermanent. Effective land taxation is difficult where food is home-consumed, the agricultural sector is largely non-monetized, and land surveys are inadequate in providing proper valuations. On the other hand, taxation is simplified in a highly open economy where imports and exports pass through major ports and thus can be readily established by tax authorities". [1]

Table 1.1: Common Bases for Taxation

Tax/Duty	Base
Excise duty	Value (in case of ad valorem duty) and quantity (in case of specific duty).
Sales tax	Sales of business.
Customs duty	Crossing of goods over national frontiers.
Inter-state sales tax	Crossing of goods over boundaries of states within a country.
Octroi/terminal taxes	Crossing of goods over boundaries of local areas within a state.
Income tax	Income earned by an assessee during an accounting year.
Gift tax	Value of gifts made by an assessee during an accounting year.

A closed economy will have no customs revenue and an agricultural economy with small business establishments cannot operate corporation tax. The relative importance of various tax bases differs in different countries and it may change in a country over a period of time. In this context, Harley Hinrichs in his book *General Theory of Tax Structure Change during Economic Development* has mentioned the following five stages through which tax structure has changed historically as economies have developed.

- **First Stage:** A traditional society relies primarily on traditional direct taxes like taxes on land, livestock, water rights etc.
- **Second Stage:** Society breaks away from old ways and indirect taxes become more important, especially external indirect taxes (i.e. taxes on foreign trade).
- **Third Stage:** Traditional direct taxes decline relative to national income and governmental revenues.
- **Fourth Stage:** Domestic commodity production increases and internal indirect taxes (excise duties and sales taxes) grow rapidly to replace customs duties.
- **Fifth Stage:** Economy gains maturity and modern direct taxes like personal income and corporate profit taxes become dominant.

1.2 Determinants of Tax Yield

Amount of money collected from a tax or a tax system is called tax yield. If the cost of collecting a tax is deducted from the gross tax yield, the resultant amount is net tax yield.

Tax yield is determined by a host of factors, the following of which are more important:

1. Coverage of the tax.

2. Exemptions/concessions.
3. Rate structure.
4. Degree of tax compliance.
5. Penal provisions.
6. Administrative efficiency.

There can be other factors also, specific to particular taxes. For example, the yield from excise duties also depends upon industrial progress and the general health of the economy. Similarly, revenue from customs duties is affected by factors like import policy, availability of foreign exchange, and international trade climate.

1.3 Objectives of Tax Policy

Why are taxes imposed? They are imposed for a variety of reasons. Tax policy has a number of functions to perform and objectives to satisfy.

Apart from its traditional functions (defence, and maintenance of law and order), a modern government undertakes welfare and developmental activities and makes provision for public goods to satisfy collective needs of the people. It has also to pay for its own administration. It needs financial resources for these purposes and taxation is one method of transferring money from private to public hands.

Taxation is a potent instrument to shape and influence the socio-economic policies of a country. It is, of course, difficult to formulate a set of universally acceptable goals of tax policy because: (a) different countries are in different stages of economic development, (b) objectives of economic policy differ in these countries, (c) priorities of economic policy are different and (d) objectives and priorities of economic policy continually change with the changing economic, social, and political milieu.

Though the concept of an ideal tax system for a country is linked with the peculiar characteristics of its economy yet tax policy is usually assigned the following four functions in the stated order in a typical developing economy:

1.3.1 Resource Mobilization: The first and foremost objective of tax policy in a country is to raise resources for public authorities for administration and development. Taxes are the main instrument for transferring resources from private to public use. By designing an appropriate tax structure, resources can be raised from those who are holding them idly or squandering them on luxury consumption.

1.3.2 Resource Allocation: Scarcity of real resources in developing countries calls for their optimum utilisation. Since the composition of investment is an important determinant of growth rate of the economy, public policy must discourage the flow of resources to *low priority* areas so that they could be diverted to *vital* sectors of the economy. By imposing high tax rates on luxuries and other low priority items (such as motor cars, air conditioners, and jewellery), the government can discourage the consumption and production of such items, ensuring in the process release of resources for high priority sectors. Conversely, production of necessities of life and employment-oriented industries can be encouraged by offering tax concessions or even subsidies.

1.3.3 Distributive Justice: Distributive justice or economic justice is an important function of tax policy. Economic justice relates largely to distribution of tax burden and benefits of public expenditure. It is a component of the broader concept of social justice which encompasses, besides distributive justice, such questions as treatment of women and children, and racial and religious tolerance in a society.

1.3.4 Stabilization: Initial developmental efforts are generally marked by inflationary tendencies in an economy. Inflation, if uncontrolled, may thwart all development plans and bring misery to the poor. A reasonable degree of price stability should be a primary concern of a government's tax policy.

1.4 Direct versus Indirect Taxes

A direct tax is one the ultimate burden of which falls on the person on whom it is levied. In other words, it is a tax that cannot be shifted from the original payer to someone else. It is contrasted with indirect tax which can readily be shifted to ultimate consumers of the commodity or service taxed.

John Stuart Mill, the celebrated British economist of the 19th century, distinguished between direct and indirect taxes as follows, "A direct tax is one which is demanded from the very person who, it is intended or desired, should pay it. Indirect taxes are those which are demanded from one person in the expectation and intention that he shall indemnify himself at the expense of another". [2]

Direct taxes, like income tax, though administratively inconvenient, are preferred because they: (a) can be related to ability-to-pay, (b) satisfy the principle of certainty, and (c) create civic consciousness.

An indirect tax is one which can be shifted from the original payer to the ultimate consumer of the commodity or service taxed. Import duties, excise levies, and sales taxes are generally regarded as indirect taxes. Thus, an excise duty on cigarettes, levied on producers, is usually passed on to the consumers in the form of higher prices.

Indirect taxes (also called hidden taxes) are convenient to collect but lack equity attribute. They do not allow considerations for the personal circumstances of taxpayers as do direct taxes. It is not possible to grant exemptions or allow deductions or to have a progressive rate schedule. Indirect taxes are borne in relation to the consumption expenditure which constitutes a higher percentage of income for lower income groups than for persons in higher income brackets. It is true that incidence of indirect taxes depends on: (a) the selection of commodities for taxation and (b) the rate of tax on them. It is desirable that luxuries and comforts are chosen for heavy taxation with necessities of life either exempted or moderately taxed. However, in poor countries the demand for luxury items is limited apart from being price elastic. Conversely, the demand for necessities is vast and price inelastic, obliging tax authorities to extend the tax net to daily needs. This has a tendency to fuel inflation.

It is almost universally accepted that indirect taxes are inferior to direct taxes in terms of equity attribute. The distribution of indirect tax burden is often, though not always, regressive and even the poorest of the poor are made to contribute to public exchequer. The chief advantage of indirect taxes is that they are convenient to collect.

The distinction between direct and indirect taxes is nebulous. The definitions of these two types of taxes have been a subject of long-drawn debate in public finance literature.

Income tax, property tax, and payroll tax are generally considered direct taxes, although many economists believe that it is possible to pass on these taxes under certain circumstances. Corporate income tax, a supposedly direct tax, is known to be shifted to consumers in many countries. [3]

Thus, demarcation between direct and indirect taxes is ambiguous because of conflicting empirical evidence of tax incidence studies. Direct taxes can be shifted under certain circumstances while taxes on commodities may stick on the producers finally. [4]

1.5 Specific versus *Ad Valorem* Taxes

This classification is relevant in the case of taxes/duties on commodities. Customs duties, excise levies, and sales taxes on commodities may take specific or *ad valorem* form.

A specific or volumetric duty represents a fixed amount of tax on a unit of the physical quantity of the product.

Specific duty is generally preferred for commodities the classifications and sub-classifications of which are not numerous, i.e. the commodity is a standardised one, e.g. sugar. A specific duty is easy to apply besides having the political and psychological advantages of obscuring the actual ratio of the tax to the selling price. It is, however, price-neutral in the sense that price changes, if any, in the commodity do not affect the revenue yield. Specific duty is quality-neutral also unless differential rates are prescribed with reference to the quality of the product.

There can be many variants of the specific form of duty. If a flat amount per unit of a commodity is levied irrespective of the price range, it is a simple specific duty. It may be simple specific with initial exemption. However, if the flat amount per unit changes with the price range of the commodity, it becomes a graduated specific duty.

An *ad valorem* (according to value) duty is imposed as a fixed percentage of the price of the product taxed. This form of duty is preferred when a commodity has many classifications and sub-classifications, e.g. textiles.

An *ad valorem* duty is responsive to price changes and thus ensures an undiminished proportion of taxes in national income. The main problem in applying *ad valorem* rate is the determination of the tax base, i.e. valuation of production.

An *ad valorem* duty may be a simple one, a duty collected as a fixed proportion of the price irrespective of the price range. As a variant of this, the commodity in question may be completely exempted till the price reaches a pre-determined maximum level. When different duty rates apply to different price brackets of a commodity, it becomes a graduated or bracketed *ad valorem* duty. So long as the price remains within a single bracket, the rate of the duty remains the same. Generally, commodities in higher price brackets bear a higher duty rate and vice versa.

Sometimes, both specific and *ad valorem* duties are levied on a single item. This pattern is called specific-cum-ad valorem duty or compound duty.

1.6 Operating Costs of a Tax

These are made up of administrative costs plus compliance costs of a tax.

1.6.1 Administrative Costs: These are costs incurred by public authorities in administering a tax. These costs (also called expense ratio) include wages of tax officials and expenditures on stores and supplies for running tax administration. They are interpreted in terms of cost-yield ratio which means cost of collection expressed as a proportion of tax revenue. A lower cost-yield ratio is considered indicative of the efficiency of tax administration. Unusually high cost-yield ratio is a drag on the public exchequer. Thus, cost-yield ratios may be used to evaluate administration of competing taxes.

The concept of cost-yield ratio suffers from various limitations and therefore needs to be used carefully as an index of tax efficiency. The ratio depends upon the nature of a tax. Generally, cost of collecting direct taxes is high as compared to indirect taxes. The ratio is also affected by the nature of tax administration. If separate administration is used for each tax, the scope for scale economies is greatly reduced. Conversely, if a single administration deals with a variety of taxes of similar nature (e.g. all direct taxes), cost-yield ratio may fall due to scale economies.

Cost-yield ratio is also influenced by the nature of an economy. The ratio is generally high in developing countries which are in the process of evolving their tax systems. Widespread illiteracy and lack of accounting practices make assessment procedures extremely difficult in these countries.

Equity considerations may demand a tax system which is poor in terms of cost-effectiveness. Thus, there may be a conflict between cost-effectiveness and equity. Pointing out another limitation, G.K. Shaw has observed, "The cost-yield ratio provides a purely static insight into the efficiency of a given tax which may be misleading in terms of the potential dynamic evolution of the tax. Thus, for example, a tax in its infancy may have high costs associated with the establishment of the appropriate administration and collection machinery and yet its future prognosis may be favourable if it is progressively based or confronts income elastic demand conditions". [5]

It is noteworthy that reduction in cost of collection which leads to ineffective enforcement and hence tax evasion, is false economy. Similarly, employment of incompetent and/or inadequate staff can result in harassment of taxpayers and multiplying appeals and hence increased cost of compliance. Properly understood, the principle of economy requires lowest possible costs consistent with effective administration and existing level of facilities to taxpayers. While interpreting cost-yield ratio, account should also be taken of compliance costs which may differ from tax to tax.

1.6.2 Compliance Costs: Compliance costs refer to costs incurred by taxpayers and/or third parties in complying with a tax, over and above the tax payment made to public authorities. The third party compliance costs are those incurred by firms in discharging their legal responsibility as tax collectors, e.g. deducting income tax from salaries and passing it on to the tax authorities.

The following three types of compliance costs may be distinguished:

- **Money Costs:** These include payment for legal advice, fees to accountants or to valuers for valuation of property (for purposes of death duties, wealth tax etc.), cost of postage, telephone calls, travelling, books, and in some cases litigation.

- **Time Costs:** These include time taken to consult tax advisers, complete tax returns, and to travel to tax offices.
- **Psychic Costs:** These refer to the worries and anxieties associated with tax payment. [6]

1.7 Excise Duties

Excise duties are imposed by a government on commodities produced or manufactured domestically. They are also known as production taxes. They are collected from the producers of excisable goods.

1.7.1 Golden Rules of Excise Taxation: The Indian Fiscal Commission, 1921-22, enunciated the following five golden rules of excise taxation, which with necessary modifications seem to be relevant to this day.

1. Excise duties should ordinarily be confined to industries which are concentrated in large factories or small areas.
2. They may properly be imposed for the purpose of checking the consumption of injurious articles and especially on luxuries coming under this category.
3. Otherwise they should be imposed for revenue purpose only.
4. While permissible on commodities of general consumption, they should not press too heavily on poorer classes.
5. When an industry requires protection, any further necessary taxation on its products may, if the other conditions are fulfilled, take the form of excise duty *plus* an additional import duty. The latter should fully countervail the former and may be pitched at a higher price. [7]

1.8 Taxation of Services

Service sector is very wide in its range. It includes, *inter alia*, health care, education, social security, leasing, entertainment, credit rating agencies, telecommunications, transport, publicity and advertising, insurance, banking, legal and financial services.

From equity point of view, services should be taxed in the same way as goods. Taxation of goods and exclusion of services distorts the relative prices of goods vis-à-vis services, encouraging artificially the demand for services. In the process, the allocation of resources is also distorted. If tax is imposed on goods and not on services, a relatively high rate of tax would be required on goods to generate a given amount of revenue. If tax is imposed both on goods and services, a moderate tax rate can yield the given revenue. Administratively, taxation of both goods and services is desirable because it would reduce disputes pertaining to distinction between goods and services.

Like goods, services can also be classified into two broad categories: essential services (e.g. health and education) and luxury services (e.g. entertainment and tourism). The rationale for exemption/lenient tax treatment of essential services is the same as for essential goods. Similarly, luxury services should be taxed at a high rate like luxury goods.

1.9 Customs Duties

These are duties on the import and export of goods levied by a national government. They become payable when the goods cross the customs boundaries of the nation. Hence, they are also called border taxes.

The term *customs duty* as an English expression originated in England during a period of disagreement between the king and the parliament over the king's right to collect it. King's supporters claimed that the sovereign had been vested with the authority to impose this levy by a long established custom. Hence, it is suggested that the term customs duty was derived. The right was claimed on the ground that customs duties were a reasonable return to the king for the protection and security he was supposed to provide on land and sea.

Customs duties are probably the most ancient form of taxation. They are as old as international trade itself. Just as domestic production flows provide the base for excise taxation so also international trade flows are the basis for customs duties. These duties are levied either on specific basis (i.e. as a stated amount per unit of weight, volume etc.) or on *ad valorem* basis (i.e. as a percentage of the value of goods imported or exported). Customs duties can be classified into two categories: import duties, and export duties.

1.9.1 Import Duties: Goods imported into a country are chargeable to a duty. The duty may be a percentage of the value of the goods (i.e. ad valorem rate) or at a specific rate. Import duties are usually levied with ad valorem rates and their base is determined by the domestic value of the imported goods calculated at the official exchange rate.

Apart from the revenue function, import duties provide a protective barrier for domestic industries. There are two main purposes of import duties: (a) to raise revenue for the government (revenue tariff) and (b) to discourage imports in order to protect a nation's domestic industry (protective tariff) or to correct disequilibrium (deficit) in its balance of payments. Other measures to protect indigenous industries from foreign competition are import licensing, import quotas, and outright import ban.

A. Countervailing Duties: These are duties in addition to the normal import duties levied on goods imported into a country. The rate of countervailing duty is generally equal to the excise duty imposed on like items produced domestically. The argument is that normal import duty represents the desirable degree of protection to internally produced goods which are not subject to excise duty. When excise duty is levied or the rate of an existing one is increased, a corresponding enhancement in import duty is required to preserve the accepted degree of protection.

B. Anti-dumping Duties: Dumping is a practice of selling goods in a foreign country at a price below their domestic selling price, after allowing for differences due to transportation expenses, tariffs, and other cost justifications. Many governments view the activity as an unfair competitive practice and frequently expose those engaged in dumping to the imposition of an anti-dumping duty. It is imposed to discourage dumping. The tariff rate is usually the difference between the normal selling price and the dumping price.

1.9.2 Export Duties: Export duties are imposed on export values expressed in domestic currency. Export duties can become an important source of revenue when a country enjoys monopoly or near-monopoly in certain products in the international market. Thus, when there is considerable disparity between the domestic and international prices of certain goods, levy of export duties is justified to mop up a part of the profits of exporters. Export duty on an item is levied after considering such factors as domestic production, likely exportable surpluses, demand for the item in the foreign markets, changes in exchange rates, and prices prevailing in the international market.

1.10 Sales Tax

Sales tax is normally an *ad valorem* levy imposed on the seller with reference to the transaction of sale. On the basis of the stage of collection, sales tax is classified into: (a) multi-point sales tax, and (b) single-point sales tax.

1.10.1 Multi-point Sales Tax: As a multi-point levy, sales tax may be applied at two or more stages of production and distribution and becomes akin to a turnover tax applicable at each transaction of purchase and sale. Multi-stage sales tax is politically expedient. A given amount of revenue can be raised at a lower rate of taxation which also reduces the temptation for tax evasion.

The chief demerit of multi-point sales tax is its encouragement to vertical integration of production and distribution processes. Thus, it discriminates against non-integrated firms. Producers of finished products prefer to produce their own materials and components, and this tendency harms the interest of independent suppliers, particularly small ones. Furthermore, multi-point sales tax discriminates against those goods, and their consumers, which have to pass through numerous transactions. In view of these disadvantages, John Due has opined, "On administrative as well as economic and equity grounds the objections to the multi-stage form are so great as to suggest its complete rejection, regardless of circumstances". [8]

1.10.2 Single-point Sales Tax: A single-point sales tax applies to one stage, either at the manufacturing, or the wholesale, or the retail level. At the manufacturing level, sales tax applies to the sale by manufacturer of finished product and is similar to excise duty. At the wholesale level, the tax applies to the last wholesale transaction, i.e. purchase by retailer. The retail sales tax applies to the final sale which means sale to the consumer.

The main advantage of single-point sales tax is that it does not discriminate against non-integrated firms as does multi-point sales tax. It, thus, discourages vertical integration and promotes horizontal integration. As regards the stage of its imposition, the retail stage is considered the most satisfactory due to the following reasons.

1. Sales tax at the retail stage is collected when final sale to the consumer takes place. Thus, it avoids what economists call the *cascading* or *pyramiding* effect of a tax. The contention is that middlemen apply fixed percentage mark-ups to purchase prices and if the purchase price include taxes (as is the case if sales tax is imposed at manufacturer's, or wholesaler's level), the mark-ups will be applicable to the tax component of the purchase prices as well, a situation which must be avoided in the interest of the consumers.

2. A given revenue can be realised by applying a lower tax rate at the retail stage as compared to other stages because the margins of all middlemen are included at the final stage of sale, meaning thereby the enlargement of the tax base at the retail stage.
3. The desired change in the ratio of tax to consumer expenditure can be achieved more effectively in case of retail-stage sales tax. This will be difficult at *other stages* because the margins of dealers on various goods, besides being applied to the tax component of the purchase prices, may differ significantly.
4. Sales tax at the retail stage can be shown separately from the price and thus made known to the purchaser, increasing tax consciousness among the taxpayers.
5. Expected changes in the rates of retail sales tax do not lead to changes in inventory position of the firms. Anticipated changes in the rates of sales tax at *other stages* may influence inventory decisions of the firms causing dislocation in trade circles.

However, retail-stage sales tax has its own problems, the chief being the large number of taxpayers in the form of small shopkeepers and scattered retail outlets. In developing countries, the problem of tax administration is more acute in view of widespread illiteracy, lack of monetisation, and poor accounting practices. From administrative viewpoint, this form of taxation is costlier and cumbersome, offering ample scope for tax evasion and corruption.

Sales tax at manufacturing or wholesale stage is administratively preferable because the number of taxpayers is small and readily identifiable. However, the problem of *cascading* will reappear. In fact, the farther we move from the retail level, the more serious the problem of *cascading* becomes. In short, the problem boils down to a trade-off between economic rationale and administrative efficiency. The relative weightage to competing objectives depends on political judgement and the economic circumstances under which the sales tax system has to operate.

1.11 Value Added Tax (VAT)

VAT, a fiscal innovation of early 1950s, has claimed world-wide attention as more and more countries are adopting it in varying degrees to reform their systems of commodity taxation.

1.11.1 Meaning and Measurement of Value Added: To understand the meaning of value added tax, it is necessary first to explain the term *value added* as used in economics.

Under the simple commodity production system of the olden days, goods were produced locally and in most cases, for local consumption. Normally, the producer himself was the seller of his products. In contrast, modern system of production is highly complex involving acute division of labour, large-scale production, and a wide market for the output. The final product as handed down to the consumer does not represent the efforts of one production unit but a host of independent manufacturers, big and small. Firms buy raw materials, components, capital goods from each other and sell their products through a chain of dealers, wholesalers, and retailers. The value of the final product as it reaches the customer represents the reward of the services of various factors of production rendered at different stages in the chain of production and distribution. The final value is the sum total of values added at different stages.

The value added at a particular stage is measured through two alternative approaches: (a) subtraction method and (b) additive method.

Both these approaches are based on the identity that total sale proceeds of a firm from its output during a given period are equal to the cost of inputs, wages, rent, interest, depreciation, and profits. Under the subtraction method, value added is measured by deducting value of inputs from the value of output (O-I). If the cost of inputs is deducted from total proceeds, the remainder represents the sum of factor incomes plus depreciation. Alternatively, additive method adds together various types of factor incomes generated, and depreciation. In practice, subtraction method is considered more workable and therefore widely relied upon.

1.11.2 Meaning and Computation of VAT: VAT is a multi-point tax with set off for tax paid on purchases. It is collected in instalments at each transaction in the production-distribution system. It does not have cascading effect due to the system of deduction or credit mechanism.

It is a tax on consumption. The final and total burden of the tax is fully and exclusively borne by the domestic consumer of goods and services. It being a tax on domestic consumption, no VAT is charged on goods exported. It is an alternative mechanism of collection of tax. Value added tax is, therefore, a multi-stage sales tax levied as a proportion of the value added, i.e. sales minus purchases, which is equivalent to wages plus profits.

Value added tax is levied on the sellers of goods and services based on value added by their respective units. The base for VAT is determined by value added at a particular stage of production or distribution. In other words, inputs of a firm are not taxed. At each point, the firm is reimbursed the tax which it has already paid at the time of purchasing the inputs. Thus, there is no cascading effect. Meaning of VAT becomes clearer when it is juxtaposed against conventional turnover tax (excise duty, sales tax) which falls on the total value of the product at each stage of production chain and is called a cascade type tax.

As already noted, subtraction method is popular one to measure value added and hence to compute VAT. There are two ways to compute VAT according to subtraction method. Under the first method, called the sales less purchases or accounts procedure, the rate of tax is multiplied by the difference of output and inputs, t (O - I). Under the second method, called the tax credit or invoice procedure, the product of the rate of tax and input is deducted from the product of the rate of tax and output, t (O) - t (I). [9] The latter is more common in practice. The VAT liability of a seller under it is equal to the tax arising from its total sales minus a credit for the tax paid by it on its purchases. The seller charges full tax from his buyer but pays to the government the difference between the tax charged and the one already paid on his (seller's) inputs.

The VAT required to be shown on any given invoice is not the seller's VAT liability with respect to that sale but which he can collect from buyer. In fact, the VAT liability is determined only at the end of the taxable period when he takes into account all of his purchases from other taxpayers. It is important to note that the ultimate burden of VAT rests on the consumer. In this connection the Indian Indirect Taxation Enquiry Committee, 1978, observed, "Since the value of a product increases as it goes through successive stages of processing or production, the tax passed on to the successive buyers keeps increasing. The final buyer, i.e. the consumer, cannot pass the tax: nor can he claim tax credit, since he is not a taxable person under VAT. The intention is that the full tax on the product, though collected in instalments from producers at different stages, should be borne by the final buyer". [10]

One distinct advantage of the invoice method is its self-enforcing characteristic because tax credit for a firm is subject to the proof of its having paid the tax to its supplier. This feature of the VAT is particularly emphasised in countries where tax compliance is rather poor.

1.11.3 Treatment of Depreciation under VAT: There are three ways to treat the cost of capital goods whose use in the production process is spread over time.

1. Since value added is defined as output minus input, it is necessary to clarify whether input includes depreciation of capital goods. One interpretation is that it does, i.e. depreciation (also called capital consumption) is excluded from the value added so that value added reflects the sum of wages, interest, rent, and profits. This is called the *income variant approach* under which the base for taxation is *net value added* by each producer. The *net value added* is defined as gross receipts minus purchases of intermediate goods and depreciation. This corresponds to the concept of net national product in national accounting.
2. The second approach is to exclude the cost of capital goods from value added instead of granting allowance for depreciation over the life of capital goods, and is called the *consumption variant approach.* Value added is now defined as gross receipts minus purchase of intermediate products and capital expenditure on machinery etc. Since producers are allowed to deduct their capital expenditures, the base for taxation is restricted to the value of production of consumer goods only.
3. Lastly, it is possible that the cost of capital goods is not allowed to be excluded when they are initially purchased and no allowance is made for depreciation when they are used in production. Value added equals gross receipts minus the cost of purchasing intermediate goods. In other words, it is the sum of wages, rent, interest, profits, and depreciation. This may be called the *gross product variant* and is the most comprehensive form of VAT. It corresponds to gross national product concept of social accounting.

The consumption variant approach permits a firm to deduct purchases of capital goods (i.e. gross investment) while income variant concept allows it to deduct depreciation only. In this sense, the base for VAT is bigger under the income variant than under the consumption variant by the amount of net investment (gross investment minus depreciation). In brief,

Income variant = Gross receipts - Costs of intermediate goods – Depreciation.

Consumption variant = Gross receipts - Costs of intermediate goods - Costs of capital goods.

Gross product variant = Gross receipts - Cost of intermediate goods.

1.11.4 Benefits and Limitations of VAT: VAT is a multi-stage tax levied on all stages of production and distribution of a commodity. It is collected in instalments on the basis of value added at each stage of production and distribution of a commodity. It is a comprehensive levy covering almost all production and distribution in its fold. It is different from excise duties which, in many cases, are selective in nature.

Under VAT, each input is taxed only once. Since an input is taxed only once, VAT avoids cascading which is the chief disadvantage of the traditional system of excise and sales taxation. Excise duties, and multi-point sales taxes levied on gross output tax the same input repeatedly as goods pass along different stages of production. [11] This type of taxation encourages vertical integration of industries, a tendency harmful to the growth of small-scale sector.

Since the cumulative effect of input taxation is absent under VAT, the cost of production increases by the amount of tax itself. Thus, by preventing unnecessary cost escalation, VAT promotes competitiveness of domestic Industries in the world market and thereby generates favourable effects on exports.

Among the various limitations of VAT, the following are more common. VAT is levied on ad valorem basis and does not admit of physical output as the basis for tax liability determination. Excise duties may be imposed on ad valorem or specific or ad valorem-cum-specific basis, or even in the form of a compounded levy.

Ideally, VAT should be imposed at a uniform rate at all stages of production and distribution so that tax credit claims can be made easily. Excise duties, as also sales taxes, are imposed at different rates depending upon the nature of the commodity taxed.

VAT is more suitable under a unitary form of government, i.e. under a single tax authority for commodity taxation. In a federation where different tiers of government enjoy overlapping commodity taxation powers, VAT is difficult to operate due to tax rivalry and lack of coordination among federal and provincial governments.

A VAT regime is theoretically meant for a unified market in which the VAT levied can always be set off against taxes already paid, irrespective of the state-wise location of the manufacturing or trading entities.

1.11.5 Rate Structure under VAT: In its ideal form VAT should be imposed at a uniform rate or at the maximum 2-3 rates. The higher the number of rates, the more complicated the operation of VAT. To quote, "Experience has shown that the introduction of several rates complicates the administration of VAT considerably. The complication arises from the fact that the taxpayer is forced to maintain separate records in order to match inputs and parts of outputs that may be taxed at different rates. The difficulties are said to be particularly felt by multi-product firms. The easiest form of VAT to administer would be one with a single rate. For various socio-economic reasons, however, governments which have adopted VAT have found it necessary to introduce more than one rate, but the number of rates has to be strictly limited". [12]

Excise taxation discriminates between necessities, comforts, and luxuries in a big way. Many necessities are either exempt or bear a very low rate of tax. Contrarily, luxuries are subject to a high rate of taxation. The underlying philosophy of this approach is that direct taxes in themselves cannot lessen economic inequalities and some degree of progression and differentiation has to be there to achieve the objective. VAT tends to be regressive in view of uniformity or limited number of rates. One way to ensure progressivity under VAT is to impose special excise duties on a select band of final commodities (luxuries) without extending the advantage of tax credit. At the other end, zero-rating or exemption may be applied in the case of necessities. [13] However, such provisions will complicate the commodity tax system of a country.

Endnotes

1. Richard Musgrave and Peggy Musgrave, *Public Finance in Theory and Practice*, New York: McGraw-Hill Book Company, 1989, p. 595.
2. *Collected Works of John Stuart Mill,* University of Toronto Press, 1965, Volume III, Book V, Chapter 3, p. 825.
3. For United States, see M. Krzyzaniak and R.A. Musgrave, *The Shifting of the Corporation Income Tax*, Baltimore: John Hopkins University Press, 1963; For India, see G.S. Laumas, 'The Shifting of Corporation Income Tax: A Study with Reference to Indian Corporations', *Public Finance*, Volume 21, No. 4, 1966, pp. 462-473.
4. For a detailed discussion on the distinction between direct and indirect taxes, see: (i) Ursula K. Hicks, "The Terminology of Tax analysis", in *Readings in the Economics of Taxation*, The American Economic Association, London: George Allen and Unwin Ltd., 1959, pp. 214-216; (ii) D. Walker, "Direct versus Indirect Taxes", in *Public Finance*, edited by D.W. Houghton, England: Penguin Books Ltd., 1972, pp. 349-375.
5. G.K. Shaw, "Leading Issues of Tax Policy in Developing Countries: The Economic Problems", in Alan Peacock and Francesco Forte (eds.), *The Political Economy of Taxation*, Basil Blackwell, Oxford, 1981, p. 153.
6. For details, see Cedric Sandford, "Economic Aspects of Compliance Costs", in Alan Peacock and Francesco Forte (eds.), *The Political Economy of Taxation*, Basil Blackwell, Oxford, 1981, pp. 163-173.
7. Government of India, *Report of the Indian Fiscal Commission* (Chairman: Ibrahim Rahimatoola), 1921-22, p. 87.
8. John F. Due, *The Problems of Tax Administration in Latin America*, Baltimore: The John Hopkins Press, 1959, p. 417.
9. Let output be ₹ 500, input ₹ 400, and VAT 10 percent. Then, t (0-I) = 1/10 (500-400) = ₹ 10, and t(0) - t(I) = 1/10 (500) - 1/10 (400) = ₹ 10.
10. Government of India, Ministry of Finance, *Report of the Indirect Taxation Enquiry Committee* (Chairman: L.K. Jha), Part II, 1978, p. 283.
11. It can be argued that double taxation of commodities can be avoided if excise duties are restricted to only final consumer goods. To compensate for the loss of revenue, rates of duty on final goods may be appropriately raised upwards.

    Several difficulties arise in adopting this approach. For one, certain goods are capable of being used as intermediate goods and also as final consumer goods as, for example, tyres and tubes. If tyres and tubes are exempted from tax, there is discrimination in favour of consumers who use them as replacement items. If these goods are subject to taxation, there is possibility of their being taxed again at the retail sales tax level, causing cascading effect. Therefore, it is not always possible to replace input taxation by tax on final output. Taxation of inputs is unavoidable and in a sense part and parcel of the indirect tax system. However, the harmful effects of this necessary evil can be lessened if appropriate methods are devised to allow refund wherever it is deemed necessary to do so. Value added tax is one such device whose scope (i.e., at what stage or how many stages) may be altered depending upon local conditions.

Furthermore, it is administratively easier to tax inputs rather than final goods produced with those inputs. It is convenient to tax aluminium than articles made of aluminium or cotton yarn than cotton fabrics.

12. *Report of the Indirect Taxation Enquiry Committee*, *op. cit*., p. 289.
13. The difference between zero-rating and exemptions is of crucial importance and has been explained by Sandford in the following words, "The difference between zero-rating and exemption is important and perhaps needs explanation. A trader selling zero-rated goods is normally a *registered* trader, part of the VAT system, recovering from Customs and Excise the whole of the input tax paid on his purchases. An exempt trader (whether by virtue of the products in which he deals or because his taxable turnover is below the threshold) is outside the system; he is not a registered trader. If his purchases are subject to VAT he will have to pay tax on them and cannot recover it from Customs and Excise, though he is at liberty to raise his prices to recoup the rise in his costs. While it is almost invariably an advantage to be zero-rated, it is not necessarily an advantage to be exempt rather than standard-rated. A trader selling almost entirely to the general public will usually gain by being exempt, but he may find exemption a disadvantage if he is selling to registered traders in competition with registered traders. His potential customers in that case will prefer to buy from other registered traders because then they can offset input tax against their output tax, which they cannot do if they are merely paying an increased price that does not technically contain VAT. For this reason provision exists for a trader (who would otherwise have been exempt because his turnover was below the threshold) to seek voluntary registration" (C.T. Sandford et al., *Costs and Benefits of VAT*, London: Heinemann Educational Books, 1981, p. 6.

2

Union Excise Duties, Modified Value Added Tax (MODVAT) and Central Value Added Tax (CENVAT)

Prior to their subsumation under the GST, excise duties were an important source of indirect tax revenue for the Central Government. They were levied on a wide range of products of the industrial sector of the economy. [1]

The excise system was leaky (riddled with extensive exemptions) and characterized by multiplicity of specific and ad valorem rates.

2.1 Post-Independence Constitutional Provisions Regarding Union Excise Duties

By virtue of powers vested in it under Entry 84 of List I (Union List) in the Seventh Schedule of the Constitution, the Central Government was authorised to impose, "duties of excise on tobacco and other goods manufactured or produced in India except: (a) alcoholic liquors for human consumption, (b) opium, Indian-hemp and other narcotic drugs and narcotics, but including medicinal and toilet preparations containing alcohol or any substance included in sub-paragraph (b) of this entry". [2]

Excise duties on liquor and other narcotics are imposed by the State Governments under provisions of Entry 51 of List II (State List) in the Seventh Schedule.

Duties of excise on medicinal and toilet preparations containing alcohol were levied by the Centre under Article 268 but they were collected and appropriated by the States within which they were leviable. These were levied by the Centre to ensure uniformity in their rate throughout the country. [3]

Apart from allocating taxation powers, the Constitution also provides for the sharing of certain taxes between the Centre and the States. Prior to the Constitution (Eightieth Amendment) Act, 2000, excise duties belonged to the category of taxes which *may* be divided between the Centre and the States (Article 272) and the subject matter of this division fell within the purview of the Finance Commission [Article 280(3)(a)]. In other words, the sharing of excise duties was permissive and therefore the States did not enjoy a constitutional right to claim a share out of the revenues from Central excises. However, successive Finance Commissions took the view that permissive sharing, contemplated under Article 272 was not only justified but even necessary in view of the growing financial needs of the States. Therefore, ever since April 1, 1952, the States got a share of the proceeds of Central excises. The Tenth Finance Commission fixed this share at 47.5 percent for the quinquennium 1995-2000. However, the Constitution (Eightieth Amendment) Act, 2000 substituted a new Article for Article 270 under which States were given a percentage share of all Central taxes and duties. However, the surcharge levied for purposes of the Union under Article 271 was excluded from the divisible pool.

Moreover, Article 272 of the Constitution was omitted by the same amendment.

2.2 Various Types of Excise Duties

In accordance with the provisions of the Constitution, various types of excise duties and cesses were imposed by the Union Government on commodities covered by the Central Excise Act, 1944 and other Acts. Before they were subsumed under GST, the important duties in operation were the following.

2.2.1 Basic Excise Duty: Levied under Section 3 of the Central Excise Act, 1944, this was the main duty commonly known as basic excise duty. This duty was fixed with reference to the value, weight, volume, unit, length or area of the excisable goods. These details were given in the Schedule of the Central Excise Tariff Act, 1985.

2.2.2 Additional Duties in Lieu of Sales Tax: These duties were imposed under the Additional Duties of Excise (Goods of Special Importance) Act, 1957, which provided for the levy and collection of additional duties on sugar, tobacco, cotton fabrics, rayon or artificial silk fabrics and woollen fabrics produced or manufactured in India. These duties were in addition to the duties payable under the Central Excises and Salt Act, 1944, and replaced, by agreement with State Governments, the sales tax levied by them on these commodities. The net proceeds from additional excise duties were distributed among the States in accordance with the principles of distribution formulated and the recommendations made by the Finance Commissions from time to time.

2.2.3 Cesses: These were levied under separate enactments on certain commodities and the revenue was earmarked for specific purposes. For example, handloom cess was levied on fabrics to raise funds for developing *khadi* and other handloom industries and for promoting the sale of *khadi* and other handloom cloth. Cesses were also levied under various Acts on tea, jute, indigenous crude oil, paper, sugar, *bidis*, automobiles, vegetable oils, and television sets.

The Central Excise Act, 1944, was the main enactment under which duties were levied on different commodities. Under Section 37 of this Act, a set of rules known as the Central Excise Rules, 1944 were framed to implement the provisions of the Act. Another set of rules under the same section dealt exclusively with the valuation of the excisable commodities and was known as Central Excise (Valuation) Rules, 1975. The Act and the Rules were amended from time to time. Broadly speaking, the Act embodied the substantive law, and the Rules contained both substantive law and procedural matters.

Although the Central Government was empowered to levy duties on agricultural products also, it refrained to do so in view of the administrative difficulties involved. Therefore, the excise system remained confined mostly to the products of the industrial sector with the notable exceptions of tea and coffee.

2.3 Different Procedures to Collect Excises

Central excise duties were assessed and collected through a vast network of offices scattered all over the country. There were various procedures to assess and collect excise duties.

2.3.1 Physical Control System: This procedure, based on personal verification of production by excise officers, was the chief procedure to realise excise duties till it was replaced by a new system called self-removal procedure from June 1, 1968. Under the physical control method, excise control was exercised by the officers of the Excise Department who were posted at the factory to keep watch over the operations in the various departments of the factory to prevent illegal disposal of the manufactured articles. The physical control procedure was based on personal verification of production, storage, and clearance of excisable goods.

The manufacturers, however, were unhappy with this direct interference in the manufacturing process. Therefore, ever since Independence in 1947 they had been demanding abolition of the physical control scheme and its replacement by a system based on audited accounts. The Taxation Enquiry Commission, 1953-54, favoured the retention of the physical control system. It observed, "It seems to us reasonable for the Government to ensure that for the period intervening between production and clearance the goods should be kept in a proper place and under adequate supervision. The procedure followed in India in this regard is also practically the same as that obtaining elsewhere. Physical supervision is considered to be necessary in such cases in almost every country". [4]

The organised sector, however, continued to build up pressure for the replacement of the physical control system and ultimately the self-removal procedure was introduced with effect from June 1, 1968. A few commodities were still subject to the physical control system including sugar, chewing tobacco, and matches.

2.3.2 Self-Removal Procedure (SRP): Under this liberal system, introduced in place of the physical control system, an assessee was allowed to take clearances on his own assessment of the duty liability without prior permission of physical checks by excise officers. This procedure was applicable to most of the commodities under the excise net. An assessee was, however, required to get his classification list approved by the excise authorities before effecting any removal. In the classification list the assessee detailed the description of the goods produced so that they could be categorised in terms of the rate of duty applicable to them.

In the case of *ad valorem* duties, the assessee was further required to submit a price list showing the prices charged along with discounts and deductions, if any. In essence, the SRP was a record-based system of duty collection relying on mutual trust and belief. Unfortunately, heavy evasion of excise duty took place under this scheme. Excise evasion under this liberal scheme was generally resorted to by following such malpractices as incorrect accounting of goods, undervaluation of goods, and flouting the conditions subject to which any goods could be exempted from duty.

2.3.3 Compounded Levy Scheme: This was another procedure for the benefit of small-scale sector and for administrative convenience. Levying of excise duties on small-scale sector was a major problem of the excise system. In many cases, small-scale sector accounted for a significant portion of the output of an industry and it became necessary to subject it to excise taxation. However, the procedures adopted for collection of excise from big firms were often found expensive and time-consuming when applied to small firms. This necessitated the adoption of special procedures suitable for small-scale sector.

Under the compounded levy scheme introduced in 1954, a lump sum payment was made on the basis of some installations, e.g. the number of looms in case of textile units. Once the compounded levy was paid, the producer became free from all excise formalities except to maintain a record of looms in operation. The scheme was applicable to small units producing *khandasari* and cotton fabrics produced on power looms. This system afforded considerable advantages to the small producers because they were saved from the cumbersome normal excise procedures and also by the fact that the fiscal burden under compounded levy was generally lower than the burden under normal procedures.

2.4 New Excise Tariff Nomenclature

The year 1986 was a landmark in the evolution of excise taxation in India. In that year a new internationally accepted harmonised system of commodity classification was introduced in place of the then existing antiquated system introduced by the British. The history of excise tariff classification dates back to the year 1944 when the Central Excises and Salt Act, 1944 was passed, consolidating separate enactments for different goods. This Act of 1944 covered 11 tariff items which were arranged in alphabetical order.

In 1960, the tariff items, the number of which had soared to 30, were rearranged in accordance with the sections of the Standard International Trade Classification (SITC). By 1986, the excise tariff schedule covered 137 tariff items and if account is taken of the sub-items, the number was well over 355 main classifications. The description of tariff commodities was based on the definitions of the Indian Standard Institution, and the descriptions and explanatory notes of the Customs Co-operation Council Nomenclature (CCCN). The domestic trade parlance was also relied upon.

On September 22, 1984, the Government set up a Technical Study Group to undertake a comprehensive review of the then existing tariff nomenclature. The Group drafted a comprehensive and elaborate tariff nomenclature broadly patterned on Harmonised System Nomenclature (HSN), fully corresponding up to 2-digit level (i.e. Chapter level) in respect of 82 of the effective 96 chapters in the HSN. It also suggested that the new tariff should be provided for by a separate Act to be called the Central Excise Tariff Act in place of the then existing system of tariff being governed by the First Schedule of the Central Excises and Salt Act, 1944.

The recommendation of the Technical Study Group as regards the new tariff nomenclature was accepted by the Government and a new Central Excise Tariff Act, 1985, was passed for the purpose. The excise tariff based on the internationally accepted harmonised commodity description and coding system came into effect from February 28, 1986, ushering a new era in excise taxation. The Schedule of the Central Excise Tariff Act, 1985, described the excisable commodities and the rate of duty leviable on them. The new tariff was spread over 91 chapters and covered around 700 four-digit headings and 1,400 six-digit headings.

2.5 Administration of Excise Taxation

There was an elaborate administrative machinery for the collection of excise duties. At the apex level was the Central Board of Excise and Customs (CBEC)—a statutory Board forming part of the Department of Revenue in the Ministry of Finance. The Board, consisting of a chairman and five members, was responsible for the proper collection of customs and Central excise duties, and framing and implementation of related fiscal policies under the control and direction of the Union Finance Minister.

Under CBEC there were 34 Commissionerates of Central excise at the field level, entrusted with the task of collecting Central excise duties. Each of the Commissionerates was headed by a Commissioner of Central Excise who was aided by a number of Additional Commissioners and Deputy Commissioners. A group of Commissionerates was headed by a Chief Commissioner.

For administrative convenience, each Commissionerate was divided into a number of divisions, each such division headed by an Assistant Commissioner. A division was further sub-divided into a number of ranges. Each range was headed by a Superintendent of Central Excise who, in turn, was assisted by a number of Inspectors.

In fact, the range was the basic unit in the administrative set up responsible for the proper assessment of Central excise duties and generation of the statistical information relating to revenue collection. The range was the primary unit which was in contact with the assessees and tried to ensure that the laws and procedures were properly followed by the production units.

To ensure that the goods were properly classified, assessable value correctly determined, and the duties correctly paid, each Commissionerate had an internal audit wing which was headed by an Additional Commissioner directly responsible to the Commissioner of Central Excise. The internal audit was in addition to the statutory audit conducted by the Comptroller and Auditor-General of India.

Each Commissionerate had an anti-evasion wing headed by an Additional Commissioner directly responsible to the Commissioner of Central Excise. The anti-evasion wing made checks on the basis of intelligence and information to ensure that duties were properly paid and there was no evasion of duties or leakage of revenue. In some Commissionerates, there was a separate Commissioner to look after the judicial and adjudication work. There were Commissioners who attended to appeals against orders passed by officers lower in rank to them.

Moreover, a number of supportive organisations under the CBEC undertook work of a specialised nature. Thus, there was the Directorate of Inspection headed by a Chief Commissioner which undertook the inspection of Central excise formations. The Directorate of Anti-Evasion had the responsibility to ensure all-India co-ordination of anti-evasion work. The National Academy of Customs, Excise and Narcotics was entrusted with the task of training officers. The Directorate of Publicity and Public Relations was responsible for printing and publicity. The Directorate of Statistics and Intelligence was responsible for compiling and updating statistical information.

2.6 Revenue Significance of Excise Duties

In the post-Independence period, the relative share of excise duties in Central Government's tax collections had increased precipitously. In 1950-51, excise duties accounted for a modest 16.8 percent of the total Central tax collections: ₹ 68 crore out of ₹ 404 crore. Within a span of 20 years, the proportionate share shot up to 54.9 percent in 1970-71. It declined to 49.3 percent in 1980-81 and further down to 42.6 percent in 1990-91. It stood at 36.3 percent in 2000-01 and 17.4 percent in 2010-11. It was estimated at 19.5 percent in the budget for 2016-17 (Table 2.1). A Government document noted the following reasons for this downward trend, "The buoyancy of excise has suffered because of a variety of factors including numerous exemptions and concessions which have given rise to substantial administrative and legal complexities. Recent years have witnessed an unprecedented increase in litigation". [5]

Table 2.1: Trends in the Relative Revenue Significance of Union Excise Duties in Gross Tax Revenues* of the Central Government: Selected Years

(₹ crore)

Central taxes	1950-51	1960-61	1970-71	1980-81	1990-91	2000-01	2010-11	2016-17#
A+B Gross tax revenues	404 (100.0)	888 (100.0)	3,206 (100.0)	13,179 (100.0)	57,576 (100.0)	1,88,603 (100.0)	7,93,072 (100.0)	16,30,888 (100.0)
A. Direct taxes	174 (43.1)	290 (32.6)	870 (27.1)	3,004 (22.8)	11,025 (19.1)	68,306 (36.2)	4,45,962 (56.2)	8,47,097 (51.9)
B. Indirect taxes of which	229 (56.7)	599 (67.5)	2,337 (72.9)	10,175 (77.2)	46,552 (80.9)	1,20,297 (63.8)	3,47,110 (43.8)	7,83,791 (48.1)
Union excise duties	68 (16.8)	414 (46.6)	1,759 (54.9)	6,500 (49.3)	24,514 (42.6)	68,526 (36.3)	1,38,299 (17.4)	3,18,670 (19.5)

* Before transferring States' share in Central taxes.
# Budget estimates.
Figures in parentheses are corresponding percentages of gross tax revenues.
Sources: Government of India, Ministry of Finance, *Explanatory Memorandum on the Budget of the Central Government* (various years); *Receipts Budget* (various years); and *Budget at a Glance*, 2016-17.

Although excise duties were imposed on a large number of commodities, a substantial proportion of revenue was derived from a limited number of items. These high revenue yielding commodities included iron and steel, motor spirit, tyres and tubes, cigarettes, cement, plastics and refined diesel oil. It is noteworthy that many of the high revenue yielding items were commodities of mass consumption and therefore the burden of excise duties fell on all sections of society.

2.7 Commodity Coverage

As already noted, excise taxation in India was fairly selective in terms of commodity coverage during the pre-Independence period. However, the need for resources required for planned economic development made it necessary to rely on excise taxation for additional funds. This was particularly so in view of the extremely narrow base for direct taxation and the dwindling relative revenue significance of customs duties owing to euphoria for import restrictions and substitution. The scope for extension of excise coverage improved considerably as development efforts were intensified for the production of industrial goods that enjoyed a relatively large and stable domestic market.

The Taxation Enquiry Commission (TEC), 1953-54, after having studied the then existing excise system, made important recommendations in terms of commodity coverage. It recommended the extension of excise coverage to sewing machines, vegetable oils, woollen textiles, biscuits, paper, dry batteries, electric lamps, aerated waters, electric fans, glass and glassware, paints and varnishes, and ceramics. In the opinion of the TEC these industries had developed sufficiently as a result of protection and it was necessary to impose excises on them to raise the much needed revenue for financing development programmes.

Consequent upon the recommendations of the TEC, the history of excise taxation in India since 1954 was one of increasing commodity coverage. Cement, footwear, rayon or artificial silk fabrics, and soap were added to the excise system in 1954. In 1955, excise duties were imposed on paints and varnishes, paper, woollen fabrics, electric batteries, electric light bulbs, and electric fans. In 1956, the excise net was extended to vegetable non-essential oils, rayon or synthetic fibres and yarn, and motor cars.

With the start of production of diesel oil and other fuel oils at the new refineries in Bombay, excise duty was imposed on a variety of petroleum products for the first time in 1956. These included refined diesel oil, diesel oil, and furnace oil. In 1959, excise duties were imposed on asphalt, bitumen, and tar.

The early 1960s witnessed another big expansion in the coverage of excise taxation in India. In 1960, eleven additional goods were subjected to excise duties including aluminium, pig iron, silk fabrics, and motor vehicles. In 1962, the number of additional products brought under the excise system was sixteen and included, *inter alia*, soda ash, caustic soda, cosmetics and toilet preparations, glass and glassware, copper and copper alloys etc. In 1962, ten more products including gases, rubber products, plywood, jute manufactures, and iron and steel products were covered under the excise net.

In 1968, duties were imposed on radio-parts, steel furniture, leather cloth, and chocolates. The biggest expansion was witnessed in 1971 when 25 additional products including linoleum, ready-made garments, vacuum flasks, and pressure cookers were brought under the excise net. The process of covering more and more items under the excise system reached its pinnacle when Tariff Item No. 68 was introduced in 1975. Tariff Item No. 68 was a catch-all item which encompassed all goods not elsewhere specified in the excise tariff. This residual tariff item was abolished with the introduction of a harmonised system of commodity classification introduced from February 28, 1986. The large assortment of commodities under this head got scattered under proper heads in the new nomenclature of excise tariff.

The Tax Reforms Committee (Chairman: Raja Chelliah), 1991, identified many items which were outside the excise net but which could be considered for levying excise duty. Some of the identified items were butter and cheese, skimmed milk powder, spices, fertilisers, feature films, wood pulp, umbrellas, bicycles, toys and sports goods, buttons, and vacuum flasks.

2.8 Excise Tariff Structure

Once the commodities for excise taxation were identified, the next step was to formulate a tariff structure for various commodities.

2.8.1 Statutory versus Effective Rates: Rates of excise duty approved by the Parliament were termed as statutory or tariff rates. However, the Government enjoyed the power to exempt, by notification, any excisable goods from the whole or any part of duty leviable on such goods. In exercise of this power, the Government determined and notified from time-to-time the effective rates of duty. The rationale for granting such powers to the executive was that during the period intervening two consecutive budgets, necessary adjustments might have to be made to regulate exports, consumption, and prices of different commodities. However, the delegation of this power to the executive led to frequent changes in excise rates, creating an unsettling atmosphere for trade and industry and problems for the administration.

Moreover, since the notifications were technically not rules, there was no obligation to place them on the table of the House. Consequently, the Parliament did not always have the information on the variations made in the rates approved by it. The determination of the operative or effective rates of duty by executive decisions led to abridgement of Parliamentary control over the excise system.

Under the Central Excise Tariff Act, 1985, the Government was empowered to enhance the rates of duty specified in the Schedule of the Act through notifications. The increase of duty was subject to certain limits and such powers were exercised only in emergent circumstances. The notifications bringing into force such increases were subject to approval by the Parliament. The said limits were: (a) in case where the rate of duty immediately before the issue of notification is nil, a rate of duty not exceeding 50 percent *ad valorem* may be specified, and (b) in any other case, the increase in the rate of duty shall not be more than twice the rate of duty in force immediately before the issue of notification.

2.8.2 Specific versus *Ad Valorem* Duties [6]: In the early days of the excise system of independent India, the emphasis was on specific rates due to administrative reasons. However, the emphasis shifted to *ad valorem* rates when the economy started experiencing frequent spells of inflation. The 1970s saw a big shift from specific rates of duty to *ad valorem* rates. While introducing the change in the 1969-70 budget, the Finance Minister observed, "...*ad valorem* duties are more rational than specific duties whose incidence declines during periods of rising prices and increases when prices fall. *Ad valorem* duties can also act as a spur to reduction in costs and prices". [7] He converted the then existing specific rates into *ad valorem* rates on cement, vegetable products, electric fans, lighting tubes and bulbs, soaps, soda, and sodium silicate. The change of duties on paper and cotton fabrics into *ad valorem* tax was effected in 1976 and on paints, varnishes, radios, and tape recorders in 1977.

However, beginning with the 1980s, the tendency to shift to *ad valorem* rates was not only halted but reversed in view of an unprecedented spurt in litigation which mainly pertained to disputes over classification and valuation of goods for purposes of excise levies. As a measure to combat tax avoidance and evasion, the basis of duty was changed from *ad valorem* to *ad valorem*-cum-specific rate or specific rate on a number of commodities. Important commodities where the shift took place (with year of change given in brackets) were: flat glass, aluminium metal (1982), paper, aerated waters, motor cars, cigarettes, sugar (1983), paper boards, tyres for buses and trucks (1984), gases, tubes and flaps of tyres, and colour television sets (1985).

The Technical Study Group on Central Excise Tariff, 1985, made estimates of the relative revenue significance of various forms of excise duty. The share of specific duties (including the specific component of *ad valorem*-cum-specific duties) was estimated at ₹ 8,242.91 crore or 66.7 percent of the total estimated excise revenue of ₹ 12,361.35 crore for the year 1985-86. The rest of the revenue was attributable to *ad valorem* duties. Broadly speaking, specific duties accounted for two-thirds of the revenue and the *ad valorem* duties for the remaining one-third. [8]

The balance further tilted in favour of specific duties as the policy of conversion from *ad valorem* rates to specific rates continued right up to 1990-91. In this connection, the Tax Reforms Committee (Chairman: Raja Chelliah), 1991, observed, "As a result of this gradual shift to more and more specific rates over the years, the share of revenue from specific-rated items has increased from a level of about 46 percent of the total revenue in 1981-82 to 65 percent in 1986-87 and has currently (presumably 1990-91) reached a level of about 70 percent". [9] The Committee examined the advantages and disadvantages of *ad valorem* and specific rates of duty and concluded, "the advantages of having *ad valorem* duties far outweigh the administrative benefits derived by switching over to specific duties. In a system of comprehensive taxation with a wide coverage of MODVAT, it would be necessary to have by and large only *ad valorem* duties in order to ensure a rational system of taxation". [10] Following the recommendations of the Committee, a modest switch over to *ad valorem* rates was made in the 1992-93 budget.

At the time of its subsumation under GST, excise duty was levied at specific rates on cigarettes, coffee, tea, sugar, beverages, mineral fuels, mineral oils, silk, man-made staple fibres, and iron and steel. *Ad valorem* rates of duty predominated for commodities including organic chemicals, pharmaceutical products, leather, footwear, ceramic products, tools and implements, machinery and mechanical appliances, electrical machinery and equipment, and miscellaneous manufactured articles. A few commodities, viz. cotton fabrics, paper and paper boards, were subject to *ad valorem*-cum-specific rates of duty.

2.9 Multiplicity of Excise Tariff

The excise rate structure was provided by the Schedule of the Central Excise Tariff Act, 1985, which included goods ranging from toys to nuclear reactors. The Schedule was divided into 20 sections covering 96 chapters. Goods falling under each chapter were divided and sub-divided into numerous headings and sub-headings. The statutory rate of duty applicable in respect of each item was shown against the appropriate commodity heading/sub-heading. These statutory rates were modified, if necessary, by Government notifications to determine effective rates of duty.

Prior to tax reforms initiated in 1991, excise taxation in India was an interesting example of the multitude of rates which were subject to frequent revisions. Numerous considerations contributed to the complexity of excise rates. The labyrinthine intricacies of the tariff often led to confusion and litigation amongst the taxpayers and revenue authorities.

Commodities such as sewing machines, water coolers, and bicycles, though on the tariff list, were completely exempt from the payment of duty. However, a host of other commodities were subject to a wide amplitude of excise rates. The rate of duty on necessities of life like food products (cheese, butter, vegetable oils), pharmaceutical products, and footwear ranged from 10 to 15 percent *ad valorem.* Rates of excise duty on semi-luxuries like washing machines, tape recorders, refrigerators, and colour televisions ranged from 25 percent to 40 percent *ad valorem.* Luxury items like cosmetics and air-conditioners suffered a high rate of duty ranging from 100 to 110 percent.

Most capital goods, classified under chapter 84 of excise tariff, were subject to duty ranging from 15 to 20 percent *ad* valorem. Some important items under this category were machine tools, cranes, agricultural machinery, textile machinery, printing machinery, calculating machines, automatic data processing machines, and other office machines.

Tobacco items were conspicuous by high rates of duty. Successive upward revision of excise duty on cigarettes was a notable feature of tobacco tariff in India. Upward revision of excise duty on cigarettes was almost an annual feature. No surprise that the commodity earned such nicknames as *annual hardy, old faithful* etc.

Broadly speaking, necessities of life were either exempt or paid a low rate of duty, semi-luxuries were moderately taxed, and luxuries and tobacco products stood out distinctly as high-rated tariff items. Capital goods were subject to a relatively low rate of duty.

2.9.1 Committee on Rationalisation and Simplification of Tax Structure (Chairman: S. Bhoothalingam), 1968: This Committee recommended, *inter alia,* a general excise duty at the rate of 10 percent *ad valorem* on all manufactured products. [11] However, this recommendation was not accepted by the Government.

2.9.2 Indirect Taxation Enquiry Committee (Chairman: L.K. Jha), 1978: This Committee also considered the problem of multiplicity of rates. It recommended a set of four excise rates. The Committee observed, "Instead of a pattern of which some product groups are very heavily taxed while others have remained either totally exempt or have been taxed at very low rates, the attempt should be to tax all consumer products, including those now falling under Tariff Item No. 68, at rates of 10, 20, 30 or 40 percent (cumulative), though some exceptional products may need to be taxed at lower or higher rates on special consideration". [12]

By suggesting a 10 to 40 percent range, the Committee virtually favoured a ceiling on excise rates. The Government disfavoured any drastic regrouping of the then existing rates. In his 1979-80 budget speech the Finance Minister observed, "A major restructuring of the excise tariff has to be ruled out in view of the need for resources and on other pragmatic considerations. Also, there is reason to apprehend that a major departure from the present pattern of excise taxation may upset the balance between different sectors of production". [13]

2.9.3 Technical Study Group on Excise Tariff (Chairman: J. Dutta), 1985: The Study Group favoured a drastic reduction in the number of duty rates to simply duty collection and compliance. The group recommended a band of five duty rates: middle rate, two rates below it and two above. Besides this, it also suggested a *zero rate* category. The middle rate (M) was defined to represent overall average incidence of excise duties. The two rates below this middle rate (L1 and L2) were suggested for adoption for inputs and important items of real mass consumption. The two rates in the upper scale (H1 and H2) could be applied to a few inputs, consumer durables and items consumed largely by the rich. The *zero rate* was recommended for products which deserved exceptional treatment on economic or social or administrative considerations.

The Group attempted only a broad and vague exercise of rate levels in terms of middle, below the middle, and above the middle rates of duty without specifying, even on a tentative basis, the duty rates in numerical terms. By leaving the actual fixation of rates to fiscal authorities, the Group left the exercise wide open.

2.9.4 Task Force on Indirect Taxes (Chairman: Vijay Kelkar), 2002: The Task Force recommended the following excise duty structure (Table 2.2).

Table 2.2: Central Excise Duty Structure Recommended by the Task Force on Indirect Taxes

Rate (percent)	Description of the commodity
0	Life-saving drugs and equipments, security items, food items, necessities and the like, and agricultural products.
6	Processed food products and matches.
14	Standard rate for all items not mentioned against other rates.
20	Motor vehicles, air-conditioners and aerated water.
Separate rates for tobacco products and their substitutes (like pan masala)	

Source: Government of India, Ministry of Finance and Company Affairs, *Report of the Task Force on Indirect Taxes*, December 2002, p. 181.

2.10 Simplification of Excise Tariff

2.10.1 Triple Rate Excise Structure: Multiple rates of commodity taxes were long considered a weakness of the indirect tax system of India. Admitting the problems created by the multiplicity of rates, the Finance Minister in his 1999-2000 budget speech observed, "The multiple rates of indirect tax are generally recognised to be a major source of misclassification, tax evasion and avoidance and cumbersome litigation. The multiplicity also encourages inefficient allocation of resources. Over a 100 countries in the world now enjoy the benefits of a value added tax (VAT) with very small number of rates in each case". [14]

Thus, in a landmark move, the Finance Minister announced in his 1999-2000 budget a triple rate excise structure. In other words, the then existing 11 major ad valorem rates were reduced to 3, viz. a central rate of 16 percent, a merit rate of 8 percent and a demerit rate of 24 percent. This was done by: (a) merging the existing rates of 5 percent, 10 percent and 12 percent into the existing 8 percent rate, (b) creating a new rate of 16 percent by merging the existing 13 percent, 15 percent and 18 percent rates into it, and (c) fixing a new rate of 24 percent in substitution of the existing rate of 25 percent. The initiative of the Finance Minister to rationalise the rate structure of excise system was widely appreciated.

2.11 Excises on Inputs and the Introduction of Modified Value Added Tax (MODVAT) and Central Value Added Tax (CENVAT)

One perennial problem of the Indian excise system was the taxation of inputs (raw materials, components, and other intermediates) and the resulting cascading effect on the prices of final products. Prior to the Second Five Year Plan (1956-61), excise coverage was limited to consumer goods with the notable exception of steel ingots. However, the need for additional resources for successive Plans necessitated extension of the excise net to capital goods and raw materials. Various inputs like internal combustion engines, aluminium, cotton yarn, woollen yarn, fertilisers, chemicals, were brought within the excise ambit. The disadvantages of input excises are well-known. [15] However, levies on inputs formed an integral part of the excise system in India for reasons of sheer administrative convenience.

2.11.1 Pre-MODVAT Arrangements: Prior to 1986, excise duty was levied on both inputs used and the output produced. This meant that an amount paid as tax on the input was subject to taxation again at the output level (with limited set offs). This was applicable to each intermediate good in the manufacturing process. This *tax on tax* led to cascading of taxes. This problem was sought to be addressed by the VAT regime under which tax paid on the inputs was deducted from the tax payable on the output. Similarly, sales tax also had a cascading effect through the distribution chain.

Prior to the introduction of MODVAT in 1986, there were provisions in the Central Excises and Salt Rules, 1944, under which certain inputs were exempted from taxation to minimise the cumulative effect of excise levies. Thus, Rule 56-A of the said Rules, introduced in 1962, allowed the manufacturers of certain notified finished excisable goods to bring excise-paid components (for example compressors for refrigerators) to take credit for the said duty in the Proforma Credit Account to get adjustment of duty on the final excisable good.

The Indirect Taxation Enquiry Committee (Chairman: L.K. Jha), 1978, which made an in-depth study of the cascading effect of input excises, recommended a wider extension of Rule 56-A to products falling under different tariff items. The same Committee recommended also the introduction of value added tax (VAT) at the manufacturing stage, called MANVAT, to tackle the problem of cascading effect of excise taxation.

The Long Term Fiscal Policy Statement (December 1985) also envisaged the extension of the Proforma Credit Scheme and observed, "The basic approach will be to move towards an extension of the present system of proforma credit to all excisable commodities with the exception of a few like petroleum, tobacco, and textile products. This programme would amount to a modified system of VAT or MODVAT for short. The programme will be implemented in a phased manner over a period of years, taking due account of the revenue implications, the need to revise administrative procedures and the lessons from experience gained in the early stages of the reform". [16]

In pursuance of the proposal made in the Long Term Fiscal Policy Statement, the Government introduced MODVAT with effect from March 1, 1986. It was introduced for a selected number of commodities and in a step-by-step manner for all commodities in terms of CENVAT in 2002-03.

2.11.2 MODVAT Scheme: Features and advantages of MODVAT scheme were as under.

MODVAT scheme provided for instant and complete reimbursement of excise duty and additional duty of customs (countervailing duty) paid on the components and raw materials when used in the manufacture of the final products. Articles which were not used as inputs in the manufacturing process were not eligible for credit under this scheme.

Initially, the MODVAT scheme covered 38 chapters of the schedule to the Central Excise Tariff Act, 1985. These chapters pertained to the products of chemical and allied industries, paints and packaging materials, plastics, glass and glassware, rubber products, base metals and articles of base metals, machinery and mechanical appliances including electrical equipment, motor vehicles, and certain miscellaneous manufactured products. In 1987, the scheme was extended to all the remaining chapters (except those relating to textiles, tobacco, and the petroleum sector). The extension covered food products, mineral products, leather and travel goods, footwear, paper and paper-board, wood and cork products, asbestos cement products, and precious metals. As long as the inputs and the final products were covered by the specified chapters, credit of duty on inputs was available. In 1994, MODVAT scheme was extended to tobacco, fibres, yarn and fabrics, and petroleum products (excluding motor spirit and high speed diesel oil) used as input.

MODVAT scheme was further expanded and rationalised in the sense that all inputs (excepting motor spirit and high speed diesel oil) and all capital goods were included in the eligible list of MODVAT scheme. However, the availability of MODVAT credit on capital goods was spread over a period of 2 years.

A. Features: The features of the MODVAT scheme were as follows:

1. The credit under MODVAT was available to a manufacturer of a final product only if the final product was dutiable. Where the final product manufactured by a manufacturer was exempt from excise duty then no credit of the duty paid on the inputs was available. Credit was allowed only after the evidence of payment of duty was received by the excise department.
2. Where the same input was used for different finished products, some of which were not dutiable, the credit of duty was allowed only for that part attributable to inputs

which were used for the manufacture of dutiable finished products.

3. Credit of the duty paid on the inputs under the MODVAT scheme could be utilised for payment of duty on the final products in which the inputs were used.
4. Under the MODVAT scheme, credit of duty was not restricted to raw materials and components only but covered all specified inputs which were used in the manufacture of final products.
5. Machines, plant, equipments, apparatus, tools or appliances used in the manufacture of the final products were not covered by the term *inputs* for the purpose of MODVAT benefits.
6. Under the MODVAT scheme, inputs could be either procured from outside or manufactured within the factory. In either case, the duty credit was available to the extent of duty actually paid.

The Government had made it clear in its Long Term Fiscal Policy Statement (1985) that the proposed MODVAT scheme was to be broadly revenue-neutral. Thus, along with the introduction of MODVAT which considerably reduced the cost of final products, the rates of duty on final products were suitably revised upwards by the Finance Act, 1986, to retain the collection of excise duties at the earlier level. This was justified on grounds of resource mobilisation for the Five Year Plans.

B. Advantages: MODVAT scheme had the following advantages:

1. It aimed at making excise levies transparent so that the effective rate of taxation on a particular commodity could be known. This information was helpful in undertaking meaningful studies of excise incidence. The results of these studies could be used to control excise burden on different commodities to ensure the desired degree of progressivity in the excise levies.
2. It sought to avoid cascading effects associated with a traditional turnover tax. In particular, it worked as a cost-saving device through the availability of instant credit of the duties paid on the inputs and the consequent reduction of the interest costs.
3. MODVAT scheme improved the competitive strength of the small-scale sector by allowing credit of duty which could be in excess of the duty actually paid on the inputs made by the small-scale units.
4. MODVAT scheme encouraged indigenisation because full set off was available when indigenous inputs were used. However, no credit of basic and auxiliary customs duties was permissible on imported materials and components. Although MODVAT scheme provided for set off of countervailing duty [17], this element of import duty was not very significant in comparison with other elements of import duty, viz. basic and auxiliary duties. As the scope of MODVAT was widened, the process of indigenisation gathered momentum.
5. MODVAT scheme was designed to encourage exports by making them more competitive in the international market. Since MODVAT allowed set off through different stages of production, the final duty became clear on final goods which could be exported without payment of duty under bond. The payment of duty drawback was swifter in view of the transparency of excise duty.

6. MODVAT checked excise evasion because credit of input duty could not be claimed unless actual production was declared to the excise authorities.
7. MODVAT scheme also helped to reduce the number of disputes—arising on account of classifications requiring lower or higher rates of duty—because the duty element on a large number of components became irrelevant for manufacturers in view of set off. Previously, a selective set off triggered disputes as regards the eligibility of an input for set off. The introduction of Harmonised System Nomenclature in 1986 further reduced the scope for ambiguities.

Some experts felt that MODVAT was old wine in a new bottle because the facility under it was practically the same as was available under Rule 56-A as mentioned above. In other words, MODVAT scheme was only an extension and liberalisation of the proforma credit facility already in operation. Though some degree of similarity did exist, the two schemes could not be termed identical. Rule 56-A scheme was restrictive and had several procedural formalities, e.g. a manufacturer had to intimate the Excise Department about the arrival of input materials for verification by the excise officials. Moreover, it was applicable on a commodity-to-commodity basis and involved discretion in taking decisions. MODVAT scheme was more comprehensive and rule-based and therefore curtailed the discretionary powers of the Excise Department. MODVAT credit on inputs could be availed on the basis of a duplicate copy of the invoice.

The Tax Reforms Committee (Chairman: Raja Chelliah), 1991, examined, *inter alia,* the scope of extending the MODVAT scheme and observed, "there is no alternative to gradually transforming the present excise tax system, consisting of two parts, namely: (a) MODVAT, and (b) excise on gross value basis with no set off for some sectors, into a genuine VAT at the manufacturing level. Manufacturing and such a VAT should include also the 'manufacture' of services although some services may be exempted on practical considerations". [18]

2.11.3 Introduction of CENVAT: As already noted, in his 1999-2000 budget, the Finance Minister had introduced three ad valorem rates of basic excise duty, namely 8 percent, 16 percent and 24 percent. Furthering the reform of excise taxation, the 2000-01 budget introduced a single rate CENVAT by converging the three ad valorem rates to a single rate of 16 percent. The 8 percent excise rate was abolished and most of the items under it were moved to 16 percent rate. Similarly, items that were mainly in the nature of raw materials or intermediates were moved from the 24 percent rate to 16 percent CENVAT. However, in addition to the 16 percent CENVAT rate, three rates of special excise, viz. 8 percent, 16 percent, and 24 percent were introduced. While the CENVAT rate was modvatable, the special excise duties were not, i.e. users could not avail of MODVAT credit of these duties. Some of the commodities on which special excise duties applied included white cement, glazed tiles, cosmetics, air conditioners, aerated water and chewing tobacco. Since these commodities were not in the nature of inputs therefore they were not modvatable.

The standard rate of excise duty (CENVAT) was brought down to 8 percent after two successive reductions in December 2008 and February 2009. It was increased to 10 percent in the Budget for 2010-11. It was further increased to 12 percent in the Budget for 2012-13 and remained the same for the financial year 2013-14 and 2014-15.

Undoubtedly, the Government provided a stable excise system to create confidence among the entrepreneurs, particularly the prospective ones, so that they could plan their investment and production without the Damocles sword of excise changes hanging over their heads. The application of CENVAT at fewer rates and the new system of CENVAT credits resulted in fewer classification disputes, reduced tax cascading, and greater neutrality of the tax. It was also hoped that CENVAT would encourage the State Governments to implement their agreed programme for converting their sales tax into VAT by April 1, 2001.

However, CENVAT was levied on goods manufactured or produced in India. This gave rise to definitional issues as to what constituted manufacturing, and valuation issues for determining the value on which the tax was to be levied. While these concepts had evolved through judicial rulings, it was recognized that limiting the tax to the point of manufacturing was a severe impediment to an efficient and neutral application of tax. Manufacturing itself formed a narrow base.

Moreover, the effective burden of tax became dependent on the supply chain, i.e. the taxable value at the point of manufacturing relative to the value added beyond this point. It was for this reason that virtually all countries had abandoned this form of taxation and replaced it by multi-point taxation system extending to the retail level.

The starting base for the CENVAT was narrow, and was further eroded by a variety of area-specific, and conditional and unconditional exemptions.

Under the Constitution, the Central Government was empowered to impose excise duty on goods produced or manufactured. It had no power to carry forward the tax up to the retail stage. Thus, CENVAT was a kind of VAT at the manufacturing stage. In any case, it paved the way for a national VAT.

2.12 Exemptions and Concessions

2.12.1 Rationale: As in other countries, exemptions and concessions were an integral part of the excise system. Excise preferences and reliefs were given to promote a wide spectrum of socio-economic objectives. Exemptions/concessions were justified on following grounds:

1. Exemptions/concessions ensured progressivity in the structure of commodity taxation.
2. They induced entrepreneurs to undertake activities which they would have otherwise shrunk, e.g. adopting labour-intensive techniques of production.
3. They were designed to promote enterprises deemed *vital* by society (though it is controversial as to which activities are *vital* and require governmental support).
4. Exemptions/concessions provided the desired flexibility to the tax system to deal with changing market situation. They were used as a corrective mechanism to stabilise demand, production, and profits of different industries.
5. Due to continuous diversification of the economy and inflation, markets for various

commodities had not remained stable in India after Independence. Because of the changing market conditions, the levels of profit in different industries had also been fluctuating and on balance had shown a rising trend. Excise rates, it was argued, should be modified upward to mop up excess profits and downward to boost sluggish demand for idle-capacity industries.

6. Exemptions were sometimes granted on administrative considerations. The duty on unmanufactured tobacco was abolished in 1979 mainly on account of the administrative difficulty of assessing and collecting duty from a large number of growers, and curers. Similarly, exemption of smaller of the small industries was also due to administrative problems. Agricultural products were also exempt owing to the same reason.

2.12.2 General Exemptions: There were various general exemptions which purported to serve a wide variety of socio-economic objectives. Thus, goods of the following description were exempt from the whole of the duty of excise leviable thereon.

1. All excisable goods, produced in a technical, educational and research institute during the course of imparting technical training of an academic or vocational nature.
2. All excisable goods donated for the welfare of defence personnel.
3. All excisable goods donated to the National Defence Fund or to the Ministry of Defence.
4. Excisable goods, supplied as stores for consumption on board a vessel of the Indian navy.
5. All excisable goods sent abroad as exhibits in any international trade fair or exhibition.

Apart from these general exemptions, excise tariff was extensively used to serve a host of other objectives including export promotion, industrial development, and mopping up a part of high profits earned by certain industries.

2.12.3 Labour-intensive Technology: Excise exemptions and concessions were particularly important in promoting labour-intensive technology and small-scale industries. Central excise law contained provisions the sole objective of which was employment generation. Products of a number of industries were exempt from excise duty if they were manufactured without the aid of power. Duty differentials were used to discourage mechanisation in certain industries.

Similarly, concessions were available to the handloom sector of the textile industry. Processed *khadi* cloth woven on handloom wholly from hand spun cotton yarn or in admixture with similar silk and/or woollen yarn enjoyed full exemption since 1969. Cotton fabrics manufactured on handlooms and processed by a factory owned by a registered handloom co-operative society enjoyed full exemption from duty.

The Expert Committee on Tax Measures to Promote Employment (Chairman: V.M. Dandekar), 1980, made estimates of the annual cost of protecting or subsidising employment through concessions in excise duties. It found that the annual cost of protecting or subsidising employment through concessions in excise duties was ₹ 523 per full-time worker in the handloom industry, ₹ 881 in *khandasari*, and ₹ 2,669 in the cottage sector of the match industry. [19]

2.12.4 Concessions to Small Industries: In line with Government's policy of encouraging small-scale industries, a wide range of concessions and exemptions from excise duty was available to small producers to enable them to stand in competition with large-scale manufacturers. Also, relatively simple and concessional procedures were followed for the assessment and collection of excises from the small-scale sector. As a part of the Comprehensive Policy Package on SSI and Tiny Sector announced by the Prime Minister on August 30, 2000, the excise exemption limit for SSI was raised from ₹ 50 lakh to ₹ 1 crore with effect from September 1, 2000.

As regards duty exemption for the small-scale sector, the Task Force on Indirect Taxes (Chairman: Vijay Kelkar), 2002 recommended as under:

- Duty exemption should be extended to only small units with a turnover of ₹ 50 lakh.
- Duty exemption limit for the larger SSI units should be gradually brought down to ₹ 50 lakh as per the following time frame: from ₹ 100 lakh to ₹ 75 lakh by the year 2004-05 and from ₹ 75 lakh to ₹ 50 lakh by the year 2005-06.

2.12.5 Problems Created by Exemptions/Concessions: These were as follows:

1. Excise concessions narrowed the tax base and therefore adversely affected government revenues.
2. Excise concessions interfered with the designing of the excise system and led to complexities in the excise law which, in turn, led to tax evasion and litigation.
3. They also obscured the evaluation of excise system, particularly from equity angle.
4. Excise concession to a particular industry led to a chain reaction (i.e. similar demands by other industries), causing unsettling effects on producers, consumers, and the administration.
5. Exemptions/concessions were often the result of persistent representations and pressure tactics by industry and trade than any economic justification.
6. It was not always possible to segregate the effects of duty reduction on production, costs, prices, and consumption because duty concessions operated in conjunction with other non-tax policy measures to affect the production process.

2.12.6 Misuse of Concessions: Though preferential treatment to small units and labour-intensive methods of production was desirable, the misuse of these concessions created doubts as regards the ultimate beneficiaries of such facilities. Concerned about the misuse of excise concessions, the Finance Minister in his 2001-2002 budget speech announced the withdrawal of exemption on certain items and observed, "Products of SSI are exempt from excise duty up to ₹ 1 crore. This exemption is intended to provide fiscal support to the genuinely small producers. I propose to withdraw this exemption in respect of the following items, in which misuse of the exemption is more than likely: (a) cotton yarn, (b) ball or roller bearings, and (c) arms and ammunition for private use". [20]

It was well-established that certain products—particularly footwear, domestic electrical appliances, electronic goods, and wires and cables—were purchased on a fairly large scale by established concerns from the exempted sector and marketed in the brand names of such concerns. However, under a scheme introduced in 1986, a small-scale manufacturer of excisable goods was allowed to clear his goods with the brand name of another manufacturer and was eligible for exemption for such clearances. Clearly, the small producers depended heavily on private marketing organisations to sell their products and this dependence needed to be reduced by strengthening and building up co-operatives and other officially sponsored marketing organisations to market the products of small sector.

Endnotes

1. Petroleum and petroleum products have been constitutionally included as *goods* under GST. However, it has also been provided that petroleum and petroleum products shall not be subject to the levy of GST till notified at a future date on the recommendation of the GST Council. The present taxes levied by the Centre and the States on petroleum and petroleum products—excise duty/CENVAT by the Centre and sales tax/VAT by the States—will continue to be levied in the interim period. The five petroleum products which have been kept in abeyance for the purpose of GST are the following: (a) petroleum crude, (b) motor spirit (petrol), (c) high speed diesel, (d) natural gas, and (e) aviation turbine fuel.
   Tobacco and tobacco products would be subject to GST. In addition, the Centre would have the power to levy Central excise duty on these products.
2. Section 17 of the Constitution (One Hundred and First Amendment) Act, 2016 substituted the following entry for the old Entry 84: "84. Duties of excise on the following goods manufactured or produced in India, namely: (a) petroleum crude; (b) high speed diesel; (c) motor spirit (commonly known as petrol); (d) natural gas; (e) aviation turbine fuel; and (f) tobacco and tobacco products.
3. Section 6 of the Constitution (One Hundred and First Amendment) Act, 2016 abolished the duties of excise on medicinal and toilet preparations.
4. Government of India, Ministry of Finance, *Report of the Taxation Enquiry Commission,* (Chairman: John Matthai), 1953-54, Vol. II, p. 323.
5. Government of India, *Long Term Fiscal Policy*, 1985, p. 25.
6. For conceptual clarifications regarding specific and ad valorem duties, see section 1.5 of chapter 1 of this book.
7. Government of India, Ministry of Finance, *Speeches of Union Finance Ministers, 1947-48 to 1984-85,* p. 313.
8. Government of India, Ministry of Finance, *Report of the Technical Study Group on Central Excise Tariff,* Part I, 1985, Table 6, p. 7.
9. Government of India, Ministry of Finance, *Interim Report of the Tax Reforms Committee,* (Chairman: Raja Chelliah), 1991, p. 113.
10. *Ibid.*, p.114.
11. Government of India, Ministry of Finance, *Final Report on Rationalisation and Simplification of Tax Structure,* (Chairman: S. Bhoothalingam), 1968, p. 8.
12. Government of India, Ministry of Finance, *Report of the Indirect Taxation Enquiry Committee,* (Chairman: L.K. Jha), Part II, 1978, p. 174.
13. *Speeches of Union Finance Ministers,* op. cit., p. 459.
14. Government of India, Ministry of Finance, *Budget Speech of the Finance Minister*, 1999-2000, Part B, p. 21.
15. Excises on inputs enhance costs and profits and therefore increase the prices of goods much more than the amount of excise collected. The cost of production increases because producers and middlemen require larger amounts of working capital to maintain the necessary stocks of inputs. Prices of finished products tend to reflect taxes imposed on inputs used. If the middlemen apply fixed percentage mark ups to purchase prices as their profit and if the

purchase prices include taxes, the mark ups will be applicable to the tax component of the purchase price as well. In other words, increase in the price of the manufactures is in excess of the excise revenue accruing from input taxes.

Further still, excises on inputs may promote vertical integration in an industry, a trend which is harmful to the growth of small-scale sector. Lastly, input excises impose an inequitable burden on different economic classes by not discriminating between essential and non-essential uses of a product. For example, an excise on aluminium hits indiscriminately the use of the product for decoration purpose as well as for making utensils (generally used by the poor).

Notwithstanding the various disadvantages of input excises, governments in many countries impose duties on inputs due to administrative convenience. Many items of inputs are the end-product of one manufacturer but merely a component for another (e.g. tyres and tubes) and are also used as replacement items. Exemption of such items will be discrimination in favour of replacement consumption and certain commodities (say motor cars) may be sold with avoidable components and accessories stripped off. Moreover, provisions can be made in tax laws to minimise the cascading effects of input excises.

16. *Long Term Fiscal Policy,* op. cit., p. 38.
17. It is an element of import duty equivalent to excise duty on domestically produced goods.
18. Government of India, Ministry of Finance, *Final Report of the Tax Reforms Committee,* (Chairman: Raja Chelliah), Part I, 1992, p. 36.
19. Government of India, Ministry of Finance, *Report of the Expert Committee on Tax Measures to Promote Employment* (Chairman: V.M. Dandekar), 1980, pp. 91, 113 and 117.
20. Government of India, Ministry of Finance, *Budget Speech of the Finance Minister, 2001-2002, Part B*, p. 27.

3

Taxation of Services by the Central Government

Service sector is very wide in its range. It includes, *inter alia*, healthcare, education, social security, leasing, entertainment, credit rating agencies, telecommunications, transport, publicity and advertising, insurance, banking, legal and financial services.

Prior to the introduction of GST, Indian tax system traditionally relied on commodity taxation for generating revenue for the Central and State Governments. The two major commodity taxes of the Central Government were excise duties and customs duties while at the level of the States, sales tax/VAT was the main commodity tax.

The extension of excise duties to more and more commodities of the industrial/manufacturing sector reached a saturation point in due course of time. However, the service sector remained outside the tax net till 1994. This pattern of tax structure development in India was contrary to the experience of most other countries where taxation of commodities and services grew hand in hand.

The introduction of service tax on a limited number of services from July 1, 1994 ushered in a major structural change in indirect taxes in the form of a wider tax base and facilitated the process of rationalization of excise duties, resulting in lower tax burden on productive sectors. Over the years, the number of services subject to tax increased and so also the rate leviable on them.

3.1 Constitutional Provisions

The Central Government had no specific powers to tax services when it introduced service tax on select services from July 1, 1994. It was done under its residual powers of taxation vide entry 97 of List I (Union List) in the Seventh Schedule of the constitution. The tax extended to the whole of India except the State of Jammu and Kashmir. The service tax being an indirect tax, its administrative control was vested with the Central Board of Excise and Customs (CBEC). The sharing of the revenue from service tax was on the basis of the recommendations of the Finance Commission, as applicable to other central taxes.

However, the Constitution (Eighty-eighth Amendment) Act, 2003 put service tax in List I (Union List) of the Seventh Schedule by inserting Entry 92C in that List. Furthermore, this amendment inserted a new Article 268A which provided for service tax to be levied by the Union and collected and appropriated by the Union and the States. The new Article was as follows:

268A. "(1) Taxes on services shall be levied by the Government of India and such tax shall be collected and appropriated by the Government of India and the States in the manner provided in clause (2).

(2) The proceeds in any financial year of any such tax levied in accordance with the

provisions of clause (1) shall be:

(a) collected by the Government of India and the States;

(b) appropriated by the Government of India and the States;

in accordance with such principles of collection and appropriation as may be formulated by Parliament by law".

Thus, Article 268A specified that the principles of collection and appropriation of taxes on services will be determined by Parliament. In other words, the revenue from taxation of services was excluded from the purview of the Finance Commission.

In this connection, the Twelfth Finance Commission remarked, "With service taxes having been excluded from the ambit of the recommendations of the finance commission, the idea of an overall shareable pool of central taxes appears to be in the process of being reversed. While service taxes are likely to prove highly buoyant in the near future, these will not be subjected to sharing with the states under the Constitution, although other statutory arrangements can be made, which can include sharing as well as assignment. It may be noted that hitherto items under Articles 268 and 269 were subjects that were generally of inter-state nature with limited revenue importance. These were wholly assigned to the states. In this context, it needs to be stressed that any legislation passed by Parliament with respect to appropriation of service tax proceeds must take care to ensure that the revenue accruing to the states through any proposed changes should not be less than the share that would accrue to them, had the entire service tax proceeds been part of the shareable pool". [1]

It is noteworthy that the above mentioned provisions (Entry 92C and Article 268A) of Constitution (Eighty-eighth Amendment) Act, 2003 were never brought into force. These two items were omitted by the Constitution (One Hundred and First Amendment) Act, 2016 to pave way for the introduction of goods and services tax (GST).

3.2 Introduction and Widening of Service Tax

In view of the need for additional resources, rising contribution of service sector to GDP and the recommendations of Tax Reforms Committee, 1991, a modest effort was made in the 1994-95 budget when a 5 percent tax was imposed on telephone and non-life insurance services and services of stock brokers with effect from July 1, 1994. The coverage of service tax was extended to advertising, courier and radio paging services from November 1, 1996.

In his 1997-98 budget speech, the Finance Minister maintained that services are products as much as manufactured goods and hence both must bear taxes. With these considerations in view he extended the service tax to the services provided by the following: transporters of goods by road, consulting engineers, custom houses, steamer and clearing and forwarding agents, air travel agents, tour operators and car rental agencies, outdoor caterers, *pandal* contractors and *mandap* keepers, and manpower recruitment agencies.

In the 1998-99 budget, service tax on the transportation of goods by road, outdoor caterers, and *pandal* contractors was abolished. However, its net was extended to services provided by architects, interior decorators, management consultants, chartered accountants, cost accountants, company secretaries, private security services, real estate agents and real estate consultants, market research agencies, credit rating agencies, underwriting agencies, and slaughter houses using mechanised means for large animals.

Acknowledging the potential of service tax, the Finance Minister in his 2000-2001 budget speech announced the setting up of an Expert Group to go into all its aspects and make suitable recommendations. The net of service tax was greatly expanded when the following 15 services were added to the list of taxable services in the 2001-02 budget.

1. Specified banking and financial services.
2. Authorised service stations for servicing of vehicles including two wheelers.
3. Port services.
4. Broadcasting services.
5. Photographic services.
6. Convention services.
7. Sound recording services.
8. Scientific and technical consulting services.
9. Telex services.
10. Telegraph services.
11. Facsimile services.
12. Online information and data base retrieval services.
13. Video tape production services.
14. Services auxiliary to insurance.
15. Services provided to lease circuit line holders.

In his 2004-05 budget speech, the Finance Minister announced the inclusion of some more services under the service tax ambit. These were the following.

1. Business exhibition services.
2. Airport services.
3. Services provided by transport booking agents.
4. Transport of goods by air.
5. Survey and exploration services.
6. Opinion poll services.
7. Intellectual property services other than copyright.
8. Brokers of forward contracts.
9. *Pandal* and *shamiana* contractors.
10. Outdoor caterers.
11. Independent TV/radio programme producers.
12. Construction services in respect of commercial or industrial constructions.
13. Life insurance services to the extent of the risk premium.

In the 2005-06 budget, the following 9 items were added to the list of taxable services.

1. Transport of goods through pipeline or other conduit.
2. Site preparation and clearance, excavation, earth moving and demolition services, other than those provided to agriculture, irrigation and watershed development.

3. Dredging services of rivers, ports, harbours, backwaters and estuaries.
4. Survey and map making other than by Government Departments.
5. Cleaning services other than in relation to agriculture, horticulture, animal husbandry or dairying.
6. Membership of clubs or associations.
7. Packaging services.
8. Mailing list compilation and mailing.
9. Construction of residential complexes having more than twelve residential units of apartments together with common areas and other appurtenances.

The 2005-06 budget also expanded the scope of certain existing services in the following manner.

1. Commercial or industrial construction services to include renovation of such building or civil structure, post-construction completion and finishing services for such building or civil structure, construction, repair, alteration, renovation or restoration of pipeline or conduits.
2. Erection, commissioning or installation services to include specified installation services.
3. Maintenance or repair services to include maintenance or management of immovable properties, maintenance or repair including reconditioning or restoration undertaken as part of any contract or agreement.
4. Broadcasting services to include charges recovered by broadcasting agencies from multi-system operator and provision of direct to home signals to the customers.
5. Sound recording to include recording of sound on any media and includes post-production services such as sound mixing or re-mixing.
6. Videotape production to include recording of any programme, event or function on any media and includes post-production services.
7. Taxable services provided by authorised service station to include reconditioning or restoration of motor cars, two wheeled and light motor vehicles.
8. Beauty parlour services to include all services provided by beauty parlours.
9. Manpower recruitment services to include supply of manpower, temporary or otherwise.
10. Franchisee services to cover all agreements by which the franchisor grants representational rights to franchise to sell or manufacture goods or provide services identified with the franchisor.
11. Business auxiliary services to include production or processing of goods for or on behalf of the client.
12. Outdoor catering services to include catering from a place or premises provided by way of tenancy or otherwise by the person receiving such services.

The budget for 2006-07 added the following new services under the service tax net.

1. Services provided by registrars to capital issues.
2. Services provided by share transfer agents.
3. Automated teller machine operations, maintenance or management.

4. Services provided by recovery agents.
5. Sale of space or time for advertisements, other than in print media.
6. Sponsorship services provided to anybody, corporate or firm, other than sponsorship of sports events.
7. Transport of passengers, other than economy class passengers, embarking on international journey by air.
8. Transport of goods in containers by rail by any person.
9. Business support services.
10. Auctioneers' services, other than auction of property under directions or orders of a court of law or auction by the Central Government.
11. Public relation services.
12. Ship management services.
13. Internet telephony services.
14. Transport of persons by cruise ship.
15. Credit card, debit card, charge card or other payment card related services.

In the 2007-08 budget, service tax net was extended to the following services.

1. Services outsourced for mining of minerals, oil or gas.
2. Renting of immovable property for use in commerce or business.
3. Development and supply of content for use in telecom and advertising purposes.
4. Asset management services provided by individuals.
5. Design services.

The budget for 2011-12 retained the service tax rate at 10 percent (increased to 12 percent in the budget for 2012-13) and focused on achieving a closer fit between the existing service tax regime and the proposed GST. This was sought to be done by: (a) adding a few new services on the ability-to-pay principle, (b) expanding or rationalizing the scope of existing services, (c) rationalizing certain provisions relating to important services and valuation, and (d) modifying provisions of the CENVAT credit scheme seeking to effect the right balance between input credits and output tax, and harmonizing the provisions of the scheme across goods and services, incentivizing honesty and penalizing dishonesty in compliance, and adoption of point of taxation rules to facilitate accrual basis of the collection.

Besides, the budget for 2011-12 imposed service tax on the following services:

1. Services provided by air-conditioned restaurants having a licence to serve alcoholic beverages in relation to serving of food and/or beverages.
2. Short-term accommodation provided by a hotel, inn, guesthouse, club or campsite, or any other similar establishment for a continuous period of less than three months.

Scope of certain existing services was expanded or altered as under:

1. Scope of *life insurance services* was widened to cover all services provided to a policy holder or any person, by an insurer, including re-insurer carrying on life insurance business. Tax to be charged on the portion of the premium other than what is allocated for investment, when the break-up of premium is shown separately in any document given to the policy holder. Rate of composition increased from 1 percent to 1.5 percent.

2. Scope of *club or association services* expanded to include services provided to non-members within its ambit.
3. Scope of the service of *authorized service stations* expanded to: (a) include services provided by any person; (b) cover all motor vehicles other than those meant for goods carriage and three-wheeler scooter (auto-rickshaws); and (c) cover decoration and other similar services in respect of vehicles along with the services already covered.
4. Definition of *business support services* amended so as to include services provided by way of operational or administrative assistance in any manner.
5. Scope of legal consultancy services expanded by bringing within their ambit: (a) services provided by a business entity to individuals in relation to advice, consultancy, or assistance in any branch of law, in any manner; (b) representational services provided by any person to any business entity (representational services provided to individuals to continue to be exempt); and (c) arbitration services provided by an arbitral tribunal to any business entity.
6. In commercial training or coaching services, the definition of *commercial training or coaching centre* amended so as to bring all unrecognized courses within the tax net, irrespective of the fact that such courses were conducted by an institute which also conducted courses that might lead to grant of a degree or diploma.

Certain exemptions were extended as follows:

1. Exemption provided to services rendered in relation to business exhibitions held abroad.
2. An abatement of 25 percent from the taxable value provided for the purpose of levy of service tax under *transport of goods through coastal and inland shipping*.
3. Exemption provided to *works contract* services rendered for construction or finishing of new residential complexes under the Jawaharlal Nehru National Urban Renewal Mission and Rajiv Awaas Yojana.
4. Exemption provided to services rendered within a port or other port or an airport under *works contract* services for specified areas.
5. Exemption provided to the Rashtriya Swasthya Bima Yojana under general insurance service.
6. Value of air freight included in the assessable value of goods for charging customs duties excluded from taxable value for the purpose of levy of service tax under *transport of goods by air* services.
7. Services related to transportation of goods by road, rail, or air when origin and destination are located outside India exempted from service tax.
8. A modified scheme introduced to refund service tax to SEZ units and developers.
9. Some existing exemptions on domestic and international travel and club or association services were withdrawn.

Keeping in view the social objectives of state policy, the Government of India refrained from taxing services in the field of health and education. [2]

3.3 Revenue Significance of Service Tax

Table 3.1 records the growth in revenue from service tax in India.

For the financial year 2016-17, the standard rate of service tax was 14 percent. In addition Swacch Bharat Cess @ 0.5 percent was also leviable. From June 1, 2016, Krishi Kalyan Cess @ 0.5 percent was also leviable.

Table 3.1: Trends in the Relative Significance of Service Tax in Gross Tax Revenues* of the Central Government: 1994-95 to 2016-17

(₹ crore)

Year	Gross Central Taxes	Revenue from Service Tax	Col. 3 as % of Col. 2
1	2	3	4
1994-95	92,297	407	0.4
1995-96	1,11,224	862	0.8
1996-97	1,29,762	1,059	0.8
1997-98	1,39,220	1,586	1.1
1998-99	1,43,797	1,957	1.4
1999-00	1,71,752	2,128	1.2
2000-01	1,88,603	2,613	1.4
2001-02	1,87,060	3,302	1.8
2002-03	2,15,905	4,122	1.9
2003-04	2,54,348	7,891	3.1
2004-05	3,04,957	14,200	4.7
2005-06	3,66,151	23,055	6.3
2006-07	4,73,513	37,598	7.9
2007-08	5,93,147	51,301	8.6
2008-09	6,05,298	60,941	10.1
2009-10	6,24,527	58,422	9.4
2010-11	7,93,072	71,016	9.0
2011-12	8,89,176	97,509	11.0
2012-13	10,36,235	1,32,601	12.8
2013-14	11,38,734	1,54,778	13.6
2014-15	12,44,885	1,67,969	13.5
2015-16	14,59,611	2,10,000	14.4
2016-17	16,30,888	2,31,000	14.2

* Before transferring States' share in Central taxes.

2015-16 = Revised estimates; 2016-17 = Budget estimates.

Sources: Government of India, Ministry of Finance, *Explanatory Memorandum on the Budget of the Central Government* (various years); *Receipts Budget* (various years); and *Budget at a Glance*, 2016-17.

3.4 Service Tax: A Critique

The expanding base of service tax provided a promising source of revenue, but there were some caveats which had to be kept in mind. First, the scope for expanding the service tax net to more and more services got narrower as the net was widened. The contribution of the expanding net, therefore, reduced over time. Second, the preponderance of small service providers below the taxable limit of turnover constrained the scope of revenue mobilization beyond a certain level.

The introduction of the service tax was a mixed blessing. While it broadened the tax base, its structure was complex. The tax was levied on specified services, classified into one hundred odd different categories. This approach spawned many disputes about the scope of each category. Unlike goods, services are malleable, and can and are often packaged into composite bundles that include taxable as well as non-taxable elements. Also, there is no standardized nomenclature for services, such as the Harmonised System Nomenclature (HSN) for goods.

Furthermore, there was a complicated rate structure. Although there was one statutory rate, in practice there were 10 other rates because of the so-called *abatement* which amounted to fixing a rate different from the standard rate and not allowing further input tax credits. Abatement was necessitated, in some part, because of uncertainty in the base, and specifically being unable to distinguish *goods* from *services*. Further, there was incomplete provision of input tax crediting for goods, and incomplete cross-crediting between goods and services. Added to this was the Central sales tax (CST) which was levied on the sale or purchase of goods in the course of inter-State trade.

The key problem with the service tax was the basic approach of levying it on specified services, each of which generated an extensive debate as to what was included in the base. Ideally, the tax base should be defined to include all services, with a limited list of exclusions (the so-called negative list). The Government was reluctant to adopt this approach for the fear that it could bring into the tax net many services that are politically sensitive. [3]

Service tax was abolished by Section 17 of Constitution (One Hundred and First Amendment) Act, 2016 to pave way for the introduction of GST.

Endnotes

1. Report of the Twelfth Finance Commission (2005-10), November 2004, pp. 15-16.
2. In the case of excise and sales tax also, commodities such as medicines and books were either exempt or taxed at very low rates.
3. As late as from July 1, 2012, the concept of taxation on services was changed from a Positive List of services to a Negative List regime. This changed the taxation system of services from tax on the specified services to tax being levied on all services, other than those mentioned in the Negative List or which were exempted by a notification.

4

State Level Sales Tax/Value Added Tax (VAT)

Prior to the introduction of GST, taxation of goods by the States was characterized by a base (sales) that extended all the way to the retail stage. Lists of exemptions, rates of taxation, compounding schemes and rules and regulations varied across States. It was a nightmare for a business entity doing business in more than one State.

4.1 Sales Tax during Pre-Independence Period

Entry 48 of List II in the Seventh Schedule of the Government of India Act, 1935, vested in the Provinces the power to levy 'taxes on the sale of goods and on advertisements'.

The Government of the Central Provinces (now Madhya Pradesh) was the first to take advantage of this provision when it levied a retail sales tax on motor spirit and lubricants in 1938. This so-called *petrol tax* was a selective sales tax imposed through the Central Provinces and Berar Sales of Motor Spirit and Lubrication Taxation Act, 1938.

In 1939, Madras levied a general multi-point sales tax through the Madras General Sales Tax Act, 1939. The tax levied at the rate of half percent was ostensibly meant to compensate the loss of revenue resulting from the policy of prohibition.

4.1.1 Initial Legal Hurdles: Since its very inception, sales tax was a controversial levy embroiled in legal wrangling. Thus, soon after its enactment, the Central Provinces Act referred above was challenged by the Central Government as unconstitutional. It may be recalled that Entry 45 of List II in Seventh Schedule of the Government of India Act, 1935 had given the Central Government the power to levy excise on tobacco and other goods manufactured or produced in India. Hence, the Central Government maintained that sales tax on motor spirit and lubricants by Central Provinces was *ultra vires* because the power to levy excise on such products belonged to it (Central Government). Deciding in favour of the Provincial Government, the Federal Court observed that such taxes were in no way connected with the production or manufacture of goods, but were imposed on their sale.

In another legal battle, the Central Government contested the Madras General Sales Tax Act, 1939 referred to above. Being a multi-point sales tax, it covered sales by manufacturers also which was challenged by the Central Government. Once again, the Federal Court decided in favour of the Provincial Government and held that it had the power to tax sales of every kind, including sales by a manufacturer or producer.

The above two judicial pronouncements made it clear that the Provinces were competent to tax sales of any commodity and at any stage. In other words, a clear-cut distinction was drawn between the two, excise to be a tax on the act of production or manufacture, and the sales tax to be a levy on the act of sale.

Initial legal squabbling over, sales tax gained rapid popularity among the Provinces with the beginning of 1940s. Bengal adopted a single-point general sales tax levied at retail level in 1941. In the same year, Punjab introduced a general sales tax broadly based on the multi-point model of Madras. A general sales tax on the lines of single-point system of Bengal was introduced by Bihar in 1944 and by Bombay in 1946. Other Provinces followed suit and by 1948, all of them were operating sales tax in one form or the other with the notable exception of Jammu and Kashmir. This State was the last to introduce sales tax in 1962.

4.1.2 Beggar-my-neighbour Policies: There was no provision in the Government of India Act, 1935, to restrict or prohibit the Provinces from levying sales tax on inter-State transactions. In other words, the Act did not require the Provinces to levy sales tax only on those transactions which exclusively took place in their respective territories.

Taking advantage of this loophole in the Act, almost all the Provincial legislatures enacted sales tax laws which enabled them to tax goods exported from one State to another. These practices led to multiple taxation of the same transaction by different Provinces. As one scholar remarked, "Perhaps, the most important problem relating to sales taxation in the pre-Constitution period was the taxation of inter-State sales. All the Provinces, with the exception of West Bengal, were collecting sales tax on goods being sent to other Provinces and were, in effect, indulging in *beggar-my-neighbour policies*. [1]

In order to sort out these problems and to ensure all-India co-ordination, the Government of India convened a conference of the Finance Ministers of States in October, 1948. At this conference, attempts were made to achieve some degree of uniformity in the taxation of inter-State sales. However, these attempts failed in view of the widespread disagreement among the States. In particular, States which produced important raw materials/manufactured goods were opposed to changes that would result in the exclusion of inter-State trade from the purview of their sales tax laws. In short, the system of sales tax during the pre-Constitution period was arbitrary and bereft of national considerations.

The problems relating to taxation of inter-State sales were considered by the Drafting Committee of the Constituent Assembly. It proposed incorporation of provisions in the Constitution restricting the powers of the State Governments in respect of the levy of sales tax in the course of foreign trade, inter-State trade, and on essential commodities. In spite of opposition from some States, these provisions were finally incorporated in the Constitution as Article 286 (described below).

4.2 Constitutional Provisions for the Regulation of Taxation of Inter-State Sales

Under Entry 54 of List II (State List) in the Seventh Schedule of the Constitution, the States were given the power to levy "a tax on sales or purchases of goods other than newspapers". This provision was quite similar to Entry 48 of List II in the Seventh Schedule of the Government of India Act, 1935. However, under the Constitution, the States' power to levy sales tax was subject to a number of restrictions. These restrictions on the sale or purchase of goods as mentioned in Article 286 of the Constitution were the following.

1. No law of a State shall impose a tax on the sale or purchase of goods where such sale or purchase takes place: (a) outside the State, or (b) in the course of import of goods into, or export of goods out of, the territory of India.
2. Except in so far as the Parliament may by law otherwise provide, no law of a State shall impose a tax on the sale or purchase of any goods where such sale or purchase takes place in the course of inter-State trade or commerce.
3. No law made by the legislature of a State imposing a tax on the sale or purchase of any such goods as have been declared by Parliament by law to be essential for the life of the community, shall have effect unless it has been reserved for the consideration of the President and has received his assent.

In simple words, the States were prevented from taxing the following transactions: (i) sales or purchases in the course of foreign trade; (ii) sales of goods delivered in another State for consumption purpose; and (iii) sales in the course of inter-State trade and commerce.

Furthermore, the power of States to levy the tax on commodities declared to be *essential* by the Parliament was made subject to the prior approval of the President (see below section 4.2.2 of this chapter).

4.2.1 Consequences of Constitutional Restrictions on Sales Tax: The first restriction resulted in considerable loss of revenue to States, which were levying sales tax on exports. The main losers in this category were Bombay, Bihar, Madhya Pradesh, Orissa, and Assam. Nevertheless, this was the least controversial provision of Article 286.

The second and third restrictions, the benefits of which applied equally to registered dealers, unregistered dealers, and consumers, led to large scale evasion and avoidance of tax and hence loss of revenue to the States in general. As the Taxation Enquiry Commission, 1953-54, observed, "Traders in one State started to sell direct to unregistered dealers and consumers in another. Similarly, consumers of valuable commodities tried to get these from dealers in another State rather than buy the articles from their local dealers. The practice grew for sales of goods within a State itself to be shown in the books of accounts as having been made to fictitious dealers outside the State and the goods having then been resold by those dealers to consumers within the State. For valuable commodities like motor vehicles, jewellery, watches, etc. this practice became very common. On transactions that could be shown to be in the course of inter-State trade, the *exporting* State was prohibited under Article 286 from levying the sales tax; and if the goods delivered as a result of these transactions were shown to be received by individual consumers or unregistered dealers neither could any tax be levied on them by the *importing* State. Thus, many of these transactions escaped sales tax altogether". [2]

The loss of revenue was more for States with single-point system as compared to States having multi-point sales taxation. This was so because the restriction was not applicable to sales in the State prior to the last point of sale for export to another State.

The constitutional restrictions led to uneconomic diversion of trade and production centres. The problems which the constitutional provisions sought to solve got further compounded *albeit* with a different nature. To quote, "The Constitutional restrictions on sales taxation greatly increased the scope for evasion. While the problem before the Constitution had been multiple taxation (by different States) on the same act of inter-State sale, the problem after the Constitution was that inter-State sales frequently escaped taxation altogether". [3]

4.2.2 Essential Goods Act, 1952: As already noted, in addition to the above restrictions, Article 286 also prevented the States from levying tax on sales or purchases of goods declared by the Parliament to be essential for the life of the community, except with the previous assent of the President. For this purpose, the Parliament enacted the Essential Goods (Declaration and Regulation of Tax on Sale or Purchase) Act, 1952, and various commodities were declared as essential including cereals and pulses, fresh and dried fruits, fresh milk, meat, fish, salt, hides and skins, iron and steel, coal, fertilisers, petroleum products, and books.

As to the desirable purpose of the Act, the Taxation Enquiry Commission, 1953-54, noted, "It is obvious that the object of restricting the power of the states to levy a tax on the sale or purchase of 'essential goods' is to achieve some degree of uniformity in the tax burden on those goods, and not necessarily or in all cases to eliminate altogether the sales tax on such goods. When the Bombay Government sought the assent of the President to tax some of the 'essential goods' under their new multi-point tax system, the assent was given on condition that the tax burden on these goods should not in any event exceed the previous tax burden under the single-point system. This seems to indicate that the policy underlying the restriction is one of freezing the existing tax levied on these goods and of ensuring that new proposals to tax them are confined within reasonable limits". [4]

In spite of its desirable objectives, the enactment of the Essential Goods Act, 1952, led to various problems and criticism from some State Governments. Since the legislation was not retrospective, the States which had been levying sales tax on *essential goods* prior to the passage of the Essential Goods Act, continued to levy the tax. However, those States which sought to levy the tax after the passage of the Act had to obtain the consent of the President. This evoked sharp resentment among the State Governments.

The resentment among the States was further fuelled by the fact that the Central Government itself was levying relatively high rates of excise/customs duties on some of the so-called *essential goods*.

4.2.3 Constitution (Sixth Amendment) Act, 1956: In view of the problems arising from constitutional restrictions on the taxation of inter-State sales, the Taxation Enquiry Commission, 1953-54, recommended as follows, "In essence, the sales tax must continue to be a State tax. However, power and responsibility of the State must end and that of the Union begin when the sales tax of one State impinges administratively and fiscally on the consumers of another State. Inter-State sales tax should be the concern of the Union". [5]

Consequently, the Constitution was amended by the Sixth Amendment Act of 1956. Under this Amendment, the Parliament was empowered to impose 'taxes on the sale or purchase of goods other than newspapers, where such sale or purchase takes place in the course of inter-State trade or commerce'. This new provision in the Constitution was made by inserting Entry 92A in List I (Union List) in the Seventh Schedule. Simultaneously, Entry 54 in List II (State List) was made subject to the provisions of the new Entry 92A of List I. Also, Article 269 of the Constitution was amended which added a new clause (1)(g) which permitted taxes on the sale or purchase of goods in the course of inter-State trade to be levied and collected by the Government of India but assigned to the States. [6] Again, clauses (2) and (3) of Article 286 of the unamended Constitution were substituted by new clauses to make it read as follows.

(1) No law of a State shall impose or authorise the imposition of a tax on the sale or purchase of goods where such sale or purchase takes place: (a) outside the State, or (b) in the course of import of goods into or export of goods out of the territory of India. [7]

(2) Parliament may by law formulate principles for determining when a sale or purchase of goods takes place in any of the ways mentioned in clause (1). [8]

(3) Any law of a State shall in so far as it imposes or authorises the imposition of a tax on the sale or purchase of goods declared by Parliament by law to be of special importance in inter-State trade or commerce, be subject to such restrictions and conditions in regard to the system of levy, rates and other incidents of the tax as Parliament may by law specify. [9]

The new Article 286(2) gave Parliament the powers to define a sale outside a State. The new Article 286(3) was different from the old Article 286(3) in the following respect: In the old provision, Parliament had the authority to restrict State taxation of commodities declared by Parliament to be *essential for the life of the community*. In the new provision, Parliament was empowered to restrict State taxation of goods declared to be of special importance in inter-State trade only. [10]

4.2.4 Central Sales Tax (CST) Act, 1956: Consequent upon the Constitution (Sixth Amendment) Act, 1956, the Central Sales Tax (CST) Act, 1956 was enacted which came into force on January 5, 1957. The following three main objectives of the CST Act were stated in the Preamble:

1. To formulate principles for determining when a sale or purchase of goods takes place in the course of inter-State trade or in the course of import into or export from India.
2. To provide for the levy, collection, and distribution of taxes on sale of goods in the course of inter-State trade or commerce.
3. To declare certain goods to be of special importance in inter-State trade and specify the restrictions to which State laws imposing taxes on the sale and purchase of such goods of special importance shall be subject.

A. Main Provisions of CST Act: The regulations contained in the CST Act provided, *inter alia,* for a degree of uniformity by prescribing a maximum rate of sales tax on certain goods considered important for the whole country. According to Section 3 of the CST Act, a sale or purchase of goods was deemed to take place in the course of inter-State trade if it: (a) occasions the movement of goods from one State to another, or (b) is effected by a transfer of documents of title to the goods during their movement from one State to another.

Section 14 of the Act declared certain goods to be of special importance in inter-State trade and commerce. These were coal, cereals, cotton, cotton yarn, cotton fabrics, crude oil, hides and skins, iron and steel, jute, oilseeds, pulses, rayon and artificial silk fabrics, sugar, tobacco, woollen fabrics. The list of *declared goods* originally covered by the Act in 1956 was expanded twice, once in 1957 to include textiles, sugar, and tobacco, and again in 1976 to include cereals (like wheat, paddy, rice etc.), crude oil, and pulses.

Section 15 of the Act laid down the rate structure. The rates were different depending upon the classes of goods and the status of the person to whom the goods were sold. Thus, goods were either *declared goods* (goods of special importance) or *non-declared goods* while a person was either a registered or a non-registered dealer. Based on these classifications, the rates of sales tax were prescribed by the Central Government though the tax was administered (i.e. assessed, collected and appropriated) by the State Governments by virtue of the powers delegated to them by the Central Government under Article 258(1) of Constitution.

The maximum prescribed rate of sales tax on *declared goods* inside a State was 2 percent of the sale price and was not leviable at more than one stage. [11] Thus, although sales tax on intra-State sales was levied by the States, taxation of intra-State sales of *declared goods* (goods of special importance) was subject to certain restrictions in terms of the nature of the levy (not to be levied at more than one stage) and the rate of tax (not more than 2 percent).

In the case of inter-State sale of such goods to registered dealers, the rate of tax was the same as applicable to the sale of such goods inside the exporting State. In respect of sale of *declared goods* to non-registered dealers (including consumers) the CST was chargeable at twice the rate applicable to the same goods inside the State, i.e. 8 percent. Where *non-declared* goods were sold in the course of inter-State trade to a registered dealer, the ceiling rate was 4 percent [12] or the rate applicable to internal sales of the concerned goods, whichever was lower. [13] However, on inter-State sale of *non-declared goods* to non-registered dealers, the rate of CST was l0 percent or the rate applicable to the sale of such goods inside the exporting State, whichever was higher. [14]

The Act further specified that when a sales tax had been levied inside a State on any *declared goods* and such goods were sold in the course of inter-State trade, the tax so levied would refunded. Provision also existed that goods which were generally and unconditionally exempt from the sales tax within a State would also be exempt from CST in the course of inter-State trade.

4.2.5 Working of CST Act: It is clear as to why some kind of Central control was necessary on sales tax for larger national interest. Had Punjab, and Haryana been free to levy sales tax on foodgrains at will, the people of food deficit States would have suffered. Similarly, uncontrolled imposition of sales tax by West Bengal, and Bihar on iron and steel, and coal would have impeded the growth of engineering industry in Gujarat and Maharashtra.

CST Act authorized a State to tax residents of other States. Lest this power should be misused to export undue tax burden to the other States, the original scheme devised in 1956 kept the rate of CST low at 1 percent ensuring some reasonable revenue for the exporting States. However, over the years the rate of CST was raised by stages to 4 percent. This trend benefited industrially advanced States (like Maharashtra, Gujarat, Tamil Nadu, and West Bengal) at the cost of industrially backward States. Since manufactures were the main items of inter-State trade, the developed States were able to export a part of their taxation to other States. In effect, it amounted to transfer of financial resources from poorer States to well-off States, much against the declared objective of regional balanced development and equitable distribution of resources among the States. Moreover, the high rate of CST hindered the free flow of trade and commerce within the country.

There were suggestions that the rate of CST should be reduced to the original level of 1 percent to safeguard the interests of poorer States. However, these suggestions met with stiff resistance from most State Governments. At the New Delhi Conference of Chief Ministers held on September 16-17, 1980, there was a unanimous opinion that the rate of CST should not be brought down from 4 percent to 1 percent. [15] However, it was agreed to constitute a panel of Chief Ministers to consider, *inter alia*, additions to the list of *declared goods*. The Conference also expressed unanimity over the need for uniform sales tax laws in the country because various variants of the sales tax posed problems for the collecting authorities as well as for the taxpayers. The Chief Ministers' Conference decided to request the Law Commission to undertake, on a high priority basis, the drafting of a model sales tax law for consideration by the States.

Originally, the rate of CST was 1 percent, which was increased first to 2 percent, then to 3 percent and with effect from July 1, 1975 to 4 percent. Later on it was reduced from 4 percent to 3 percent with effect from April 1, 2007 and from 3 percent to 2 percent with effect from June 1, 2008. These reductions were done as a precursor to the introduction of GST, as CST was inconsistent with the concept and design of GST. CST was an origin-based tax and hence inconsistent with GST (a value added tax) which is destination-based tax with inherent input tax credit refund.

CST was a state-level tax, applied to inter-state sales of goods, based on the origin principle. The tax law (including the base, rates, and the procedures) was enacted by Parliament, but the entire revenue accruing under the levy of CST was collected and kept by the State in which the sale originated. The Act excluded taxation of imports and exports. It was a perfect example of absolute harmonization, with the States enjoying the risks and rewards of ownership of the tax.

CST was subsumed under GST when the latter came into force on July 1, 2017.

4.3 Additional Duties of Excise (Goods of Special Importance) Act, 1957

Another landmark in the evolution of sales tax in India was the year 1956 when, following a voluntary agreement between the Centre and the States at a meeting of the National Development Council (NDC) held in December, 1956, it was decided to replace sales tax on textiles, tobacco, and sugar by additional duties of excise and to distribute revenues derived therefrom among the States. The agreement provided also that the share accruing to each State shall not in any case be less than the revenue realised from the levy of sales tax on these goods for the financial year 1956-57 in that State. The Council's decision was implemented through the Additional Duties of Excise (Goods of Special Importance) Act, 1957, the First Schedule of which prescribed the rates of additional duties of excise and the Second Schedule the scheme of distribution of the net proceeds among the States.

The Act did not debar States from the levy of sales tax on the specified commodities, but it did provide that if in any year any State levied and collected a tax on the sale or purchase of such commodities, no sum would be paid to that State in that year by way of share out of the net proceeds of the additional duties of excise, unless the Central Government by special order decided otherwise. The commodities covered under the scheme (textiles, tobacco, and sugar) were declared goods of special importance in inter-State trade so that no State could find it worthwhile to opt out of the voluntary agreement not to impose sales tax on these goods. [16] The revenue derived from additional duties of excise, levied and collected by the Centre, was distributed among the States in accordance with the formula prescribed by the Finance Commission. The Fourth Finance Commission described it as a *tax rental arrangement.* [17]

4.3.1 Rationale of the Scheme: The scheme of additional duties of excise in lieu of sales tax had the following advantages:

1. It minimized tax evasion by levying the tax at first point and saving industry, trade, and consumers from administrative complexities involved in the collection and payment of sales tax.
2. It helped in maintaining uniformity in the prices of widely consumed goods throughout the country.
3. Such an arrangement contributed to the development of an integrated market by facilitating movement of goods across State borders.
4. Rationalisation of commodity taxation at the national level became easy.
5. Cost of collection is reduced.

4.3.2 Views of the State Governments: While the business community demanded extension of this scheme to other commodities, the States generally remained disinclined in this regard. The distrust between the Centre and the States regarding the operation of this scheme by the Central Government was an irritant in Centre-State relations. States had argued that: (a) sales tax was the only elastic source of revenue available to them and in view of its regional applicability it was also the only effective instrument for shaping their economic policies, (b) replacement of it by Central levy encroached on their constitutional rights leading to erosion of their financial autonomy, and (c) if taxes were levied and collected by a State itself then it was more conscious of its responsibilities towards the taxpayers. Subventions from the Centre may lead to reckless spending, causing fiscal indiscipline.

As regards the working of the scheme, the dissatisfaction of State Governments was borne out of their belief that revenue potential of additional duties of excise was not fully exploited by the Centre. Their complaint was that the growth of revenue from additional excise duties on textiles, sugar, and tobacco lagged behind the growth in revenue from basic excise duties on the same commodities. The States complained that once sales tax on the three commodities was replaced by additional excise duties, the Centre did not feel the need for consultation with the States for reviewing the working of the scheme. They claimed that the growth rate of their sales tax revenue was much higher than the growth rate of the yield from additional excise duties.

4.3.3 Decisions of the National Development Council (NDC): Following complaints from the States, the whole issue was reconsidered by the NDC in its meeting held on December 28, 1970. The Council decided to continue the scheme with the following conditions: (a) that the incidence of additional duties would be stepped up to 10.8 percent of the value of clearances within a period of two or three years, (b) that a ratio of 2:1 between basic and additional excise duties would be achieved and maintained, (c) that specific duties would be converted into *ad valorem* duties except in regard to unmanufactured tobacco. It was also agreed that a Standing Review Committee consisting of representatives of the Central and State Governments with the Economic Adviser, Planning Commission, as convenor, would be set up and the same would meet at least once a year to review the working of the new arrangement and make such recommendations as may be necessary for its further improvement.

As a follow up action, specific duties were replaced by *ad valorem* rates and significant enhancements were made in additional excise duties in the Central budgets for the three consecutive years 1971-72 to 1973-74. The Standing Review Committee met for the first time in February 1981 and appointed a sub-committee which recommended that the incidence of 10.8 percent should be achieved in three stages: 8.5 percent by 1984-85; 9.75 percent by 1987-88; and 10.8 percent by 1989-90. The Ninth Finance Commission was informed by the Union Finance Ministry that the incidence achieved by the end of 1988-89 was 10.7 percent. The Commission hoped that the committed level of 10.8 percent would actually be achieved by the end of 1989-90. In a significant move, the Commission recommended that during its award period (1990-95), if in any year the incidence of additional excise duties fell short of the level of 10.8 percent of the value of clearances, the shortfall would be made good by the Centre by providing an equivalent amount by way of grants-in-aid to be distributed among the States in the same manner as recommended for sharing the proceeds of additional excise duties. [18] As regards the ratio between basic excises and additional excises, the Centre fulfilled its obligations by achieving the stipulated 2:1 ratio by 1981-82.

4.3.4 Expert Committee on Replacement of Sales Tax by Additional Excise Duty, 1983: As already noted, sales tax on textiles, tobacco, and sugar was replaced by additional duties of excise in 1957. The scheme of additional excise duties was proposed to be extended to some more commodities in 1980. At a conference of the Chief Ministers convened by the Centre on September 16-17 of that year, it was resolved to bring *vanaspati*, and life-saving drugs under additional excise duties in lieu of sales tax. It was also decided to constitute a committee of Chief Ministers to consider what other items could be added to the list for additional excise duties. However, the non-Congress (I) States viz. Kerala, Tamil Nadu, Tripura, and West Bengal did not agree with the resolution passed at the Chief Ministers Conference.

The matter was further examined at another conference of Chief Ministers held in February 1981, which recommended the appointment of an expert committee by the Central Government to look into this matter. The expert committee under the Chairmanship of Mr. Kamlapati Tripathi submitted its report [19] in January 1983. It recommended the replacement of sales tax by additional excise duty on *vanaspati*, drugs and medicines, cement, paper and paper board, and petroleum products. The recommendations were considered in a conference of Chief Ministers held on November 2, 1983. However, the six Chief Ministers of the non-Congress (I) States, viz. Andhra Pradesh, Jammu and Kashmir, Karnataka, Tamil Nadu, Tripura, and West Bengal opposed the Centre's initiative to implement the recommendations. The recommendations of the Tripathi Committee were further discussed at a conference of Chief Ministers held in New Delhi on February 9-10, 1989. However, no progress could be made in this regard and the matter remained in limbo ever afterwards.

The opposition of non-Congress (I) States was based on the belief that implementation of the scheme would erode their revenue position. However, a close perusal of the recommendations of the Tripathi Committee suggested that it evolved elaborate formulae for protecting the financial interests of the States. In the case of three commodities, namely paper and paper board, *vanaspati*, and drugs and medicines, it suggested that the annual growth rate of the amount to be collected by way of additional excise duty in lieu of sales tax would be related to the future annual growth rate of sales tax revenue of all the States. For petroleum products and cement, which were substantially subject to administered prices, the Committee recommended and worked out linkages between the amount to be collected by way of additional excise duty from year-to-year and value of consumption on which normal sales tax would be leviable.

In spite of these safeguards, the apprehension of some States that their resource position would be adversely affected reflected their lack of confidence in the Centre in implementing the scheme sincerely. Thus, an important tax reform became a casualty of the distrust between the Central and the State Governments.

It is pertinent to mention here that during the first two decades of Independence (1947-67), the Congress party ruled, with some exceptions, both at the Centre and in the States. This political homogeneity facilitated taxation agreements between the two tiers of the Government, e.g. the agreement reached in 1957 regarding substitution of sales tax by excise duties on sugar, textiles, and tobacco. Since 1967, the politics of confrontation pursued by different political parties ruling at the Centre and in the States has hindered the process of rationalisation and harmonisation of commodity taxation. In fact, reform of commodity taxation is closely interwoven with the political process.

Additional duties of excise in lieu of sales tax were subsumed under GST when the latter came into force on July 1, 2017.

4.4 Constitution (Forty-sixth Amendment) Act, 1982 and Consignment Tax

Consequent upon the Sixth Amendment of the Constitution, the Central Sales Tax

(CST) Act was passed in 1956. Section 14 of the Act declared certain goods to be of special importance in inter-State trade while section 15 of the Act laid down the rate structure.

However, the CST Act left out of its ambit the consignments (or despatches or stock-transfers) from a company to its branch located in a different State. Since no sale was involved, it was called in-house transaction by a company. The loophole came in handy for unscrupulous parties to evade sales tax by showing virtual sales as consignments from one State to another. By this method, the payment of CST was avoided. Only local sales tax became payable. Therefore, through the Constitution (Forty-sixth Amendment) Act, 1982, the Parliament was empowered to levy 'taxes on the consignment of goods (whether the consignment is to the person making it or to any other person), where such consignment takes place in the course of inter-State trade or commerce'. This was done by inserting Entry 92B in List I (Union List) of the Seventh Schedule and simultaneously amending Article 269 by inserting sub-clause 269 (1) (h). Consignment tax was a levy on inter-State transfer of goods.

The States had been pressing the Centre to levy the tax, the net proceeds of which were entirely assignable to States under Article 269. The proposed tax was intended to check avoidance of CST. The Commission on Centre-State Relations, 1988, also impressed upon the Government to "bring in suitable legislation in this regard without further loss of time". [20]

Though the necessary legislation was still to be enacted, industrial and commercial circles expressed grave concern about the deleterious effects of the impending levy. Trade circles maintained that consignments were necessary in view of seasonal fluctuations in the demand for goods as well as frequent transport bottlenecks. Commercial practices like *branch transfer* or *transfer on consignment basis* also helped manufacturer-supplier to reduce avoidable costs of holding high levels of inventory.

4.5 Intra-State Sales Tax

As already noted, under Entry 54 of List II (State List) in the Seventh Schedule of the Constitution, the States were given the power to levy "a tax on sale or purchases of goods other than newspapers". Enjoying this Constitutional right, different State Governments levied sales tax on a wide range of commodities at different rates with diverse procedures and rules for its collection. The Central Government also entered the field in so far as it prescribes the ceiling rate of sales tax on goods in inter-State trade. In the case of three important commodities, viz. textiles, sugar, and tobacco, additional duties of excise were imposed in lieu of sales tax, the proceeds of which were distributed among the States.

Different States adopted different variants of the sales tax due to a number of reasons including administrative convenience, ad hoc measures to increase tax revenues, and to attract enterprise in their respective areas. Sales tax in a State could take the form of a single point, double-point and/or multi-point levy. However, single-point was the main type of sales tax imposed on most commodities in all States. In most States, a significant part of sales tax revenue originated from first-point levy, i.e. at the manufacturer's level. Some States also levied surcharges on sales tax as an ad hoc measure to augment their resources.

The rate structure of sales tax was further complicated in view of different lists of exemptions/concessions, numerous nominal rate categories, and different administrative procedures in each of the States. These variations caused disparities in the effective rate of sales tax on similar commodities in different States. Agricultural commodities like cereals and pulses were either exempted or subjected to low rate of sales tax, ranging from 2 to 3 percent. For most commodities, the rate of single-point levy varied between 4 to 8 percent. However, in the case of luxury items (like motor cars and refrigerators), the rate could go up to even 15 percent in some States. The rate of multi-point levy hovered around 4 percent.

4.5.1 Revenue Significance of Sales Tax: An outstanding development in the sphere of State finances after Independence in 1947 was the precipitous growth in the relative revenue significance of sales tax levied under Entry 54 of List II (State List) in the Seventh Schedule of the Constitution. It grew considerably in depth and coverage, and formed the mainstay of States' tax revenue. It was levied not only on consumer goods but also on raw materials and capital goods. In 1950-51, the relative share of sales tax was 26.1 percent: ₹ 58 crore out of a total collection of ₹ 222 crore from States' taxes. Recording a precipitous growth in relative revenue significance, sales tax was estimated to contribute 62.0 percent to States' own tax revenues in the 2015-16 budgets of the State Governments (Table 4.1). It is noteworthy that sales tax was replaced by State-VAT—sales tax with set-off provisions. Haryana was the first state to replace its sales tax by VAT on April 1, 2003. Other States followed suit. State-VAT, in turn, has been subsumed under GST.

Table 4.1: Trends in the Relative Revenue Significance of Sales Tax in Total Revenue from States' Own Taxes: Selected Years

(₹ crore)

State taxes	1950-51	1960-61	1970-71	1980-81	1990-91	2000-01	2010-11	2015-16
A+B Revenue from States' own taxes	222 (100.0)	455 (100.0)	1,546 (100.0)	6,665 (100.0)	30,145 (100.0)	1,16,717 (100.0)	4,78,594 (100.0)	9,69,594 (100.0)
A. Direct taxes	55 (24.7)	110 (24.2)	140 (9.1)	271 (4.1)	1,230 (4.1)	3,457 (2.9)	12,307 (2.6)	21,774 (2.2)
B. Indirect taxes of which	167 (75.3)	345 (75.8)	1,406 (90.9)	6,394 (95.9)	28,915 (95.9)	1,13,260 (97.1)	4,66,287 (97.4)	9,47,820 (97.8)
1. Sales tax	**58 (26.1)**	**158 (34.7)**	**755 (48.8)**	**3,887 (58.3)**	**16,476 (54.6)**	**68,386 (58.6)**	**2,90,682 (60.7)**	**6,00,851 (62.0)**

2015-16 Budget estimates

Figures in parentheses indicate corresponding percentages of the total revenue from States' own taxes.

Sources: Reserve Bank of India, *Report on Currency and Finance,* Volume II, (various years); and Government of India, Ministry of Finance, *Indian Public Finance Statistics, 2015-2016,* Tables 1.7 and 3.2 (excerpted).

4.5.2 Problems Created by Sales Tax: Perhaps no other tax impinged on so large a number of interests as sales tax. Firstly, it impacted the consumers who ultimately bore its burden. Next, there were the dealers from whom it was collected, and in many cases the producers also come in its ambit in case it was levied at the manufacturer's level. Then there were the State Governments, always anxious to extend its scope and retain their hold on it. Furthermore, the Central Government decided the rate of sales tax on goods of special importance in inter-State trade. Consequently, the operation of sales tax created a host of problems which may be summarised as follows.

1. Sales tax was a levy on commodities which, in most cases, were also subject to excise duties. As excise duty and sales tax were levied by different layers of Government, it became difficult to determine judiciously the impact of these levies on production, investment, and the consumers. No attempt to rationalise commodity tax system could succeed if the Centre and States acted independently without co-ordination among themselves.
2. A closely related problem was the taxation of inputs and capital goods, by the Central and State Governments, through excise duties and sales tax respectively. Apart from generating cascading effect, sales tax on inputs benefited comparatively richer States at the cost of poorer States. To quote, "The (sales) taxation of inputs also means that its burden falls on consumers outside the State. While procedures exist for refund of excise duties on a product when it is exported outside the country, the sales tax paid on inputs is not rebated. In consequence, the more developed States which have attained high levels of agricultural or industrial production are able to derive additional resources, by taxing consumers in other States, while the resource mobilisation capacity of the less developed States, which have to depend on most of their needs being met by imports from other States, is weakened". [21] This reverse flow of funds was further strengthened by the frequent hikes in the rate of Central sales tax (CST).

   Originally at 1 percent, CST rate steadily increased to 4 percent, thereby imposing undue burden on the importing States and defeating, in the process, the very objective of Central Sales Tax Act of 1956.

   To tackle the problem of cascading effect associated with the taxation of intermediate goods, reforms at the Central level provided instant credit of excise duty paid on inputs under the modified value added tax (MODVAT) scheme. Although State laws did provide relief through exemptions in regards to sales tax when inputs are sold to manufacturers, such concessions were limited and lacked uniformity. This lacuna in the sales tax system hindered reform of indirect tax system in India.
3. In order to attract trade and industry to their respective areas, some States indulged in a kind of *rate war* (competitive reductions in sales tax rates). It is true that some States lacked infrastructural facilities and to compensate for that sales tax concessions came handy to attract industries, but this shortcut eroded the resource-base of the States, so vital for the development of infrastructure which alone could guarantee their speedy development on permanent footing.

4. Differential rates of sales tax on the same set of commodities in different States often led to uneconomic diversion of trade as well as production centres. It was not uncommon for people of one State making purchases in other States to avoid or reduce sales tax liability. Apparently, purchases from lower tax States to those where rates were higher were beneficial so long as the cost of transporting goods was lower than the tax differential. Purchase of truck chassis in Daman (a Union Territory levying a low rate of 3 percent) by the residents of a far off State of Jammu and Kashmir was a popular case in point.
   Similarly, rate differentials caused flight of capital and enterprise from high to low tax rate States thereby distorting natural selection of production centres based on geographical advantages, leading to unnecessary transportation of raw materials and finished goods and hence cost escalations. Such a misallocation of resources undermined economic efficiency and thereby retarded developmental efforts.
5. Sales tax had another disadvantage in that it discouraged horizontal integration and on the contrary encouraged vertical integration in industries. Firms tried to produce their own components in order to avoid sales tax. This tendency harmed the growth of ancillary units which were mainly in the small-scale sector.
6. Different types of sales tax (multi-point, double-point, and single point) with varying procedures and rules in different States caused difficulties for the traders, particularly small ones, leading to harassment, corruption, and litigation.

4.5.3 Alternative Remedies Suggested: To deal with the foregoing weaknesses of the sales tax system, fiscal experts put forward various suggestions from time-to-time. Some of these were as under:

A. Sales Tax as Central Levy: It was argued that through a constitutional amendment, the levy of sales tax could be made a Central subject and thereafter a rationalised system of indirect taxation of domestic production and consumption could be administered by the Centre. This was a drastic suggestion which did not find favour with statesmen. The Taxation Enquiry Commission (TEC), 1953-54, was quite categorical in rejecting this suggestion. Emphasising the impracticability of centralisation of sales tax the Commission observed, "On account of its yield and flexibility, sales tax has come to occupy a large and indispensable place in the State financial systems. Centralisation of the tax must be ruled out. Difficulties which confront the tax administrations vary considerably in character and composition from State to State and taken together present a large and almost bewildering variety of problems". [22]

The views of the TEC appeared to be valid considering the fiscal arrangements and political equations in the country. Thus, a constitutional amendment to make sales tax a Central subject was ruled out.

B. Complete Substitution of Sales Tax by Excise Duty: It was suggested, particularly by the business community, that in place of sales tax corresponding enhancements could be made in Central excises the proceeds of which could be earmarked for distribution among the States. This would facilitate rationalisation of commodity taxation and also reduce the cost of collection apart from saving the business community from harassment from the differing sales tax practices of the various States.

Was a complete substitution of sales tax by excise duties possible? Probably not! Like sales tax, excise duties could not become universal in scope because of administrative reasons. For instance, the Centre had the legal power to impose excises on agricultural products but it refrained from doing so. Similarly, small and tiny units of the industrial sector were left out because of administrative reasons.

However, what was small for excise duty was large for the purpose of sales tax. The Indirect Taxation Enquiry Committee, 1977, estimated that nearly ₹ 500 crore of sales tax was being collected on goods not subject to excise duties such as agricultural products, articles of jewellery which for administrative or other reasons could not be reached by excises. It concluded, "The consequence of a simple abolition of sales tax from the angle of resource mobilisation would be a substantial loss of revenue to compensate for which something like a 50 percent increase in excise duties on the average would be necessary, given the present base of excise taxation". [23]

Since excise duties were of all-India nature, they could not take into account regional variations in the levels of income and patterns of consumption. However, different rates of sales tax in individual States permitted consideration of regional factors. Moreover, if sales tax was levied at the retail stage, the value base of the tax was large and even low rates of tax could yield sufficient revenues.

C. Partial Substitution of Sales Tax by Excise Duty: The approach towards substitution of sales tax by excise duties could have been selective. Some arrangements already existed in this regard in the form of additional duties of excise in lieu of sales tax on three important commodities, namely textiles, tobacco, and sugar. The extension of this arrangement to certain other commodities as recommended by Tripathi Committee has already been discussed in section 4.3.4 of this chapter.

4.6 Replacement of Sales Tax by Value Added Tax (VAT)

The replacement of the state sales taxes by VAT in 2005 marked a significant step forward in the reform of domestic trade taxes in India. Implemented by the Empowered Committee of State Finance Ministers (Chairman: Asim Dasgupta) [24], it addressed the distortions and complexities associated with the levy of tax at the first point of sale under the erstwhile system and resulted in a major simplification of the rate structure and broadening of the tax base. The consensus reached among the States for uniformity in the VAT rates brought an end to the harmful tax competition among them. It also lessened the cascading of tax.

In mid-1990s, most states had agreed to phase out the incentive-related exemptions and implement floor rates of sales tax. As part of the nation wide efforts to redesign commodity taxation and the implementation of CENVAT at the level of the Centre, many States modified their sales tax regimes to launch a state level VAT under the scheme prepared by the Empowered Committee of State Finance Ministers for this purpose.

4.6.1 Minimum Rate Agreement among States, 1989: As already noted, some States had been indulging in a sort of *rate-war* to attract trade and industry to their respective regions. To avoid this unhealthy competition, the Chief Ministers agreed, at their conference in New Delhi on February 9-10, 1989, that all the States would adopt the minimum floor level rates as recommended by the Committee of Sales Tax Commissioners in its report of 1984 in respect of 29 identified items. The Chief Secretaries of northern States (Punjab, Haryana, Himachal Pradesh, Rajasthan, Delhi, and Uttar Pradesh) had recommended in May 1994 that there should not only be a uniform rate of sales tax but the slabs of this tax be reduced in these States.

In this connection the Tax Reforms Committee, 1991, observed, "As regards sales tax, the Committee is of the view that this tax could be converted into a form of State VAT within the manufacturing sector. There may be no need for levying sales tax at more than two rates since the distributional and other non-revenue objectives could be left to be performed by the Central taxes which apply uniformly throughout the country". [25]

4.6.2 State Finance Ministers' Conference, 1994: The State Finance Ministers' Conference held in New Delhi on May 27, 1994 failed to arrive at a consensus on the replacement of indirect taxes at the State level by a value added tax. The matter was deferred indefinitely by appointing a ten-member Committee of State Finance Ministers to go into this and related questions.

4.6.3 Preliminary Discussion on State-level VAT, 1995: The first preliminary discussion on State-level VAT took place in a meeting of Chief Ministers convened by Dr. Manmohan Singh, the then Union Finance Minister in 1995. In this meeting, the basic issues on VAT were discussed in general terms and this was followed up by periodic interactions of State Finance Ministers.

4.6.4 Chief Ministers Conference, 1999: In a significant meeting of all the Chief Ministers, convened on November 16, 1999 by Shri Yashwant Sinha, the then Union Finance Minister, two important decisions, among others, were taken. First, before the introduction of State-level VAT, the unhealthy sales tax *rate war* among the States must end, and sales tax rates would need to be harmonised by implementing uniform floor rates of sales tax for different categories of commodities with effect from January 1, 2000. Secondly, on the basis of achievement of the first objective, steps would be taken by the States for introduction of State-level VAT after adequate preparation. For implementing these decisions, a Standing Committee of State Finance Ministers was formed which was then made an Empowered Committee of State Finance Ministers.

4.6.5 Report of Empowered Committee, 2001: The Empowered Committee met regularly. All the decisions were taken on the basis of consensus. On the strength of these repeated discussions and collective efforts, involving the Ministers and the concerned officials, it was possible within a period of about a year and a half to achieve nearly 98 percent success in the first objective, namely harmonisation of sales tax structure through implementation of uniform floor rates of sales tax.

After reaching this stage, steps were initiated for systematic preparation for introduction of State level VAT. Again, in order to avoid any unhealthy competition among the States which might lead to distortions in manufacturing and trade, attempts were made from the very beginning to harmonise the VAT design in the States, keeping also in view the distinctive features of each State and the need for federal flexibility. This was done by the States collectively agreeing, through discussions in the Empowered Committee, to certain common points of convergence regarding VAT, and allowing at the same time certain flexibility to accommodate the local characteristics of the States.

Along with these measures, steps were taken for necessary training, computerization and interaction with trade and industry. While these preparatory steps were taken, the Empowered Committee got a significant support from Shri P. Chidambaram, the then Union Finance Minister, when he responded positively in providing Central financial support to the States in the event of loss of revenue in transitional years of implementation of VAT.

The Empowered Committee, through its deliberations over the years, finalised a design of VAT to be adopted by the States. The model design sought to retain the essential features of VAT, while at the same time, providing a measure of flexibility to the States, to enable them to meet their local requirements. The main features of the VAT design finalised by the Empowered Committee were the following:

1. Rates of VAT on various commodities were to be uniform for all the States/UTs. There were 2 basic rates of 4 percent and 12.5 percent, besides an exempt category and a special rate of 1 percent for a few selected items. The items of basic necessities were put in the zero-rate bracket or the exempted schedule. Gold, silver and precious stones were put in the 1 percent schedule. There was also a category with 20 percent floor rate of tax, but the commodities listed in this schedule were not eligible for input tax rebate/set off. This category covered items like motor spirit (petrol), diesel, aviation turbine fuel, and liquor.
2. Model VAT design made provision for eliminating the multiplicity of taxes. In fact, all the State taxes on purchase or sale of goods (excluding entry tax in lieu of octroi) were required to be subsumed in VAT.
3. Provision was made for allowing input tax credit, which was the basic feature of VAT. However, since the VAT being implemented was intra-State VAT only and did not cover inter-State sale transactions, input tax credit was not made available on inter-State purchases.
4. There were provisions to make the system more business-friendly. For instance, there was provision for self-assessment by the dealers. Similarly, there was provision of a threshold limit for registration of dealers in terms of annual turnover of ₹ 5 lakh. Dealers with turnover lower than this threshold limit were not required to obtain registration under VAT and were exempt from payment of VAT. There was also provision for composition of tax liability up to annual turnover limit of ₹ 50 lakh.
5. Regarding the industrial incentives, the States were allowed to continue with the existing incentives, without breaking the VAT chain. However, no fresh sales tax/VAT-based incentives were permitted.
6. Exports were zero-rated, with credit given for all taxes on inputs/purchases related to such exports.

It was emphasised that the States must think in terms of economic development of the country as a whole and encourage the free flow of trade and commerce in the economy.

At a Conference of Chief Ministers and Finance Ministers of various States held on July 5, 2001 in New Delhi, the Report of the Empowered Committee of State Finance Ministers on VAT (Chairman: Asim Kumar Dasgupta), was accepted and adopted for the introduction of VAT with effect from April 1, 2002. The VAT design recommended by the Empowered Committee was geared to achieve the following objectives:

1. Eliminate the cascading burden of taxation by setting off the tax paid on inputs against that on output.
2. Reduce distortions in the economy caused by double taxation.
3. End market fragmentation with a uniform regime of taxation followed in all the States.
4. Ensure one category of tax-exempted commodities for all the States.
5. Ensure two VAT rates: a uniform 4 percent for all States on goods of basic necessities and a uniform floor rate of 10 percent for other commodities (except a few items such as bullion and liquor).
6. Ensure uniform set of procedures for VAT assessment to be followed by all the States, including the use of permanent account number (PAN) as a common business identifier.
7. Ensure that States implemented uniform floor rates of sales tax by July-end 2001, failing which faulting States could be penalised by discontinuing Central Government assistance.

In view of the apprehensions expressed by a large number of States about possible revenue losses in the initial years of introduction of VAT, an assurance was given to the States that the Government of India would compensate the States to the extent of 100 percent of revenue loss in the first year (2002-03), 75 percent of the loss in the second year (2003-04) and 50 percent of the loss in the third year (2005-06). A Committee of State Finance Secretaries was appointed to evolve clear and measurable criteria for judging revenue loss, if any, due to the introduction of VAT.

4.6.6 Agreement of January 23, 2002: At the Conference of State Finance Ministers held on January 23, 2002 a final decision was taken that all States and Union Territories would introduce VAT from April 2003. This position was reiterated by all States at the Conference of State Chief Ministers held on October 18, 2002. Empowered Committee of State Finance Ministers endorsed the suggestion that every State Legislation on VAT should have a minimum set of common features. Accordingly, a model VAT Bill was circulated to all the States.

4.6.7 Meeting of State Finance Ministers, 2003: Again, at a meeting of the Finance Ministers of all States/Union Territories on January 17, 2003, States and Union Territories again reiterated their firm commitment to introduce VAT from April 1, 2003. It was decided that the VAT legislations of all States and UTs would have common provisions in respect of all important matters and that a simple VAT legislation with maximum convergence would be implemented. It was also agreed that along with the introduction of VAT, the origin-based Central Sales Tax (CST) would be phased out. It was also agreed that the Additional Duties of Excise (Goods of Special Importance) Act would be suitably amended to empower States to levy sales tax/VAT on sugar, textiles and tobacco with a ceiling rate of 4 percent. This would be done without affecting the existing levy of Additional Duties of Excise on these items by the Union Government.

The Empowered Committee of State Finance Ministers agreed upon the following sequence of steps to ensure introduction of VAT in place of retail sales tax system in States.

1. Passing of VAT legislation and framing of rules and regulations.
2. Computerisation of dealers who would fall within the ambit of VAT.
3. Training of tax officials, traders and consumer associations.
4. Publicity for consumers.
5. Implementation of VAT, assigning VAT identification numbers to tax payers.
6. Implementing transitional measures for introduction of VAT.

4.6.8 Agreement of June 2004: At a meeting of the State Finance Ministers with the Union Finance Minister on June 18, 2004, it was decided that all States would introduce a uniform VAT from April 1, 2005. The proposed VAT would replace the taxes levied by different States like sales tax and octroi. Coinciding with the introduction of VAT, the Central Government would bring down the Central Sales Tax (CST) rate from 4 percent to 2 percent. The CST would be phased out in 2006-07. It was also decided that traders with an annual turnover up to ₹ 5 lakh would be exempt from VAT. This decision was aimed at ending traders' opposition to VAT. It may be recalled that States had missed at least five deadlines for the introduction of VAT, mainly due to resistance from trading community.

As a consequence of all these steps, the States started implementing VAT beginning April 1, 2005. After overcoming the initial difficulties, all the States and Union Territories were able to implement VAT. The Empowered Committee monitored closely the process of implementation of State-level VAT.

4.6.9 Role of the Central Government: Introduction of State VAT was an important reform measure at the State level. The State VAT replaced the earlier sales tax systems of the States. VAT, being a 'tax on sale or purchase of goods within a State' was a State Subject by virtue of Entry 54 of List II (State List) of the Seventh Schedule of the Constitution of India. Since sales tax/VAT was a State subject, the Central Government played the role of a facilitator for successful implementation of VAT. Some of the steps taken by the Central Government in this regard were as follows:

1. A package for payment of compensation to States for any revenue loss on account of introduction of VAT was implemented.
2. Financial support under Mission Mode Project (MMP) was provided to States/UTs in order to enable them to take up computerization of their tax departments.
3. A separate project for computerization of tax administration of Himachal Pradesh and Jammu and Kashmir was sanctioned.
4. 50 percent funding was provided to the Empowered Committee of State Finance Ministers for implementation of the TINXSYS Project for tracking of inter-State transactions.

4.6.10 Shortcomings of State VAT: Complexities under the State VAT related primarily to classification of goods to different tax rate schedules. Theoretically, one might expect that the lower tax rates would be applied to basic necessities that are consumed largely by the poor. This was not the case under the State VAT. The lowest rate of 1 percent applied to precious metals and jewellery, and related products—unacceptable from the distributional perspective. The middle rate of 4 percent applied to selected basic necessities and also a range of industrial inputs and IT products. In fact, basic necessities fell into three categories—exempted from tax, taxable at 4 percent, and taxable at the standard rate of 12.5 percent. The classification was arbitrary, with no well-accepted theoretical underpinning. Whatever the political merits of this approach, it was not conducive to lower compliance costs. Most retailers found it difficult to determine the tax rate applicable to a given item without referring to the legislative schedules. Consumers were even less aware of the tax applicable to various items. This gave rise to leakages and rent-seeking.

Another source of complexity under the State VAT was determining whether a particular transaction constituted a sale of goods or not. This problem was most acute in the case of software products and intangibles such as the right to distribute/exhibit movies or time slots for broadcasting advertisements.

The issue of cascading taxation was partly addressed when all the states adopted the concept of VAT for state sales tax. Several central and state taxes were excluded from VAT. Sectors such as real estate, oil and gas production etc. were exempt from VAT. Further, goods and services were taxed differently, thereby making the taxation of products complex.

Broadly speaking, the experience of implementing VAT was quite encouraging. The new system was received well by all the stakeholders, and the transition was quite smooth with the Empowered Committee (EC) constantly reviewing the progress of implementation. The EC advised the States to constantly interact with trade and industry to remove their apprehensions, if any, and to ensure that the benefits of VAT due to input tax credit and reduction in tax rates (wherever applicable) were passed on to the consumers.

Introduction of VAT in the States was a more challenging exercise in a federal country like India, where each State, in terms of constitutional provision, is sovereign in levying and collecting State taxes. In the sales tax regime (before the introduction of VAT), apart from the problem of multiple taxation and burden of adverse cascading effect of taxes, there was also no harmony in the rates of sales tax on different commodities among the States. Not only were the rates of sales tax numerous (often more than ten in several States), and different from one another for the same commodity in different States, but there was also an unhealthy competition among the States in terms of sales tax rates—so-called *rate war*—often resulting in revenue loss.

It is in this background that attempts were made by the States to introduce a harmonious VAT in the States, keeping at the same time in mind the issue of sovereignty of the States regarding the State tax matters.

Sales tax was abolished (except on a few commodities) by Section 17 of Constitution (One Hundred and First Amendment) Act, 2016. [26]

Endnotes

1. Walter Mahler, *Sales and Excise Taxation in India*, New Delhi: Orient Longman Ltd., 1970, p. 151.
2. Government of India, Ministry of Finance, *Report of the Taxation Enquiry Commission, 1953-54* (Chairman: John Matthai), Vol. III, p. 26.
3. Walter Mahler, *Sales and Excise Taxation in India*, New Delhi: Orient Longman Ltd., 1970, p. 154.
4. *Report of the Taxation Enquiry Commission,* 1953-54, Vol. III, op. cit., p. 30.
5. *Ibid.*, p. 519.
6. Under Article 258(1), the Union has the power to delegate to any State Government any of its executive functions (including the power to assess and collect sales tax on inter-State trade). Thus, the power to levy and collect sales tax on inter-State trade belongs to the Centre [Article 269(1)(g)] though it has delegated the power to collect it to the States.
7. Clause (1) of Article 286 was amended by Section 13 of the Constitution (One Hundred and First Amendment) Act, 2016 in the following manner: (a) for the words "the sale or purchase of goods where such sale or purchase takes place", the words "the supply of goods or of services or both, where such supply takes place" shall be substituted; (b) in sub-clause (b), for the word "goods", at both the places where it occurs, the words "goods or services or both" shall be substituted.
8. Clause (2) of Article 286 was amended by Section 13 of the Constitution (One Hundred and First Amendment) Act, 2016 in the following manner: for the words "sale or purchase of goods takes place", the words "supply of goods or of services or both" shall be substituted.
9. Clause (3) of Article 286 was omitted by Section 13 of the Constitution (One Hundred and First Amendment) Act, 2016.
10. Clause (3) of Article 286 was further amended by the Constitution (Forty-sixth Amendment) Act, 1982. In its present form it is as follows. Any law of a State shall in so far as it imposes, or authorises the imposition of: (a) a tax on the sale or purchase of goods declared by Parliament by law to be of special importance in inter-State trade or commerce; or (b) a tax on the sale or purchase of goods, being a tax of the nature referred to in sub-clause (b), sub-clause (c) or sub-clause (d) of clause (29-A) of Article 366, be subject to such restrictions and conditions in regard to the system of levy, rates and other incidents of the tax as Parliament may by law specify.
11. In 1956, when the Central Sales Tax Act was passed the rate was fixed at 1 percent. Subsequently, it was raised to 2 percent, 3 percent, and 4 percent in 1958, 1966, and 1975 respectively. It was reduced to 3 percent and 2 percent in 2007 and 2008 respectively.
12. Originally, the rate was fixed at 1 percent in 1956. It was raised to 2 percent, 3 percent, and 4 percent in 1963, 1966, and 1975 respectively.
13. It means the States are free to fix the rate of sales tax on the internal sales of non-declared goods but there is a ceiling rate of 4 percent on the sale of such goods in inter-State trade. For example, if the rate of sales tax on internal sale is 6 percent, it will be 4 percent for inter-State trade, being lower of the two.
14. In other words, the rate of CST is a minimum of 10 percent. For example, if general sales tax is charged at the rate of 5 percent on the sale of colour television in a State, the rate of CST on the same will be 10 percent, being higher of the two rates. In 1956, the minimum rate was fixed at 7

percent but was raised to 10 percent by the Central Sales Tax (Amendment) Act, 1963.

15. To prepare for the implementation of national level Goods and Services Tax (GST), Central Government has also begun a phased reduction of Central Sales Tax (CST). The Central Government has brought down the level of CST over the last few years from 4 percent to 2 percent as a precursor to rolling out GST. This is because CST, which is an origin-based tax, is inconsistent with value added taxes, which are destination based—the two should not co-exist.
16. Internal as well as inter-State sales tax on goods of special importance is governed by the Central Sales Tax Act, 1956. The present rate of CST is 4 percent.
17. India's federal system of government creates a dual polity based on divided governmental functions and taxation powers. Taxation laws of the Central Government extend to the whole of the country while those of State Governments are applicable within their respective jurisdictions. A tax belonging to the States may be imposed with a varying base and/or rate in different States. Even the procedures and rules for its collection may differ from State to State. The lack of uniformity in the imposition of State tax laws can cause difficulties for traders and consumers and thus hinder inter-State trade. To overcome these problems, arrangements could be made to transfer from the States, the legal right to levy the tax, to the Centre with the proviso that revenue collected will be assigned to the States. This is known as 'tax rental arrangement'.
18. *Second Report of the Ninth Finance Commission,* December 1989, p. 34.
19. Government of India, Ministry of Finance, *Report of the Expert Committee on Replacement of Sales Tax by Additional Excise Duty,* (Chairman: Kamlapati Tripathi), January 1983.
20. Government of India, *Report of the Commission on Centre-State Relations,* (Chairman: Justice R.S. Sarkaria), 1988, Part I, p. 293.
21. Government of India, Ministry of Finance, *Report of the Indirect Taxation Enquiry Committee,* (Chairman: L.K. Jha), 1977, Part I, p. 50.
22. *Report of the Taxation Enquiry Commission,* 1953-54, Vol. III, op. cit., p. 519.
23. *Report of the Indirect Taxation Enquiry Committee,* 1977, Part I, op. cit., p. 49.
24. See endnote 5 of chapter 7 of this book for a note on Empowered Committee.
25. Government of India, Ministry of Finance, *Tax Reforms Committee-Final Report*, Part I, (Chairman: Raja Chelliah), August 1992, p. 174.
26. See Entry 54 in Table 6.2 of chapter 6 of this book.

5

Problems Created by Multiple Taxation of Goods and States' Exclusion from Taxing Services

Prior to the implementation of GST, indirect tax system of India was inefficient, complicated and fragmented. For example, State level sales tax/VAT was a levy on commodities which, in most cases, were also subject to excise duties imposed by the Centre. As excise duty and sales tax were levied by different layers of Government, it became difficult to determine judiciously the impact of these levies on production, investment, and the consumers. Since the Centre and States acted independently without co-ordination among themselves, there was hardly any possibility to rationalize commodity tax system successfully.

5.1 Tax Cascading

Tax cascading was the most serious flaw of the pre-GST system. It increased the cost of production and put Indian suppliers at a competitive disadvantage in the international markets. It created a bias in favour of imports, which did not bear the hidden burden of taxes on production inputs. It also detracted from a neutral application of tax to competing products. Although the statutory rate was uniform, the effective tax rate (i.e. statutory rate on finished products and the implicit or hidden tax on production inputs) varied from product to product depending on the magnitude of the hidden tax on inputs used in their production and distribution. The intended impact of government policy towards sectors or households was negated by the indirect or hidden taxation in a cascading system of taxes.

Prior to the introduction of MODVAT/CENVAT at the level of Centre and VAT at the level of States, there was a burden of multiple taxation in the form of Central excise duty and the States' sales tax systems. Before any commodity was produced, inputs were first taxed, and then after the commodity got produced with input tax load, output was taxed again. This was causing a burden of multiple taxation (i.e. *tax on tax*) with a cascading effect. Moreover, in the sales tax structure, there was also a system of multi-point sales taxation at subsequent levels of distributive trade, thus aggravating the cascading effect further.

Tax cascading occurred under both the Central and State taxes. The most significant contributing factor to tax cascading was the partial coverage of Central and State taxes. Oil and gas production, mining, agriculture, wholesale and retail trade, real estate construction, and a range of services remained outside the ambit of excise duties/CENVAT and the service tax levied by the Centre. The exempt sectors were not allowed to claim any credit for the excise duties/CENVAT or the service tax paid on their inputs.

Similarly, under the State sales tax/VAT, no credits were allowed for the inputs of the exempt sectors, which included the entire service sector, real estate sector, agriculture, oil and gas production and mining.

No credit of excise duty and service tax paid at the stage of manufacture was available to the traders while paying the State level sales tax or VAT, and vice-versa. Further, no credit of State taxes paid in one State could be availed in other States. Hence, the prices of goods and services got artificially inflated to the extent of this *tax on tax*.

Another major contributing factor to tax cascading was the Central Sales Tax (CST) on inter-state sales, collected by the originating state and for which no credit was allowed by any level of government.

In any case, CENVAT and State VAT were much better than the system that prevailed earlier. Notable among the improvements made were the following:

1. Rationalization of the CENVAT rates by reducing their multiplicity and replacing many of the specific rates by ad valorem rates based on the maximum retail price (MRP) of the products.
2. Introduction of the service tax by the Centre, and a substantial expansion of its base over the years.
3. Replacement of the single-point state sales taxes by the VAT in all of the States and Union Territories.
4. Reduction in the Central Sales Tax (CST) rate to 2 percent, from 4 percent, as part of a complete phase out of the tax.

These changes yielded significant dividends in economic efficiency of the tax system, ease of compliance, and growth in revenues.

5.2 Multiplicity of Taxes and Rates

The multiplicity of taxes at the Central and State levels resulted in a complex indirect tax structure in the country that was ridden with hidden costs for the trade and industry. There was no uniformity of tax rates and structure across States.

Differential rates of sales tax on the same set of commodities in different States often led to uneconomic diversion of trade as well as production centres. It was not uncommon for people of one State making purchases in other States to avoid or reduce sales tax liability. In order to attract trade and industry to their respective areas, some States indulged in a kind of *rate war* (competitive reductions in sales tax rates).

Likewise, rate differentials caused flight of capital and enterprise from high to low tax rate States thereby distorting natural selection of production centres based on geographical advantages, leading to unnecessary transportation of raw materials and finished goods and hence cost escalations.

It is noteworthy that GST has subsumed under it 17 indirect taxes (8 Central and 9 State taxes). GST is a single tax on the supply of goods or services or both, right from the manufacturer to the consumer. Credits of input taxes paid at each stage are available in the subsequent stage of value addition, which makes GST essentially a tax only on value addition at each stage.

5.3 Complexity of Administration

In spite of the improvements made in the tax design and administration, the systems at both the Central and State levels remained complex. Their administration left a lot to be desired. There were often disputes and court challenges, and the process for resolution of disputes was slow and expensive. At the same time, the systems suffered from substantial compliance gaps, except in the highly organized sectors of the economy. There were several factors contributing to this unsatisfactory state of affairs. The most significant cause of complexity was the existence of exemptions and multiple rates, and the irrational structure of the levies. These deficiencies were the most glaring in the case of the CENVAT and the service tax.

Compounding the structural or design deficiencies of each of the taxes was the poor or archaic infrastructure for their administration. Taxpayer services were virtually non-existent or grossly inadequate under both Central and State administrations. Many of the administrative processes were still manual, not benefiting from the efficiencies of automation. All this not only increased the costs of compliance, but also undermined revenue collection.

5.4 States' Exclusion from Taxing Services

During the pre-GST system, States were precluded from taxing services. This arrangement posed difficulties in taxation of goods supplied as part of a composite works contract involving a supply of both goods and services, and under leasing contracts, which entailed a transfer of the right to use goods without any transfer of their ownership. While these problems were addressed by amending the Constitution to bring such transactions within the ambit of the State taxation [1], services per se remained outside the scope of state taxation powers. This limitation was unsatisfactory from two perspectives.

First, the advancements in information technology and digitization have blurred the distinction between goods and services. Under Indian jurisprudence, goods are defined to include intangibles, e.g. copyright, and software, bringing them within the purview of state taxation. However, intangibles are often supplied under arrangements which have the appearance of a service contract. For example, software upgrades (which are goods) can be supplied as part of a contract for software repair and maintenance services. Software development contracts could take the character of contracts for manufacturing and sale of software goods or for rendering software development services, depending on the roles and responsibilities of the parties. The so-called value added services (VAS) provided as part of telecommunication services include supplies some of which could be considered goods. An on-line subscription to newspapers could be viewed as a service, but online purchase and download of a magazine or a book could constitute a purchase of goods. This blurring also clouds the application of tax to transactions relating to tangible property. For example, disputes have arisen whether leasing of equipment without transfer of possession and control to the lessee would be taxable as a service or as a deemed sale of goods.

The traditional distinctions between goods and services found in the Indian Constitution have become archaic. In markets today, goods, services, and other types of supplies are being packaged as composite bundles and offered for sale to consumers under a variety of supply-chain arrangements. Under the pre-GST division of taxation powers, neither the Centre nor the States could apply the tax to such bundles in a seamless manner. Each could tax only parts of the bundle, creating the possibility of gaps or overlaps in taxation.

The second major concern with the exclusion of services from the state taxation powers was its negative impact on the buoyancy of State tax revenues. With the growth in per capita incomes, services account for a growing fraction of the total consumer basket, which the states could not tax. With no powers to levy tax on incomes or the fastest growing components of consumer expenditures, the States had to rely almost exclusively on compliance improvements or rate increases for any buoyancy in their *own-source revenues*.

Despite a certain degree of success, there were still certain shortcomings in the structure of VAT both at the Central and at the State level. The shortcoming in CENVAT of the Centre lied in non-inclusion of several Central taxes in the overall framework of CENVAT, such as additional customs duty, surcharges etc., and thus keeping the benefits of comprehensive input tax and service tax set-off out of reach for manufacturers/dealers. Moreover, no step was taken to capture the value-added chain in the distribution trade below the manufacturing level in the scheme of CENVAT.

In the State-level VAT structure there were also certain shortcomings. There were several taxes in the nature of indirect tax on goods and services—such as luxury tax, entertainment tax etc.—and yet not subsumed in the VAT.

The design of the CENVAT and state VAT was dictated by the constraints imposed by the constitution, which allowed neither the Centre nor the States to levy taxes on a comprehensive base of all goods and services and at all points in their supply chain. The Centre was constrained from levying the tax on goods beyond the point of manufacturing, and the States in extending the tax to services. This division of tax powers made both the CENVAT and the state VAT partial in nature and contributed to their inefficiency and complexity.

In short, pre-GST indirect tax system of India was mired in multi-layered taxes levied by the Central and State Governments at different stages of the supply chain. GST has subsumed a profusion of Central and State indirect taxes to create a single unified market. It is slated to make India a seamless national market, boosting trade and industry and hence growth rate.

GST is a tax on goods and services with comprehensive and continuous chain of set-off benefits from the producer's point and service provider's point up to the retailer's level. It is essentially a tax only on value addition at each stage, and a supplier at each stage is permitted to set-off, through a tax credit mechanism, the GST paid on the purchase of goods and services. The final consumer only bears the GST charged by the last dealer in the supply chain.

Endnote

1. Section 4 of the Constitution (Forty-sixth Amendment) Act, 1982, inserted the following clause 29A in Article 366 of the Constitution to deem a tax on the following six items to be a tax on the sale or purchase of goods.
   [(29A). "tax on the sale or purchase of goods" includes:
   (a) a tax on the transfer, otherwise than in pursuance of a contract, of property in any goods for cash, deferred payment or other valuable consideration;
   (b) a tax on the transfer of property in goods (whether as goods or in some other form) involved in the execution of a works contract;
   (c) a tax on the delivery of goods on hire-purchase or any system of payment by instalments;
   (d) a tax on the transfer of the right to use any goods for any purpose (whether or not for a specified period) for cash, deferred payment or other valuable consideration;
   (e) a tax on the supply of goods by any unincorporated association or body of persons to a member thereof for cash, deferred payment or other valuable consideration; and
   (f) a tax on the supply, by way of or as part of any service or in any other manner whatsoever, of goods, being food or any other article for human consumption or any drink (whether or not intoxicating), where such supply or service, is for cash, deferred payment or other valuable consideration, and such transfer, delivery or supply of any goods shall be deemed to be a sale of those goods by the person making the transfer, delivery or supply and a purchase of those goods by the person to whom such transfer, delivery or supply is made].

Part II
Structure, Administration and Implications of GST

6

Constitutional Provisions Pertaining to Taxes in India

This chapter explains the constitutional provisions pertaining to taxation powers of different tiers of government in India. The Constitution makes elaborate, albeit complex, arrangements relating to the distribution, between the Union and the States, of taxes, the power of borrowing, and provision for grants-in-aid by the Union to the States. The underlying philosophy of these arrangements is to place at the disposal of the two tiers of government adequate financial resources to enable them to discharge their respective responsibilities under the Constitution.

6.1 Distribution of Taxation Powers

Article 265 of the Constitution specifically states that no taxes shall be levied or collected except by the authority of law.

Article 246 (read with Seventh Schedule of the Constitution) mentions the matters on which the Centre and the States can legislate. Thus, the Centre has exclusive powers to legislate in respect of matters contained in List I (Union List) of the Seventh Schedule. Entries 82 to 92C of this list refer to taxation powers of the Union Government (Table 6.1). Similarly, the States have exclusive powers to legislate in respect of matters contained in List II (State List) of the Seventh Schedule. Entries 45 to 63 of this list refer to taxation powers of the States (Table 6.2). Furthermore, the Centre and the States have concurrent powers to make laws on any matter contained in List III (Concurrent List) of the Seventh Schedule. However, this list does not contain any head of taxation.

The residual powers of taxation, as in general legislation, belong to the Union vide Article 248 read with Entry 97 of List I (Union List) in the Seventh Schedule. The Article reads, "(1) Subject to Article 246A, Parliament has exclusive power to make any law with respect to any matter not enumerated in the Concurrent List or State List.

(2) Such power shall include the power of making any law imposing a tax not mentioned in either of those Lists".

For example, gift tax was imposed by the Union Government in 1958 under these residual powers (gift tax was abolished in 1998). Similarly, prior to the Constitution (Eighty-eighth Amendment) Act, 2003, service tax was imposed under these residual powers.

As regards Union Territories, the Parliament has the power to impose any tax included in the State List.

A scrutiny of the taxation powers contained in List I Union List) and List II (State List) of the Seventh Schedule of the Constitution reveals that major and elastic sources of tax revenue belong to the Centre while relatively inelastic sources of revenue come under the purview of State Governments.

Table 6.1: Taxes within Union Jurisdiction as Enumerated in List I (Union List) in the Seventh Schedule (Read with Article 246) of the Constitution of India

Entry No. in List I	Description of the Tax/Duty	
	Before Constitution (One Hundred and First Amendment) Act, 2016	**After Constitution (One Hundred and First Amendment) Act, 2016**
82	Taxes on income other than agricultural income.	Same
83	Duties of customs including export duties.	Same
84	Duties of excise on tobacco and other goods manufactured or produced in India except: (a) alcoholic liquors for human consumption; (b) opium, Indian hemp and other narcotic drugs and narcotics, but including medicinal and toilet preparations containing alcohol or any substance, included in sub-paragraph (b) of this entry.	Duties of excise on the following goods manufactured or produced in India, namely: (a) petroleum crude; (b) high speed diesel; (c) motor spirit (commonly known as petrol); (d) natural gas; (e) aviation turbine fuel; and (f) tobacco and tobacco products.
85	Corporation tax.	Same
86	Taxes on the capital value of assets, exclusive of agricultural land, of individuals and companies, taxes on the capital of companies.	Same
87	Estate duty in respect of property other than agricultural land.	Same
88	Duties in respect of succession to property other than agricultural land.	Same
89	Terminal taxes on goods or passengers carried by railway, sea or air; taxes on railway fares and freights.	Same
90	Taxes other than stamp duties on transactions in stock exchanges and future markets.	Same
91[1]	Rates of stamp duty in respect of bills of exchange, cheques, promissory notes, bills of lading, letters of credit, policies of insurance, transfer of shares, debentures, proxies, and receipts.	Same
92	Taxes on the sale or purchase of newspapers and on advertisements published therein.	Omitted

Contd...

92A[2]	Taxes on the sale or purchase of goods other than newspapers, where such sale or purchase takes place in the course of inter-State trade or commerce.	Same
92B[3]	Taxes on the consignment of goods (whether the consignment is to the person making it or to any other person), where such consignment takes place in the course of inter-State trade or commerce.	Same
92C[4]	Taxes on services.	Omitted
97[5]	Any other matter not enumerated in List II or List III including any tax not enumerated in either of these lists.	Same

1. To be read with Article 268.
2. Inserted by the Constitution (Sixth Amendment) Act, 1956; to be read with Article 269.
3. Inserted by the Constitution (Forty-sixth Amendment) Act, 1982; to be read with Article 269.
4. Inserted by the Constitution (Eighty-eighth Amendment) Act, 2003.
5. To be read with Article 248.

Source: Government of India, Ministry of Law, Justice and Company Affairs, *The Constitution of India,* Seventh Schedule, List I (Union List).

6.2 Special Provisions with Respect to Goods and Services Tax

Article 246A of the Constitution [1] makes special provision with respect to goods and services tax by the Centre and the States. It reads, "246A. (1) Notwithstanding anything contained in Articles 246 and 254, Parliament, and, subject to clause (2), the Legislature of every State, have power to make laws with respect to goods and services tax imposed by the Union or by such State. (2) Parliament has exclusive power to make laws with respect to goods and services tax where the supply of goods, or of services, or both takes place in the course of inter-State trade or commerce.

Explanation—The provisions of this article, shall, in respect of goods and services tax referred to in clause (5) of Article 279A, take effect from the date recommended by the Goods and Services Tax Council".

6.3 Restrictions on the Taxation Powers of the States

Constitution also imposes certain restrictions on the taxation powers of the States. Although a State legislature enjoys the power to levy Goods and Services Tax (GST) under Article 246A and any of the taxes mentioned in List II (State List) of the Seventh Schedule, in the case of certain taxes, this power is subject to restrictions imposed by substantive provisions of the Constitution. Some examples of these restrictions are as follows.

6.3.1 Restriction on States to Impose Tax on the Supply of Goods or Services or Both: Article 286 ensures that taxes imposed by the States do not interfere with imports and exports or inter-State trade and commerce which are matters of national importance. The Article reads as under:

Table 6.2: Taxes within State Jurisdiction as Enumerated in List II (State List) in the Seventh Schedule (Read with Article 246) of the Constitution of India

Entry No. in List II	Description of the Tax/Duty	
	Before Constitution (One Hundred and First Amendment) Act, 2016	**After Constitution (One Hundred and First Amendment) Act, 2016**
45	Land revenue, including the assessment and collection of revenue, the maintenance of land records, survey for revenue purposes and records of rights, and alienation of revenues.	Same
46	Taxes on agricultural income.	Same
47	Duties in respect of succession to agricultural land.	Same
48	Estate duty in respect of agricultural land.	Same
49	Taxes on lands and buildings.	Same
50	Taxes on mineral rights subject to any limitations imposed by Parliament by law relating to mineral development.	Same
51	Duties of excise on the following goods manufactured or produced in the State and countervailing duties at the same or lower rates on similar goods manufactured or produced elsewhere in India: (a) alcoholic liquors for human consumption; (b) opium, Indian hemp and other narcotic drugs and narcotics but not including medicinal and toilet preparations containing alcohol or any substance included in sub-paragraph (b) of this entry.	Same
52	Taxes on the entry of goods into a local area for consumption, use or sale therein.	Omitted
53	Taxes on the consumption or sale of electricity.	Same
54*	Taxes on the sale or purchase of goods other than newspapers, subject to the provisions of Entry 92A of List I.	Taxes on the sale of petroleum crude, high speed diesel, motor spirit (commonly known as petrol), natural gas, aviation turbine fuel and alcoholic liquor for human consumption, but not including sale in the course of inter-State trade or commerce or sale in the course of international trade or commerce of such goods.

Contd...

55**	Taxes on advertisements other than advertisements published in the newspapers (and advertisements broadcast by radio or television).	Omitted
56	Taxes on goods and passengers carried by road or on inland waterways.	Same
57	Taxes on vehicles, whether mechanically propelled or not, suitable for use on roads, including tramcars subject to the provisions of Entry 35 of List III.	Same
58	Taxes on animals and boats.	Same
59	Tolls.	Same
60***	Taxes on professions, trades, callings and employment.	Same
61	Capitation taxes.	Same
62	Taxes on luxuries, including taxes on entertainment, amusements, betting and gambling.	Taxes on entertainments and amusements to the extent levied and collected by a panchayat or a municipality or a regional council or a district council.
63	Rates of stamp duty in respect of documents other than those specified in the provisions of List I with regard to rates of stamp duty.	Same

*Substituted by the Constitution (Sixth Amendment) Act, 1956: ** The words 'and advertisements broadcast by radio or television' inserted by the Constitution (Forty-second Amendment), Act, 1976: *** The scope of these taxes is spelt out in Article 276, clause (2) of which fixes the amount payable by a person on account of these taxes.

Source: Government of India, Ministry of Law, Justice and Company Affairs, *The Constitution of India*, Seventh Schedule, List II (State List).

"286. (1) No law of a State shall impose, or authorise the imposition of, a tax on the supply of goods or services or both, where such supply takes place: (a) outside the State; or (b) in the course of the import of the goods or services or both into, or export of the goods or services or both out of, the territory of India.

(2) Parliament may by law formulate principles for determining when a supply of goods or of services or both takes place in any of the ways mentioned in clause (1).

6.3.2 Exemption from State Taxes on Electricity Consumed by the Government of India (Article 287): The Article reads: "287. Save in so far as Parliament may by law otherwise provide, no law of a State shall impose, or authorise the imposition of, a tax on the consumption or sale of electricity (whether produced by a Government or other persons) which is:

(a) consumed by the Government of India, or sold to the Government of India for consumption by that Government; or (b) consumed in the construction, maintenance or operation of any railway by the Government of India or a railway company operating that railway, or sold to that Government or any such railway company for consumption in the construction, maintenance or operation of any railway, and any such law imposing, or authorising the imposition of, a tax on the sale of electricity shall secure that the price of electricity sold to the Government of India for consumption by that Government, or to any such railway company as aforesaid for consumption in the construction, maintenance or operation of any railway, shall be less by the amount of the tax than the price charged to other consumers of a substantial quantity of electricity".

6.3.3 Monetary Limit on Taxes on Professions etc.: A State legislature is empowered to levy a tax on professions, trade, calling or employment vide Entry 60 of List II. However, the total amount payable in respect of any one person to the State by way of such tax is not to exceed ₹ 2,500 per annum [Article 276(2)].

6.4 Exemption of Property of the Union from State Taxation

The property of the Centre is exempt from State taxation under Article 285(1) which reads as follows: "285. (1) The property of the Union shall, save in so far as Parliament may by law otherwise provide, be exempt from all taxes imposed by a State or by any authority within a State. (2) Nothing in clause (1) shall, until Parliament by law otherwise provides, prevent any authority within a State from levying any tax on any property of the Union to which such property was immediately before the commencement of this Constitution liable or treated as liable, so long as that tax continues to be levied in that State".

6.5 Exemption of Property and Income of a State from Union Taxation

Under Article 289 the property and incomes of the States are exempt from Union taxes, except that Parliament may by law provide for Central taxation of any trading activities of a State which are not incidental to the ordinary functions of Government. Article 289 reads as follows: "289. (1) The property and income of a State shall be exempt from Union taxation. (2) Nothing in clause (1) shall prevent the Union from imposing, or authorising the imposition of, any tax to such extent, if any, as Parliament may by law provide in respect of a trade or business of any kind carried on by, or on behalf of, the Government of a State, or any operations connected therewith, or any property used or occupied for the purposes of such trade or business, or any income accruing or arising in connection therewith. (3) Nothing in clause (2) shall apply to any trade or business, or to any class of trade or business, which Parliament may by law declare to be incidental to the ordinary functions of Government".

6.6 Sharing of Central Taxes

All the taxes and duties levied by the Union are not meant entirely for the purpose of the Union. In fact, revenues from certain taxes and duties leviable by the Union are totally assigned to States [2] or shared with them to supplement their revenues in accordance with their needs. It is a tribute to the foresight of the founding fathers that they realised that the sources of revenue allocated to the States may not prove sufficient in view of their growing welfare, maintenance, and developmental activities. Hence, specific provisions were made to set apart a portion of Central revenues for the benefit of States. These provisions indicate the flexibility of India's Constitution in terms of distribution of financial resources between different layers of the Government. They also make a distinction between the legislative power to *levy* a tax and the power to *appropriate* the proceeds of a tax so levied.

6.6.1 From Itemised Sharing to Global Sharing: Prior to the Constitution (Eightieth Amendment) Act, 2000, two main Central taxes were shared with the states, namely income tax (other than corporation tax) and the Union excise duties. The sharing of the income tax was mandatory under Article 270 while that of the Union excise duties was discretionary under Article 272. There were also two tax rental arrangements with the States, where the Union Government collected the tax on behalf of the States and then distributed the proceeds among the States on the basis of criteria recommended by the Finance Commission. These were: (i) additional duties of excise in lieu of sales tax on textiles, tobacco and sugar, and (ii) grant in lieu of tax on railway passenger fares.

The Constitution (Eightieth Amendment) Act, 2000, significantly changed the manner of distribution of Central tax collections between the Central and State Governments. It substituted a new Article for Article 270 and omitted the old Article 272. The new Article 270 provides for the sharing of the net proceeds of all Union taxes and duties with the States, subject to the provisions of Article 271 (explained below). In other words, all central taxes were brought into a shareable pool and it became mandatory to assign a share from each central tax to the States. Eleventh Finance Commission was the first to make recommendations in accordance with the new provisions of the Constitution.

It is noteworthy that only *net proceeds* are to be shared, and as such *cost of collection* has to be deducted to obtain the net proceeds as prescribed under Article 279. The proceeds are to be distributed among the States where the central taxes are *leviable* in *that year*.

Article 270 reads as follows: "270. (1) All taxes and duties referred to in the Union List, except the duties and taxes referred to in Articles 268, 269 and 269A, respectively, surcharge on taxes and duties referred to in Article 271 and any cess levied for specific purposes under any law made by Parliament shall be levied and collected by the Government of India and shall be distributed between the Union and the States in the manner provided in clause (2).

(1A) The tax collected by the Union under clause (1) of Article 246A shall also be distributed between the Union and the States in the manner provided in clause (2).

(1B) The tax levied and collected by the Union under clause (2) of Article 246A and Article 269A, which has been used for payment of the tax levied by the Union under clause (1) of Article 246A, and the amount apportioned to the Union under clause (1) of Article 269A, shall also be distributed between the Union and the States in the manner provided in clause (2).

(2) Such percentage, as may be prescribed, of the net proceeds of any such tax or duty in any financial year shall not form part of the Consolidated Fund of India, but shall be assigned to the States within which that tax or duty is leviable in that year, and shall

be distributed among those States in such manner and from such time as may be prescribed in the manner provided in clause (3).

(3) In this article, "prescribed" means—(i) until a Finance Commission has been constituted, prescribed by the President by order, and (ii) after a Finance Commission has been constituted, prescribed by the President by order after considering the recommendations of the Finance Commission".

The objective of the Constitution (Eightieth Amendment) Act, 2000 was to construct a pool of all central taxes for sharing so that a holistic view could be taken and both sides could share in the aggregate buoyancy of the central tax revenues.

6.7 Surcharges on Certain Duties and Taxes for the Purposes of the Union (Article 271)

The Article reads, "271. Notwithstanding anything in Articles 269 and 270, Parliament may at any time increase any of the duties or taxes referred to in those articles [except the goods and services tax under Article 246A [3] by a surcharge for purposes of the Union and the whole proceeds of any such surcharge shall form part of the Consolidated Fund of India".

6.8 Duties Levied by the Union but Collected and Appropriated by the States (Article 268)

These include such stamp duties as are mentioned in Entry 91 of List I (Union List) of the Seventh Schedule. The Article reads as follows: "268. (1) Such stamp duties as are mentioned in the Union List shall be levied by the Government of India but shall be collected: (a) in the case where such duties are leviable within any Union Territory by the Government of India, and (b) in other cases, by the States within which such duties are respectively leviable. (2) The proceeds in any financial year of any such duty leviable within any State shall not form part of the Consolidated Fund of India, but shall be assigned to that State".

Stamp duties are leviable on bills of exchange, cheques [4], promissory notes, bills of lading, letters of credit, policies of insurance, transfer of shares, debentures, proxies, and receipts. These documents are executed in the course of business and trade and they find place in the Union List to ensure uniformity of rates throughout the country for the smooth conduct of commercial and related transactions. Inter-State disparities in their rates and tax regulations can hinder, and even disrupt, the free flow of trade and commercial activities. The levy and collection of stamp duty is governed by the Indian Stamp Duty Act, 1899 which was last amended in 1976 when rates of stamp duty on certain instruments were revised. [5]

6.9 Taxes Levied and Collected by the Union but Assigned to the States (Article 269)

Article 269 reads as follows: "269. (1) Taxes on the sale or purchase of goods and taxes on the consignment of goods, except as provided in Article 269A, shall be levied and collected by the Government of India but shall be assigned and shall be deemed to have been assigned to the States on or after the 1st day of April, 1996 in the manner provided in clause (2).

Explanation—For the purposes of this clause: (a) the expression "taxes on the sale or purchase of goods" shall mean taxes on sale or purchase of goods other than newspapers, where such sale or purchase takes place in the course of inter-State trade or commerce and (b) the expression "taxes on the consignment of goods" shall mean taxes on the consignment of goods (whether the consignment is to the person making it or to any other person), where such consignment takes place in the course of inter-State trade or commerce.

(2) The net proceeds in any financial year of any such tax, except in so far as those proceeds represent proceeds attributable to Union territories, shall not form part of the Consolidated Fund of India, but shall be assigned to the States within which that tax is leviable in that year, and shall be distributed among those States in accordance with such principles of distribution as may be formulated by Parliament by law.

(3) Parliament may by law formulate principles for determining when a sale or purchase of, or consignment of, goods takes place in the course of inter-State trade or commerce".

The above two taxes correspond to Entries 92A and 92B in List I (Union List) of the Seventh Schedule. [6]

It is noteworthy that out of these two taxes only one was being levied till recently, viz. inter-State sales tax (Entry 92A). Central Sales Tax (CST) on inter-State sales was subsumed under GST.

6.9.1 Philosophy of Articles 268 and 269: Taxation arrangements under Articles 268 and 269 of the Constitution are of special importance. They place under the charge of the Union the taxes and duties which have inter-State character and require uniformity in rate structure for the smooth conduct of business and trade activities throughout the country. These two Articles mention taxes/duties which shall be levied by the Centre but assigned completely to the States within which they are leviable. [7]

6.10 Levy and Collection of Goods and Services Tax in the Course of Inter-State Trade or Commerce (Article 269A)

Inserted by Section 9 of the Constitution (One Hundred and First Amendment) Act, 2016 this new Article reads as follows: "269A. (1) Goods and services tax on supplies in the course of inter-State trade or commerce shall be levied and collected by the Government of India and such tax shall be apportioned between the Union and the States in the manner as may be provided by Parliament by law on the recommendations of the Goods and Services Tax Council.

Explanation—For the purposes of this clause, supply of goods, or of services, or both in the course of import into the territory of India shall be deemed to be supply of goods, or of services, or both in the course of inter-State trade or commerce.

(2) The amount apportioned to a State under clause (1) shall not form part of the Consolidated Fund of India.

(3) Where an amount collected as tax levied under clause (1) has been used for payment of the tax levied by a State under Article 246A, such amount shall not form part of the Consolidated Fund of India.

(4) Where an amount collected as tax levied by a State under Article 246A has been used for payment of the tax levied under clause (1), such amount shall not form part of the Consolidated Fund of the State.

(5) Parliament may, by law, formulate the principles for determining the place of supply, and when a supply of goods, or of services, or both takes place in the course of inter-State trade or commerce".

6.11 Goods and Services Tax Council (GST Council) (Article 279A)

Section 12 of the Constitution (One Hundred and First Amendment) Act, 2016 inserted a new Article 279A in the Constitution to provide for the constitution of Goods and Services Tax Council (GST Council) to make recommendations to the Union and the States on various aspects of the Goods and Services Tax (GST). The new Article reads as follows: "279A. (1) The President shall, within sixty days from the date of commencement of the Constitution (One Hundred and First Amendment) Act, 2016, by order, constitute a Council to be called the Goods and Services Tax Council.

(2) The Goods and Services Tax Council shall consist of the following members, namely: (a) the Union Finance Minister…Chairperson; (b) the Union Minister of State in charge of Revenue or Finance…Member; (c) the Minister in charge of Finance or Taxation or any other Minister nominated by each State Government…Members.

(3) The Members of the Goods and Services Tax Council referred to in sub-clause (c) of clause (2) shall, as soon as may be, choose one amongst themselves to be the Vice-Chairperson of the Council for such period as they may decide.

(4) The Goods and Services Tax Council shall make recommendations to the Union and the States on: (a) the taxes, cesses and surcharges levied by the Union, the States and the local bodies which may be subsumed in the goods and services tax; (b) the goods and services that may be subjected to, or exempted from the goods and services tax; (c) model Goods and Services Tax Laws, principles of levy, apportionment of Goods and Services Tax levied on supplies in the course of inter-State trade or commerce under Article 269A and the principles that govern the place of supply; (d) the threshold limit of turnover below which goods and services may be exempted from goods and services tax; (e) the rates including floor rates with bands of goods and services tax; (f) any special rate or rates for a specified period, to raise additional resources during any natural calamity or disaster; (g) special provision with respect to the States of Arunachal Pradesh, Assam, Jammu and Kashmir, Manipur, Meghalaya, Mizoram, Nagaland, Sikkim, Tripura, Himachal Pradesh and Uttarakhand; and (h) any other matter relating to the goods and services tax, as the Council may decide.

(5) The Goods and Services Tax Council shall recommend the date on which the goods and services tax be levied on petroleum crude, high speed diesel, motor spirit (commonly known as petrol), natural gas and aviation turbine fuel.

(6) While discharging the functions conferred by this article, the Goods and Services Tax Council shall be guided by the need for a harmonised structure of goods and services tax and for the development of a harmonised national market for goods and services.

(7) One-half of the total number of Members of the Goods and Services Tax Council shall constitute the quorum at its meetings.

(8) The Goods and Services Tax Council shall determine the procedure in the performance of its functions.

(9) Every decision of the Goods and Services Tax Council shall be taken at a meeting, by a majority of not less than three-fourths of the weighted votes of the members present and voting, in accordance with the following principles, namely: (a) the vote of the Central Government shall have a weightage of one-third of the total votes cast, and (b) the votes of all the State Governments taken together shall have a weightage of two-thirds of the total votes cast, in that meeting.

(10) No act or proceedings of the Goods and Services Tax Council shall be invalid merely by reason of: (a) any vacancy in, or any defect in, the constitution of the Council; or (b) any defect in the appointment of a person as a Member of the Council; or (c) any procedural irregularity of the Council not affecting the merits of the case.

(11) The Goods and Services Tax Council shall establish a mechanism to adjudicate any dispute: (a) between the Government of India and one or more States; or (b) between the Government of India and any State or States on one side and one or more other States on the other side; or (c) between two or more States, arising out of the recommendations of the Council or implementation thereof."

Section 15 of the Constitution (One Hundred and First Amendment) Act, 2016 also amended Article 368 of the Constitution which pertains to power of Parliament to amend the Constitution and procedure therefore. Thus, Article 279A (pertaining to GST Council) was included in the list of items amendments to which require ratification by the legislatures of not less than one-half of the States.

6.12 Taxes and Duties in List I (Union List) of the Seventh Schedule not being Levied at Present

These taxes/duties are discussed below individually along with the logic for retaining them with the Centre.

6.12.1 Entries 87 and 88: These two entries pertain to estate duty, and succession duty in respect of property other than agricultural land respectively. Since the incidence of both estate duty, and succession duty is on the same object, viz. property passing on the death of the owner to his successors, they are essentially similar in nature. However, while in the case of the estate duty, the value of the whole estate, even if situated in more than one State, is the base for taxation, the succession duty is relatable to the value of individual shares (i.e. parts of an estate) passing on to the successors.

The desirability of retaining both these duties with the Centre is self-evident. An individual may have properties located in more than one State and a total assessment of his estate can better be undertaken by the Union Government. Similarly, if succession duty is levied by the States, the persons inheriting properties in different States will have to deal with different tax rates and procedures. Moreover, if estate/succession duties are levied by the States, it may trigger unhealthy competition among the States, resulting into harassment of the assessees and hence litigation. On efficiency criterion (i.e. cost of collection) also it is desirable if these duties are levied and administered by the Union, thus avoiding duplication of tax administration. Moreover, the Union has better access to information and otherwise also it is in larger national interest to ensure uniformity with respect to these duties. It may be noted that estate duty was first imposed in India in 1953 when the Estate Duty Act of that year imposed a duty on the capital value of all property passing on the death of any person on or after October 15, 1953. It was abolished with effect from March 16, 1985.

6.12.2 Entry 89: It relates to terminal taxes on goods and passengers carried by railway, sea or air. However, under Entry 56 of List II, States are empowered to levy taxes on goods and passengers carried by road or on inland waterways. Thus, the taxation powers in regard to the services of the major means of transport rest with the Union.

In a developing and diversifying economy like India, the importance of transport sector is self-evident. The growth of this vital infrastructure enlarges the size of the market and determines, *inter alia,* the level of private enterprise. Lest the free flow of inter-State trade should be hampered by differential State levies, the taxation of transport services is, by and large, with the Union Government. The Fifth and the Eighth Finance Commissions examined the scope for levying these taxes but expressed themselves against their imposition on grounds of administrative difficulties and meagre revenue potential. It is noteworthy that there already exists a terminal tax on passengers carried by railway from or to certain places of pilgrimage or where fairs or exhibitions are held. The proceeds of the tax are credited to the Consolidated Fund of the concerned States. The tax is restrictive and limited in scope and not a general terminal tax on passengers carried by railways to all places.

Entry 89 also refers to taxes on railway fares and freights. The Eighth Finance Commission favoured levying tax on railway passenger fares but not until the present arrangement of giving grants in lieu of such a tax continues to exist.

6.12.3 Entry 90: It pertains to 'taxes other than stamp duties on transactions in stock exchanges and future markets'. Since stock exchanges and future markets [8] are at a formative stage and have an inter-State character therefore it is desirable to retain these taxes with the Union. The Eighth Finance Commission did not think it advisable to levy taxes on transactions in stock exchanges and future markets.

6.12.4 Entry 92: It refers to 'taxes on the sale or purchase of newspapers and on advertisements published therein'. This tax is retained with the Union to protect the freedom of the press, and avoid undue tax burden on newspaper industry, particularly the regional language newspapers. Since newspaper reading habit is not sufficiently developed and widespread in the country, it is not desirable to impose a tax on the sale or purchase of newspapers. Both the Fifth and the Eighth Finance Commissions did not recommend a tax on the sale or purchase of newspapers. However, both the Commissions opined that there was scope for tax on advertisements published in newspapers. The Eighth Commission cautioned that a tax on advertisement, if levied, should be borne by the advertisers themselves and not passed on to the newspapers and journals.

It is noteworthy that Entry 92 was omitted by Section 17 of the Constitution (One Hundred and First Amendment) Act, 2016.

6.13 Taxation Powers to Local Governments

The Constitution does not provide for any taxation powers to local governments. However, the implication of Article 276 is that the taxes on professions, trades, callings or employment are for the benefit of a State or of a municipality, district board, local board or any other local authority. The States on their own may assign any of the taxes in the State List to the local bodies. The taxes generally assigned to local governments are property taxes, and taxes on vehicles.

6.14 Powers of District Councils to Levy Taxes in Tribal Areas

Sixth Schedule of the Constitution [read with Articles 244 (2) and 275 (1)] pertains to provisions as to the administration of tribal areas in the States of Assam, Meghalaya, Tripura and Mizoram. Sub-paragraph (3) of paragraph 8 of the Sixth Schedule relates to powers of the District Council for an autonomous district to levy and collect all or any of the following taxes within such district: (a) taxes on professions, trades, callings and employments; (b) taxes on animals, vehicles and boats; (c) taxes on the entry of goods into a market for sale therein, and tolls on passengers and goods carried in ferries; (d) taxes for the maintenance of schools, dispensaries or roads; and (e) taxes on entertainment and amusements.

6.15 Freedom as to Payment of Taxes for Promotion of any Particular Religion

According to Article 27 of the Constitution of India, "No person shall be compelled to pay any taxes, the proceeds of which are specifically appropriated in payment of expenses for the promotion or maintenance of any particular religion or religious denomination".

6.16 Rationale for Constitutional Arrangements

The distribution of taxation powers between the Centre and the States is meant to minimise tax problems in a federal set up such as double taxation, tax rivalry among States, duplicate tax administration, and tax evasion. Constitutional division of taxation powers between the Union and the States in India rests on economic and administrative considerations. Taxes with an inter-State base, and those in the case of which uniformity in rates is desirable, are vested in the Central Government. Also, taxes which the taxpayer can evade by shifting his habitat, or where the place of residence is not a correct guide to the true incidence of the tax, belong to the Centre. Taxes which are location-specific and relate to subjects of local consumption are with the States.

Commenting upon the soundness of the constitutional arrangements regarding division of taxation powers, the Commission on Centre State Relations, 1988, observed, "A well balanced distribution of heads of taxation based on economic and administrative rationale between the Union and the States and adequate arrangements for sharing of resources is vital for the proper functioning of the two-tier polity. We are of the firm view that the basic scheme of the Constitution dividing the field of taxation between the Union and the States and incorporating adequate arrangements for sharing of resources between them, is sound and no major modifications in it are called for". [9]

Similarly, the Sixth Finance Commission made the following observations in this regard, "We must bear in mind that the country as a whole and every part thereof has gained significantly from the maintenance of a vast unified market within which there is free movement of goods and men. Having regard to the trends all over the world even for independent political entities to come together to forge closer economic links in the form of common markets and economic groupings, our best hopes of accelerated economic development lie in the further strengthening of our national market and in the promotion of fiscal arrangements that are most conducive to the effective functioning of this market. Given this basic fact, there can be no room for argument that the levy and administration of taxes with wide economic base such as income tax, corporation tax, Union excise duties and of course also import and export duties will have to remain with the Union Government. In fact the architects of our Constitution drew on the experience of some of the other federations in which the assignment of taxes with wide economic base to units had led to intractable problems of conflicting tax jurisdictions. They wisely averted the possibility of such conflicts by assigning such taxes right from the beginning to the Union Government. At the same time, the framers of our Constitution rightly allocated to the States' subjects such as agriculture, education, medical care, public health, irrigation and law and order that touch intimately the lives of the people. These can be efficiently administered in a vast country only by the State Governments which are closer to the people and are more keenly alive to their problems and needs. The heads of revenue and responsibilities were distributed on the basis of whether the Centre or the State was better equipped to deal with the particular head". [10]

6.17 Definitions

In relation to taxation, the Constitution provides the following definitions:

6.17.1 Goods: According to clause 12 of Article 366 of the Constitution, *goods* include all materials, commodities, and articles.

6.17.2 Goods and Services Tax: According to clause 12A [11] of Article 366 of the Constitution, *goods and services tax* means any tax on supply of goods, or services or both except taxes on the supply of the alcoholic liquor for human consumption.

6.17.3. Services: According to clause 26A [12] of Article 366 of the Constitution, *services* means anything other than goods.

6.17.4 State: According to clause 26B [13] of Article 366 of the Constitution, *State* with reference to Articles 246A, 268, 269, 269A and Article 279A includes a Union Territory with legislature.

6.18 Summary of Constitutional Provisions Pertaining to Taxes

Provisions regarding taxes in the Constitution of India are summarized in Table 6.3.

Table 6.3: Constitutional Provisions Pertaining to Taxes

Article	Brief Description
27	Freedom as to payment of taxes for promotion of any particular religion.
246 (read with Seventh Schedule of the Constitution)	Subject-matter (including taxes) of laws made by Parliament and by the Legislatures of States.
246A	Special provisions with respect to Goods and Services Tax (GST).
248 [read with Entry 97 of List I (Union List) of the Seventh Schedule]	Residuary powers of legislation, including taxes.
265	No tax shall be levied or collected except by authority of law.
268 [read with Entry 91 of List I (Union List) of the Seventh Schedule]	Duties levied by the Union but collected and appropriated by the States.
269 [read with Entries 92A and 92B of List I (Union List) of the Seventh Schedule]	Taxes levied and collected by the Union but assigned to the States.
269A	Levy and collection of Goods and Services Tax (GST) in the course of inter-State trade or commerce.
270	Taxes and duties levied and collected by the Union but distributed between the Union and the States.
271	Surcharges on certain duties and taxes for the purpose of the Union.
276(2)	Monetary limit on taxes on professions, trade, calling or employment.
279A	Goods and Services Tax Council (GST Council).
285(1)	Exemption of property of the Union from State taxation.
286	Restriction on States to impose tax on the supply of goods or services or both, where such supply takes place: (a) outside the State; or (b) in the course of the import of the goods or services or both into, or export of the goods or services or both out of, the territory of India.
287	Exemption from State taxes on electricity consumed by the Government of India.
289	Exemption of property and income of a State from Union taxation.
244(2) and 275(1) [read with sub-paragraph (3) of paragraph 8 of the Sixth Schedule	Powers of District Councils to levy taxes in tribal areas.
366(12)	Definition of *goods.*
366(12A)	Definition of *goods and services tax.*
366(26A)	Definition of *services.*
366(26B)	Definition of *state* with reference to Articles 246A, 268, 269, 269A and 279A.

Endnotes

1. Article 246A was inserted in the Constitution by Section 2 of the Constitution (One Hundred First Amendment) Act, 2016.
2. See sections 6.8 and 6.9 of this chapter.
3. Inserted by Section 11 of Constitution (One Hundred and First Amendment) Act, 2016.
4. Stamp duty was payable on cheques prior to 1927 but was withdrawn in that year.
5. **Indian Stamp Act:** The Indian Stamp Act, 1899 is a fiscal statute laying down the law relating to tax levied in the form of stamps on instruments recording transactions and stamp duties on instruments specified in Entry 91 of List I (Union List) of the Seventh Schedule of the Constitution. Because of large scale changes in the usage of the instruments since the Indian Stamp Act, 1899 was introduced, a need to amend a good number of provisions of this Act is being felt for quite some time. Law Commission in its 67th report submitted in 1976 made extensive recommendations in this regard. Serious efforts are now being made to bring in large scale amendments in Indian Stamp Act, 1899 to bring this law in tune with the times. Stamp duties on instruments other than those mentioned in Entry 91 of List I above are levied by the States as per Entry 63 of List II (State List). Thus, stamp duty and registration fees are levied on the registration of property or other conveyances. Provisions other than those relating to rates of duty fall within the legislative power of both the Union and the States by virtue of Entry 44 of List III (Concurrent List) of the Seventh Schedule. Stamp duties on all the instruments are collected and kept by the concerned States.

   Till recently, the stamp duty rates were quite high in most states and the procedures for evaluating the conveyances were also complicated. In this context, the Tenth Five Year Plan (2002-07) remarked, "Stamp duty needs to be paid on all documents which are registered and the rate varies from state to state. With stamp duty rates of 13 percent in Delhi, 14.5 percent in Uttar Pradesh and 12.5 percent in Haryana, India has perhaps one of the highest levels of stamp duty. Some states even have double stamp incidence, first on land and then on its development. In contrast the maximum rate levied in most developed markets whether in Singapore or Europe is in the range of 1-2 percent. Even the National Housing and Habitat Policy, 1998, recommended a stamp duty rate of 2-3 percent. Most of the methods to avoid registration are basically to avoid payment of high stamp duty.

   Another fall out of high stamp duty rates is the understatement of the proceeds of a sale. This is also linked to payment of income tax and capital gains tax. When registration has not been effected, a transfer is not deemed to have taken place and hence capital gains tax can be totally avoided. Thus, the present provisions in various laws and their poor implementation have led to a situation where there is considerable financial loss to the exchequer on account of understatement of sale proceeds, non-registration and consequent non-payment of stamp duty and avoidance of capital gains tax". [Government of India, Planning Commission, *Tenth Five Year Plan* (2002-07), Volume II, pp. 833-834.]

   Of late, states have undertaken reforms by reducing the duty rates and streamlining procedures for evaluation of property. After the reduction of rates, the general experience has been revenue-augmenting due to improved compliance of law.
6. Prior to the Eightieth Amendment of the Constitution, provisions of Article 269 were as follows.

   Taxes Levied and Collected by the Union but Assigned to the States (Article 269): These were: (a) duties in respect of succession to property other than agricultural land, (b) estate duty in respect of property other than agricultural land, (c) terminal taxes on goods or passengers carried by railway, sea or air, (d) taxes on railway fares and freights, (e) taxes other than stamp duties on transactions in stock exchanges and future markets, (f) taxes on the sale or purchase of newspapers and on advertisements published therein, (g) taxes on the sale or purchase of goods other than newspapers, where such sale or purchase takes place in the course of inter-State trade or commerce, and (h) taxes on the consignment of goods (whether the consignment is to the person making it or to any other person), where such consignment takes place in the course of inter-State trade or commerce. These taxes corresponded to Entries 87, 88, 89, 90, 92, 92A and 92B in the Union List.

7. **Assignment of Taxes:** Assignment of a tax means transfer of taxation power from a higher level to a lower level of government. Taxation power includes the following: the right to levy the tax, collect the tax, and appropriate the proceeds from the tax. Thus, there can be three interpretations of assignment of a tax. In the first case, the higher level government may levy and collect a tax but handover the entire proceeds to a lower level government. Taxes levied by the Government of India under Article 269 of the Constitution are a case in point. Secondly, the higher level government may levy a tax but allow the lower level government to collect it and retain fully the proceeds therefrom. Taxes levied by the Government of India under Article 268 of the Constitution fall under this category. Finally, the higher level government may transfer a tax to a lower level government lock, stock and barrel, a situation which defines assignment of a tax in its strictest sense.

   Assignment of taxes should not be unconditional. Along with the determination of tax domain for a state, the central government ought to prescribe conditions so that the underlying purpose of assignment is adequately served. Thus, it should be obligatory on the part of a state to levy the tax assigned to it. Not only this, the state should not have powers to alter the basic structure of the assigned tax. The state may enjoy flexibility in fixing the tax rates within a minimum and maximum range prescribed by the central government. Tax exemptions/concessions should be minimum because a state is not expected to serve national objectives through its tax policy. As at other levels, tax default through disputes should be discouraged by requiring full payments prior to disputing an assessment.

8. Future trading refers to contracts for sale and purchase of goods at a future date primarily with a view to avoid price fluctuations. Presently, future trading is allowed at specific centres in respect of four commodities, viz. jute products, paper, turmeric, and *gur*.
9. Government of India, *Report of the Commission on Centre State Relations* (Chairman: Justice R.S. Sarkaria) Part I, 1988, p. 271.
10. *Report of the Sixth Finance Commission*, 1973, p. 5.
11. Inserted by section 14 of the Constitution (One Hundred First Amendment) Act, 2016.
12. Ibid.
13. Ibid.

7

Early Thoughts and Preparations for GST

After an arduous journey of 12 years—beginning with the mention of Goods and Services Tax (GST) by the Finance Minister Shri P. Chidambaram in his budget speech for 2005-06 on February 28, 2005— GST finally became operative on July 1, 2017. The historic tax reform saw various ups and downs during this period.

7.1 The Genesis

GST was first recommended by the Task Force on Implementation of the Fiscal Responsibility and Budget Management Act, 2003 (Chairman: Vijay Kelkar). The Report of the Task Force observed, "The introduction of the GST at both Central and State levels should be accompanied by the withdrawal of all cascading taxes such as octroi, Central Sales Tax, state level sales taxes, entry tax, stamp duties, telecom license fees, turnover taxes, tax on consumption or sale of electricity, taxes on transportation of goods and passengers etc. This removal of inefficient and distortionary taxes would constitute a major milestone for reforms in Indian public finance.

The Central Excise Act and the taxation of services by the Finance Act, 1994, will be subsumed under the central goods and services tax. This should be implemented through a legislation which may be named Indian Goods and Services Act. The States will need to simultaneously introduce corresponding legislation for taxation of goods and services which will subsume their existing State-level cascading taxes. Under this proposed *grand bargain*, the States obtain revenues from taxation of services, and from access to GST on imports. More importantly, India would obtain the full efficiencies of a single national VAT, while retaining a federal structure." [1]

The idea of moving towards the GST was first mooted by the then Union Finance Minister Shri P. Chidambaram in his budget speech for 2005-06 on February 28, 2005. He observed, "In the medium to long-term, it is my goal that the entire production-distribution chain should be covered by a national VAT, or even better, a goods and services tax, encompassing both the Centre and the States." [2] Reiterating the desirability of switching over to GST, he remarked in his budget speech for 2006-07, "It is my sense that there is a large consensus that the country should move towards a national level Goods and Services Tax (GST) that should be shared between the Centre and the States. I propose that we set April 1, 2010 as the date for introducing GST. World over, goods and services attract the same rate of tax. That is the foundation of a GST. People must get used to the idea of a GST". [3, 4]

7.2 Role of the Empowered Committee (EC) of State Finance Ministers

While declaring its intention to introduce GST from April 1, 2010, the Central

Government had indicated that the Empowered Committee (EC) of State Finance Ministers [5] would work with the Central Government to prepare a road map for the introduction of GST. Hence, EC—which had formulated the design of State level VAT—prepared a report on a Model and Road Map for GST. Pursuant to this, on May 10, 2007, EC set up a Joint Working Group consisting of representatives of the EC and the Government of India.

This Joint Working Group got itself divided into three Sub-Groups and had several rounds of internal discussions as well as interaction with experts and representatives of Chambers of Commerce and Industry. On the basis of these discussions and interaction, the Sub-Groups submitted their reports which were then integrated and consolidated into the report of Joint Working Group (November 19, 2007).

7.2.1 Model and Road Map for GST: This report was discussed in detail in the meeting of the EC on November 28, 2007, and the States were also requested to communicate their observations on the report in writing. On the basis of these discussions in the EC and the written observations, certain modifications were considered necessary and were discussed with the representatives of the Department of Revenue, Ministry of Finance, Government of India. With the modifications duly made, a final version of the views of EC resulted in the preparation of *A Model and Road Map for Goods and Service Tax in India* (April 30, 2008). The model and roadmap, while recommending that a dual GST be put in place, also provided preliminary views on the Central and State taxes to be subsumed within the GST.

The *model* detailed the operational issues which needed to be addressed, including the number of rates, exemptions and exclusions from GST, as well as the treatment of inter-state transactions.

The *roadmap* outlined the legal and administrative steps which needed to be taken in order to comply with the April 1, 2010 deadline.

These views of EC were then sent to the Government of India, and the comments of Government of India were received on December 12, 2008. These comments were duly considered by the EC (December 16, 2008), and it was decided that a Committee of Principal Secretaries/Secretaries of Finance/Taxation and Commissioners of Trade Taxes of the States should be set up to consider these comments, and submit their views.

The Committee held detailed deliberations on January 5-6, 2009, and submitted its recommendations to the Empowered Committee. The Empowered Committee considered these recommendations in its meeting held on January 21, 2009 and accepted them in-principle.

7.2.2 First Discussion Paper on GST: As a follow-up of this in-principle acceptance, a Working Group consisting of the concerned officials of the State Governments was formed who, in association with senior representatives of Government of India, submitted their recommendations in detail on the structure of GST.

After taking into account a detailed view on the recommendations of the Working Group of officials and other related matters, EC released the *First Discussion Paper on Goods and Services Tax in India* (November 10, 2009, for discussion with industry, trade, agriculture and people at large. The comments of Government of India on the proposed design of GST were sent to the Empowered Committee in January 2010. A joint group of officers was constituted to prepare draft Constitutional Bill, Central GST legislation, model State GST legislation and rules required to introduce GST. To operationalize the GST, the Constitution (One Hundred and Fifteenth Amendment) Bill was introduced in the Lok Sabha in March 2011 to enable Parliament and State Legislatures to make laws for levying GST on every transaction of supply of goods or services or both. Some goods, namely crude petroleum, diesel, petrol, aviation turbine fuel, natural gas and alcohol were not to come under the purview of the GST.

The Discussion Paper was divided into 4 sections. Section 1 gave a brief reference to the process of introduction of VAT by the Centre and the States and also indicated the precise points where there was a need for further improvement. This section also showed how GST could bring about this improvement. With this as the background and justification for GST, section 2 then described the process of preparation for GST. Thereafter, section 3 presented in detail the comprehensive structure of the GST model. For illustrating this GST model further, there was in the end an annexure on frequently asked questions and answers.

7.3 Summary of Recommendations of the First Discussion Paper (FDP)

7.3.1 Goods and Services Tax Model for India: FDP took note of the significant administrative issues involved in designing an effective GST model in a federal system with the objective of having an overall harmonious structure of rates. Together with this, it emphasized the need for upholding the powers of Central and State Governments in their taxation matters. Further, it underlined the need to propose a model that would be easily implementable, while being generally acceptable to stakeholders.

A dual GST structure with defined functions and responsibilities of the Centre and the States was recommended. An appropriate mechanism that would be binding on both the Centre and the States would be worked out whereby the harmonious rate structure along with the need for further modification could be upheld, if necessary with a collectively agreed constitutional amendment.

Salient features of the model recommended by FDP were as follows:

1. GST should have two components—one levied by the Centre (referred to as Central GST), and the other levied by the States (referred to as State GST). Rates for Central GST and State GST would be prescribed appropriately, reflecting revenue considerations and acceptability. This dual GST model would be implemented through multiple statutes (one for CGST and SGST statute for every State). However, the basic features of law such as chargeability, definition of taxable event and taxable person, measure of levy including valuation provisions, basis of classification etc. would be uniform across these statutes as far as practicable.
2. Central GST and the State GST would be applicable to all transactions of goods and services made for a consideration except the exempted goods and services, goods which remain outside the purview of GST and the transactions which are below the

prescribed threshold limits.

3. Central GST and State GST are to be paid to the accounts of the Centre and the States separately. It would have to be ensured that account-heads for all services and goods would have indication whether it relates to Central GST or State GST (with identification of the State to whom the tax is to be credited).
4. Since the Central GST and State GST are to be treated separately, taxes paid against the Central GST shall be allowed to be taken as input tax credit (ITC) for the Central GST and could be utilized only against the payment of Central GST. The same principle would be applicable for the State GST. A taxpayer or exporter would have to maintain separate details in books of account for utilization or refund of credit. Further, the rules for taking and utilization of credit for the Central GST and the State GST would be aligned.
5. Cross utilization of ITC between the Central GST and the State GST would not be allowed except in the case of inter-State supply of goods and services under the IGST mode.
6. Ideally, the problem related to credit accumulation on account of refund of GST should be avoided by both the Centre and the States except in the cases such as exports, purchase of capital goods, input tax at higher rate than output tax etc. where, again refund/adjustment should be completed in a time bound manner.
7. To the extent feasible, uniform procedure for collection of both Central GST and State GST should be prescribed in the respective legislation for Central GST and State GST.
8. Administration of the Central GST to the Centre and for State GST to the States was recommended. This would imply that the Centre and the States would have concurrent jurisdiction for the entire value chain and for all taxpayers on the basis of thresholds for goods and services prescribed for the States and the Centre.
9. FDP noted that existing threshold prescribed in different State VAT Acts—below which VAT was not applicable—varied from State to State. A uniform State GST threshold across States was desirable and, therefore, it was recommended that a threshold of gross annual turnover of ₹10 lakh—both for goods and services for all the States and Union Territories—may be adopted with adequate compensation for the States (particularly, the States in North-Eastern Region and Special Category States) where lower threshold had prevailed in the VAT regime. Keeping in view the interest of small traders and small-scale industries and to avoid dual control, the threshold for Central GST for goods may be kept at ₹ 1.5 crore and the threshold for Central GST for services may also be appropriately high.
10. Composition/compounding scheme for the purpose of GST should have an upper ceiling on gross annual turnover and a floor tax rate with respect to gross annual turnover. In particular, there should be a compounding cut-off at ₹ 50 lakh of gross annual turn over and a floor rate of 0.5 percent across the States. The scheme should also allow option for GST registration for dealers with turnover below the compounding cut-off.

11. Taxpayer would need to submit periodical returns, in common format as far as possible, to both the Central GST authority and to the concerned State GST authorities.
12. Each taxpayer would be allotted a PAN-linked taxpayer identification number with a total of 13/15 digits. This would bring the GST PAN-linked system in line with the prevailing PAN-based system for Income tax, facilitating data exchange and taxpayer compliance.
13. Keeping in mind the need of tax payer's convenience, functions such as assessment, enforcement, scrutiny and audit would be undertaken by the authority which is collecting the tax, with information sharing between the Centre and the States.

7.3.2 Subsumation of Central and State Taxes under GST: The various Central, State and Local levies were examined to identify their possibility of being subsumed under GST. While identifying these levies, the following principles were kept in mind:

1. Taxes or levies to be subsumed should be primarily in the nature of indirect taxes, either on the supply of goods or on the supply of services.
2. Taxes or levies to be subsumed should be part of the transaction chain which commences with import/manufacture/production of goods or provision of services at one end and the consumption of goods and services at the other.
3. Subsumation should result in free flow of tax credit in intra and inter-State levels.
4. Taxes, levies and fees that are not specifically related to supply of goods and services should not be subsumed under GST.
5. Revenue fairness for both the Union and the States individually would need to be attempted.

On application of the above principles, FDP recommended that the following Central taxes should be, to begin with, subsumed under the GST:

1. Central excise duty.
2. Additional excise duties.
3. Excise duty levied under the Medicinal and Toiletries Preparation Act.
4. Service tax.
5. Additional customs duty, commonly known as countervailing duty (CVD).
6. Special additional duty (SAD) of customs.
7. Surcharges.
8. Cesses.

Following State taxes and levies, to begin with, were recommended for subsumation under GST:

1. VAT/sales tax.
2. Entertainment tax (unless it is levied by the local bodies).
3. Luxury tax.
4. Taxes on lottery, betting and gambling.
5. State cesses and surcharges in so far as they relate to supply of goods and services.
6. Entry tax not in lieu of octroi.

7.3.3 Purchase Tax: Some of the States were getting substantial revenue from purchase tax and, therefore, they were not in favour of its subsumation under GST while majority of the States were of the view that no such exemptions should be given. The difficulties of the foodgrains producing States and certain other States were appreciated as substantial revenue was being earned by them from purchase tax and it was, therefore, felt that in case purchase tax had to be subsumed then adequate and continuing compensation should be provided to such States. This issue was discussed in consultation with the Government of India.

7.3.4 Tax on Items Containing Alcohol: Alcoholic beverages would be kept out of the purview of GST. Sales tax/VAT can be continued to be levied on alcoholic beverages as per the existing practice. In case it has been made VATable by some States, there is no objection to that. Excise duty, which is presently being levied by the States may not be also affected.

7.3.5 Tax on Tobacco Products: Tobacco products would be subjected to GST with ITC. Centre may be allowed to levy excise duty on tobacco products over and above GST without ITC.

7.3.6 Tax on Petroleum Products: As regards petroleum products, it was decided that the basket of petroleum products, i.e. crude, motor spirit (including ATF) and HSD would be kept outside GST as is the prevailing practice in India. Sales tax could continue to be levied by the States on these products with prevailing floor rate. Similarly, Centre could also continue its levies. A final view whether natural gas should be kept outside the GST would be taken after further deliberations.

7.3.7 Inter-State Transactions of Goods and Services: IGST model for taxation of inter-State transaction of goods and services would be adopted. The scope of IGST Model is that Centre would levy IGST which would be CGST plus SGST on all inter-State transactions of taxable goods and services with appropriate provision for consignment or stock transfer of goods and services. The inter-State seller would pay IGST on value addition after adjusting available credit of IGST, CGST, and SGST on his purchases. The Exporting State would transfer to the Centre the credit of SGST used in payment of IGST. The Importing dealer would claim credit of IGST while discharging his output tax liability in his own State. The Centre would transfer to the importing State the credit of IGST used in payment of SGST. The relevant information would also be submitted to the Central Agency which would act as a clearing house mechanism, verify the claims and inform the respective governments to transfer the funds.

7.3.8 GST Rate Structure: FDP suggested a two-rate structure—a lower rate for necessary items and goods of basic importance and a standard rate for goods in general. It also recommended a special rate for precious metals and a list of exempted items. For upholding of special needs of each State as well as a balanced approach to federal flexibility, and also for facilitating the introduction of GST, it was discussed whether the exempted list under VAT regime including goods of local importance be retained in the exempted list under State GST in the initial years. It was also deliberated whether the Government of India may adopt, to begin with, a similar approach towards exempted list under the CGST.

The States were of the view that for CGST relating to goods, the Government of India may also have a two rate structure, with conformity in the levels of rate under the SGST. For taxation of services, there may be a single rate for both CGST and SGST. The exact value of the SGST and CGST rates, including the rate for services, would be made known duly in course of appropriate legislative actions.

7.3.9 Zero Rating of Exports: Exports would be zero-rated. Similar benefits may be given to special economic zones (SEZs). However, such benefits would only be allowed to the processing zones of the SEZs. No benefit to the sales from an SEZ to domestic tariff area (DTA) should be allowed.

7.3.10 GST on Imports: The GST will be levied on imports with necessary Constitutional Amendments. Both CGST and SGST should be levied on import of goods and services into the country. The incidence of tax would follow the destination principle and the tax revenue in case of SGST would accrue to the State where the imported goods and services are consumed. Full and complete set-off would be available on the GST paid on import on goods and services.

7.3.11 Special Industrial Area Scheme: After the introduction of GST, the tax exemptions, remissions etc. related to industrial incentives should be converted, if at all needed, into cash refund schemes after collection of tax, so that the GST scheme on the basis of a continuous chain of set-offs is not disturbed. Regarding Special Industrial Area Schemes, it was clarified that such exemptions, remissions etc. would continue up to legitimate expiry time both for the Centre and the States. Any new exemption, remission etc. or continuation of earlier exemption, remission etc. would not be allowed. In such cases, the Central and the State Governments could provide reimbursement after collecting GST.

7.3.12 Compensation during Implementation of GST: Despite the sincere attempts made by the Empowered Committee on the determination of GST rate structure, revenue neutral rates, it was difficult to estimate accurately as to how much the States would gain from service taxes and how much they would lose on account of removal of cascading effect, payment of input tax credit and phasing out of CST. In view of this, it would be essential to provide adequately for compensation for loss that might emerge during the process of implementation of GST for the next 5 years. The payment of this compensation will need to be ensured in terms of special grants to be released to the States duly in every month on the basis of neutrally monitored mechanism.

7.4 Constitutional Requirements and Measures

Why did the introduction of GST require a Constitutional amendment? The Indian Constitution demarcates the powers of taxation between the Central and State Governments. The Constitution provides for delineation of power to tax between the Centre and States. Prior to the enactment of Constitution (One Hundred and First Amendment) Act, 2016, while the Centre was empowered to tax services and goods up to the production stage, the States had the power to tax sale of goods. The States did not have the power to levy a tax on the supply of services while the Centre did not have power to levy tax on the sale of goods. Thus, the Constitution did not vest express power either in the Central or State Government to levy a tax on the *supply of goods and services*. Moreover, the Constitution also did not empower the States to impose tax on imports. All these and other issues need to be addressed.

Under the GST regime, all goods and services are simultaneously taxed by both the Central and State Governments.

7.4.1 Constitution (One Hundred and Twenty-second Amendment) Bill, 2014: On March 22, 2011, the Constitution (One Hundred and Fifteenth Amendment) Bill, 2011 was introduced in Parliament to enable the levy of GST. However, the Bill lapsed with the dissolution of the 15th Lok Sabha. Subsequently, on December 19, 2014, the Constitution (One Hundred and Twenty-second Amendment) Bill, 2014 was introduced in the Lok Sabha to address various issues related to GST.

Main Features: The salient features of the Bill were as follows:

1. Conferring simultaneous power upon Parliament and the State Legislatures to make laws governing goods and services tax.
2. Subsuming of various Central indirect taxes and levies.
3. Subsuming of various indirect taxes and levies of State Governments.
4. Dispensing with the concept of *declared goods of special importance* under the Constitution.
5. Levy of integrated goods and services tax on inter-state transactions of goods and services.
6. GST to be levied on all goods and services, except alcoholic liquor for human consumption. Petroleum and petroleum products to be subject to the levy of GST on a later date notified on the recommendation of the GST Council.
7. Compensation to the states for loss of revenue arising on account of implementation of GST for a period of five years.
8. Creation of GST Council to examine issues relating to goods and services tax and make recommendations to the Union and the States on parameters like rates, taxes, cesses and surcharges to be subsumed, exemption list and threshold limits, model GST laws etc.

The Bill needed to be passed by a two-third majority in both Houses of Parliament and subsequent ratification by at least half of the State Legislatures.

The Bill was passed by the Lok Sabha on May 6, 2015. The Bill was referred to the Select Committee of Rajya Sabha on May 12, 2015. The Select Committee submitted its Report on the Bill on July 22, 2015. Rajya Sabha passed the Bill with 9 amendments on August 3, 2016. Lok Sabha passed the modified Bill on August 8, 2016 approving all the 9 amendments by the Rajya Sabha.

After getting approval of half of the States, it was sent to the President for his assent which was given on September 8, 2016. The Constitution (One Hundred and Twenty-second Amendment) Bill, 2014 was notified as the Constitution (One Hundred and First Amendment) Act, 2016 with effect from September 16, 2016.

The outer limit for GST rollout was mid-September 2017 given that the Constitution amendment provided a one-year window. In other words, due to constitutional compulsion, the GST had to be rolled out by September 16, 2017 as the existing indirect taxes would have come to an end, and it would not have been possible for either the Centre or the states to collect indirect taxes.

After passage of the Bill by both Houses of Parliament, ratification by State legislatures and receipt of assent by the President, the process of enactment was completed and the road to GST rollout was cleared.

7.5 Legislative Requirements for the Introduction of GST

Suitable legislations for the levy of GST drawing powers from the Constitution were needed to be passed by the Parliament and the State Legislatures. Unlike the constitutional amendment which required 2/3rd majority, the GST Bills needed to be passed by a simple majority. Obviously, the levy of the tax could commence only after the GST laws had been enacted by the Parliament and respective Legislatures.

Moreover, unlike the State VAT, the date of commencement of GST had to be synchronized across the Centre and the States. This was so because the IGST model could not have functioned unless the Centre and all the States participated in it simultaneously.

In short, both the Centre and States had to pass Central GST and State GST Bills respectively and rules had to be made under them.

7.5.1 Central Legislations: On March 20, 2017, the Union Cabinet approved the following 4 draft laws on GST which were needed to implement India's biggest tax reform:

1. Central Goods and Services Tax (CGST) Bill, 2017.
2. Integrated Goods and Services Tax (IGST) Bill, 2017.
3. Union Territory Goods and Services Tax (UT-GST), Bill, 2017.
4. Goods and Services Tax (Compensation to States), Bill, 2017.

All the 4 GST-related bills were taken up as money bills in the Parliament. Finance Minister Shri Arun Jaitley introduced the 4 GST-related Bills in the Lok Sabha on March 27, 2017 which were passed on March 29, 2017.

All the 4 GST-related Bills were passed by the Rajya Sabha on April 6, 2017. It is noteworthy that Rajya Sabha cannot reject a money bill as it only has powers to make recommendations on such legislation, which the Lok Sabha can choose to accept or reject.

All the 4 GST-related Bills passed by the Parliament received the assent of the President on April 12, 2017 and were notified on the same date.

It is noteworthy that the GST Council had already cleared all the 5 draft laws (the above 4 and the SGST law).

A brief explanation of the 4 GST-related enactments is as under:

A. Central Goods and Services Tax (CGST) Act, 2017: It makes provisions for the levy and collection of tax on intra-state supply of goods or services or both by the Central Government. It extends to the whole of India except the state of Jammu and

Kashmir. The CGST Act, 2017 is divided into 21 chapters which deal with matters connected with the levy, collection and administration of GST.

B. Integrated Goods and Services Tax (IGST) Act, 2017: It makes provisions for the levy and collection of tax on inter-state supply of goods or services or both by the Central Government. It extends to the whole of India except the state of Jammu and Kashmir.

C. Union Territory Goods and Services Tax (UT-GST), Act, 2017: It makes provisions for the levy and collection of tax on intra-UT supply of goods or services or both in the Union Territories without legislature. Thus, it extends to the Union territories of: (a) Andaman and Nicobar Islands, (b) Lakshadweep, (c) Dadra and Nagar Haveli, (d) Daman and Diu and (e) Chandigarh.

D. Goods and Services Tax (Compensation to States), Act, 2017: It provides for compensation to the states for loss of revenue arising on account of implementation of GST for first 5 years as per the provisions of Constitution (One Hundred and First Amendment) Act, 2016. It extends to the whole of India.

Compensation law provides for the levy of cess on top of the peak rate of approved tax on paan masala, tobacco, aerated waters, luxury cars and coal to create a fund for compensating states. Such cess has been capped at 135 percent in case of pan masala, ₹ 4,170 per thousand cigarette sticks or 290 percent on value (ad valorem), ₹ 400 per tonne on coal and 15 percent on aerated water and luxury cars. The compensation to states will be paid bi-monthly and the amount due would be calculated after considering a 14 percent growth rate in taxes over the base year of 2015-16.

7.5.2 State Legislations: Telangana was the first State to pass the SGST Act followed by Bihar, Rajasthan, Jharkhand, Chhattisgarh, Uttarakhand, Madhya Pradesh, Haryana, Gujarat, and Goa. Jammu and Kashmir was the last to do so and that too post-GST implementation. Table 7.1 presents the enactment of SGST Acts by the States in chronological order.

Although the dual GST model is being implemented through multiple statutes, the basic features of law—such as chargeability, definition of taxable event and taxable person, measure of levy including valuation provisions, basis of classification etc.— are uniform across these statutes as far as practicable.

7.6 Taxes Subsumed under GST

7.6.1 Central Taxes Subsumed under GST: These are as under:

1. **Central Excise Duty:** After the Constitution (One Hundred and First Amendment) Act, 2016 all Union duties of excise were abolished except those on petroleum products and tobacco. [6]
2. **Duties of Excise (Medicinal and Toilet Preparations):** Duties on medicinal and toilet preparations were imposed under the Medicinal and Toilet Preparations (Excise Duties) Act, 1955. They included a range of medicinal items which were important from the viewpoint of public health policy. They had inter-State significance and therefore uniformity in regard to taxation was in larger national interest.

Table 7.1: SGST Acts Enacted by the States in Chronological Order

S. No.	State	Date on which Act was Passed	S. No.	State	Date on which Act was Passed
1.	Telangana	April 9, 2017	17.	Maharashtra	May 22, 2017
2.	Bihar	April 24, 2017	18.	Tripura	May 24, 2017
3.	Rajasthan	April 26, 2017	19.	Sikkim	May 25, 2017
4.	Jharkhand	April 27, 2017	20.	Mizoram	May 26, 2017
5.	Chhattisgarh	April 28, 2017	21.	Nagaland	May 27, 2017
6.	Uttarakhand	May 2, 2017	22.	Himachal Pradesh	May 27, 2017
7.	Madhya Pradesh	May 3, 2017	23.	Delhi	May 31, 2017
8.	Haryana	May 4, 2017	24.	Manipur	June 5, 2017
9.	Gujarat	May 9, 2017	25.	Meghalaya	June 12, 2017
10.	Goa	May 9, 2017	26.	West Bengal*	June 15, 2017
11.	Odisha	May 11, 2017	27.	Karnataka	June 16, 2017
12.	Assam	May 11, 2017	28.	Punjab	June 19, 2017
13.	Arunachal Pradesh	May 12, 2017	29.	Tamil Nadu	June 19, 2017
14.	Uttar Pradesh	May 16, 2017	30.	Kerala*	June 21, 2017
15.	Andhra Pradesh	May 16, 2017	31.	Jammu & Kashmir	July 7, 2017
16.	Puducherry	May 17, 2017			

*Through ordinance route.

3. **Additional Duties of Excise (Goods of Special Importance):** These duties were imposed under the Additional Duties of Excise (Goods of Special Importance) Act, 1957 on sugar, tobacco, and textiles in lieu of sales tax. The net proceeds from additional excise duties were distributed among the States in accordance with the principles of distribution formulated and the recommendations made by the Finance Commissions from time to time. [7]
4. **Additional Duties of Excise (Textiles and Textile Products):** The Additional Duties of Excise (Textiles and Textile Articles) Act, 1978 was enacted on December 6, 1978 with an intention to impose and collect extra excise duties on some textiles and textile products. The Act shall come into effect on October 4, 1978.
5. **Additional Duty of Customs [Commonly Known as Countervailing Duty (CVD)]:** Under Section 3(1) of the Customs Tariff Act, 1975, an additional duty on goods imported into the country was leviable. The rate of this duty was equal to the excise duty on like articles if produced or manufactured in India. The underlying philosophy of a countervailing duty is to ensure that the protection provided by the import duty to domestic industry is not reduced. [8]
6. **Special Additional Duty of Customs (SAD):** This duty was also known as special CVD and was levied under Section 3(5) of the Customs Tariff Act, 1975. This duty was in addition to basic customs duty and CVD levied under Sections 3(1) and 3(3)

respectively of the said Act. It was equal to sales tax/VAT, local tax or any other charge on a like article on its sale, purchase or transportation in India.

7. **Service Tax:** In view of the need for additional resources, rising contribution of service sector to GDP, service tax was introduced in India with effect from July 1, 1994 on a limited number of services. Its coverage was increased to more and more services from time to time. Service tax was abolished by Section 17 of Constitution (One Hundred and First Amendment) Act, 2016 to pave way for the introduction of GST. [9]
8. **Central Surcharges and Cesses Related to Supply of Goods and Services**

7.6.2 State Taxes Subsumed under GST: These are as under:

1. **State Sales Tax/VAT:** Under Entry 54 of List II (State List) in the Seventh Schedule of the Constitution, the States were given the power to levy "a tax on sale or purchases of goods other than newspapers". Enjoying this Constitutional right, different State Governments levied sales tax on a wide range of commodities at different rates with diverse procedures and rules for its collection. Later on the States switched over to VAT. Sales tax was abolished (except on a few commodities) by Section 17 of Constitution (One Hundred and First Amendment) Act, 2016. [10]
2. **Central Sales Tax (CST):** CST was a state-level tax, applied to inter-state sales of goods, based on the origin principle. The tax law (including the base, rates, and the procedures) was enacted by Parliament, but the entire revenue accruing under levy of CST was collected and kept by the State in which the sale originated. The Act excluded taxation of imports and exports. [11]
3. **Purchase Tax:** It was a tax paid to the VAT department on purchase of goods from unregistered dealers. See also section 7.3.3 of this chapter.
4. **Luxury Tax:** Luxury tax could mostly be seen in the usage bills of hotels, spas and specific resorts. Interestingly, this tax was chargeable on the room rented or the overall stay charges of the hotel, resort or spa, but not on the food and beverages served. The rate of luxury tax varied from state to state. Luxury tax for any state generally fell under the jurisdiction of the Commercial Taxes Department or the Excise Department. The duty of handling such taxes fell to different departments in different states but it was normally those institutions that also handled the imposition and collection of VAT, entertainment tax and service tax.
5. **Entry Tax (all forms):** Entry tax, an important source of revenue for local bodies, was a tax on the entry of goods into a local area from other areas for the purpose of consumption or sale. It was mentioned in Entry 52 of List II (State List) in the Seventh Schedule. Industry and trade circles had criticised the continuation of entry tax (octroi) and termed it as a retarding factor in the growth of business and commerce in the country. By obstructing the free movement of vehicles carrying goods, the levy of octroi caused delays and thus hampered industrial progress. Entry tax was abolished by Section 17 of the Constitution (One Hundred and First Amendment) Act, 2016.
6. **Entertainment and Amusement Tax (except when levied by the local bodies):** Under Entry 62 of List II (State List) in the Seventh Schedule of the Constitution,

States were empowered to levy 'taxes on luxuries, including taxes on entertainment, amusements, betting and gambling'. In the changed scenario, taxes on entertainments and amusements can be levied and collected by panchayat etc. [12]

7. **Taxes on Advertisements.** These were imposed under Entry 55 of List II (State List) of the Seventh Schedule of the Constitution.
8. **Taxes on Lotteries, Betting and Gambling:** These were imposed under Entry 62 of List II (State List) of the Seventh Schedule of the Constitution.
9. **State Surcharges and Cesses Related to Supply of Goods and Services**
   Taxes such as stamp duty, toll tax, road tax, electricity duty etc. are not part of GST.

The GST Council shall make recommendations to the Union and States on the taxes, cesses and surcharges levied by the Union, the States and the local bodies which may in future be subsumed under GST.

7.7 Phasing out of Central Sales Tax (CST)

While making preparation for GST, it was also necessary to phase out the CST, because the latter did not carry any set-off relief and there was a distortion in the VAT regime due to export of tax from one State to other State.

The Empowered Committee accordingly took a decision to phase out CST on the understanding with the Centre that—since phasing out of CST would result in a loss of revenue to the States on a permanent basis—an appropriate mechanism to compensate the States for such loss would be worked out.

The rate of CST had already been reduced from 4 percent to 2 percent and it was phased out with effect from the date of introduction of GST, i.e. July 1, 2017. CST, which was an origin-based tax, was inconsistent with GST which is a destination-based value added tax.

7.8 GST in Recent Budget Speeches of the Finance Ministers

Hoping for the early implementation of the GST, Finance Minister Shri P. Chidambaram in his 2013-14 budget speech observed, "Hon'ble Members will recall that I had first mentioned the Goods and Services Tax (GST) in the Budget speech for 2007-08. At that time, it was thought that GST could be brought into effect from 1.4.2010. Alas, that was not to be, although all States swear by the benefit of GST.

However, my recent meetings with the Empowered Committee of State Finance Ministers has led me to believe that the State Governments—or, at least, the overwhelming majority—are agreed that there is need for a Constitutional amendment; there is need for State Governments and the Central Government to pass a GST law that will be drafted by the State Finance Ministers and the GST Council; and there is need for the Centre to compensate the States for loss due to the reduction in the CST rate.

I hope we can take this consensus forward in the next few months and bring to this House a draft Bill on the Constitutional amendment and a draft Bill on GST. Hope inspires courage. I propose to take the first decisive step by setting apart, in the Budget, a sum of ₹ 9,000 crore towards the first instalment of the balance of CST compensation. I appeal to the State Finance Ministers to realise the serious intent of the Government to introduce GST and come forward to work with the Government and bring about a transformational change in the tax structure of the country". [13]

In his budget speech to the Parliament on June 10, 2014, Finance Minister Shri Arun Jaitley made the following observations regarding GST, "The debate whether to introduce a Goods and Services Tax (GST) must now come to an end. We have discussed the issue for the past many years. Some States have been apprehensive about surrendering their taxation jurisdiction; others want to be adequately compensated.

I have discussed the matter with the States both individually and collectively. I do hope we are able to find a solution in the course of this year and approve the legislative scheme which enables the introduction of GST. This will streamline the tax administration, avoid harassment of the business and result in higher revenue collection both for the Centre and the States. I assure all States that government will be more than fair in dealing with them". [14]

In his budget speech to the Parliament on February 28, 2015, Finance Minister Shri Arun Jaitley observed on GST as follows, "We need to revive growth and investment to ensure that more jobs are created for our youth and benefits of development reach millions of our poor. We need an enabling tax policy for this.

I have already introduced the Bill to amend the Constitution of India for Goods and Services Tax (GST) in the last Session of this august House. GST is expected to play a transformative role in the way our economy functions. It will add buoyancy to our economy by developing a common Indian market and reducing the cascading effect on the cost of goods and services. We are moving in various fronts to implement GST from the next year". [15]

GST was finally implemented from July 1, 2017.

7.9 Chronology of Events that Led to the Introduction of GST

The long journey of GST commenced on February 28, 2005 when Union Finance Minister Shri P. Chidambaram proposed it in his 2005-06 budget speech to the Parliament. Major milestones in the journey of GST are presented in Table 7.1 in chronological order.

Table 7.1: Major Milestones in the Journey of GST

Date/month/year	Event
2003	Vijay Kelkar Task Force on Implementation of the Fiscal Responsibility and Budget Management Act, 2003 suggests a comprehensive Goods and Services Tax (GST) based on VAT principle.
February 28, 2005	Finance Minister Shri P. Chidambaran in his Budget Speech for the year 2005-06 states, as his medium to long-term goal, "...a goods and services tax, encompassing both the Centre and the States".

Contd...

February 28, 2006	Finance Minister Shri P. Chidambaran in his Budget Speech for the year 2006-07 moots a proposal to introduce a National Level Goods and Services Tax (GST) by April 1, 2010. Since the proposal involved reform/restructuring of not only indirect taxes levied by the Centre but also the States, the responsibility of preparing a Design and Road Map for the implementation of GST is assigned to the Empowered Committee (EC) of State Finance Ministers. EC duly prepares a report on a Model and Road Map for GST.
May 10, 2007	EC sets up a Joint Working Group consisting of representatives of the EC and the Government of India for an in-depth study of the report prepared by it.
November 19, 2007	The Joint Working Group submits its report based on discussions and interactions with stakeholders.
November 28, 2007	EC discusses in detail the report of the Joint Working Group.
April 30, 2008	EC releases the final version of its views in the document titled, *A Model and Road Map for Goods and Services Tax in India.* The *model* detailed the operational issues which needed to be addressed, including the number of rates, exemptions and exclusions from GST, as well as the treatment of inter-state transactions. The *roadmap* outlined the legal and administrative steps which needed to be taken in order to comply with the April 1, 2010 deadline.
December 12, 2008	EC receives the comments of the Government of India on the above-mentioned document.
December 16, 2008	EC takes note of the comments of the Government of India and appoints a Committee to consider these comments in detail.
January 5-6, 2009	The Committee holds detailed deliberations and submits its recommendations to EC.
January 21, 2009	EC considers the recommendations of the Committee and accepts them in-principle. It forms a Working Group of concerned officials to submit their recommendations in detail on the structure of GST.
November 10, 2009	Based on the recommendations of the Working Group, EC releases the *First Discussion Paper on Goods and Services Tax in India.*
March 22, 2011	Constitution (One Hundred and Fifteenth Amendment) Bill, 2011 is introduced in the Parliament. The Bill lapses with the dissolution of the 15th Lok Sabha.
December 19, 2014	Constitution (One Hundred and Twenty-second Amendment) Bill, 2014 is introduced in the Lok Sabha.
May 6, 2015	The above Bill is passed by the Lok Sabha.

Contd...

May 12, 2015	The Bill is referred to the Select Committee of Rajya Sabha.
July 22, 2015	Select Committee of Rajya Sabha submits its Report.
August 3, 2016	The Bill is passed by the Rajya Sabha with 9 amendments.
August 8, 2016	Lok Sabha passes the modified Bill approving all the 9 amendments by the Rajya Sabha.
September 8, 2016	After being approved by half of the States, President gives his assent to the Bill.
September 16, 2016	The Constitution (One Hundred and Twenty-second Amendment) Bill, 2014 is notified as the Constitution (One Hundred and First Amendment) Act, 2016.
March 20, 2017	Union Cabinet approves the 4 GST-related draft laws.
March 27, 2017	The 4 GST-related Bills are introduced in the Lok Sabha.
March 29, 2017	The 4 GST-related Bills are passed by the Lok Sabha.
April 6, 2017	The 4 GST-related Bills are passed by the Rajya Sabha.
July 1, 2017	GST is rolled out.

Endnotes

1. Government of India, Ministry of Finance, *Report of the Task Force on Implementation of the Fiscal Responsibility and Budget Management Act, 2003* (Chairman: Vijay Kelkar), July 16, 2004, p. 7.
2. Government of India, Ministry of Finance, *Budget Speech of the Finance Minister,* 2005-06, Part A, para 94.
3. Government of India, Ministry of Finance, *Budget Speech of the Finance Minister,* 2006-07, Part B, p. 26.
4. While presenting the budget for 2010-11 to the Parliament on February 26, 2010, Minister of Finance Shri Pranab Mukherjee, rescheduled the time limit for the implementation of GST and expressed the hope that GST, along with the Direct Tax Code (DTC), would be introduced from April 1, 2011.
5. Empowered Committee of State Finance Ministers (EC) was originally set up on July 17, 2000 by the Government of India with the State Finance Ministers of West Bengal, Karnataka, Madhya Pradesh, Maharashtra, Punjab, Uttar Pradesh, Gujarat, Delhi and Meghalaya as members with an objective to monitor the implementation of uniform floor rates of sales tax by States and Union territories, to monitor the phasing out of the sales-tax based incentive schemes, to decide milestones and methods of States to switch over to VAT and to monitor reforms in the Central Sales Tax system existing in the country. Subsequently, State Finance Ministers of Assam, Tamil Nadu, Jammu and Kashmir, Jharkhand and Rajasthan were also notified as the members of the Empowered Committee. On August 12, 2004, the Government of India decided to reconstitute the Empowered committee with State Finance/Taxation Ministers of all States as its members.
   The body was later registered as a Society under the Societies Registration Act (XXI of 1860). The registration certificate was issued on August 17, 2004. Presently, all the Ministers in-charge of Finance/Taxation of all State Governments and Union Territories with legislatures, Additional Secretary (Revenue), Government of India and Member Secretary, Empowered Committee are the members of the Empowered Committee. The Empowered

Committee has its office in Delhi Sachivalaya, I.P. Estate, New Delhi where Government of NCT of Delhi has provided accommodation and other facilities. The Society has been receiving contribution from the State Government and Government of India to meet its administrative expenditure and undertake various other activities.

Recently, in order to strengthen the EC, Thirteenth Finance Commission recommended that a grant of ₹ 30 crore be made to EC, so that they can pursue GST related research work and enhance capacities. Amount of ₹ 30 crore has accordingly been released to EC for creating a corpus of for this purpose.

6. See Entry 84 in Table 6.1 of chapter 6 of this book. For a detailed discussion on Union excise duties before their abolition, see chapter 2 of this book.
7. For details, see section 4.3 of chapter 4 of this book.
8. Since the GST Council has not taken final decision regarding the inclusion of petroleum products under GST therefore additional duty of customs would continue to be levied on imports of petroleum and tobacco products.
9. For a detailed discussion on service tax before its abolition, see chapter 3 of this book.
10. See chapter 4 of this book for a detailed discussion on sales tax/VAT before its subsumation under GST.
11. For details, see section 4.2.4 of chapter 4 of this book.
12. See Entry 62 in Table 6.2 of chapter 6 of this book.
13. Government of India, Ministry of Finance, *Budget Speech of the Finance Minister, 2013-14.*
14. Government of India, Ministry of Finance, *Budget Speech of the Finance Minister, 2014-15.*
15. Government of India, Ministry of Finance, *Budget Speech of the Finance Minister, 2015-16,* para *96.*

8

Goods and Services Tax Council (GST Council)

GST Council was created under the Constitution. GST Council is a joint forum of the Centre and the States. The recommendations made by the Council act as benchmark or guidance to Union as well as State Governments.

8.1 GST Council: Constitutional Provisions

The Constitution (One Hundred and Twenty-second Amendment) Bill, 2014, for introduction of Goods and Services Tax (GST) in the country, was accorded assent by the President on September 8, 2016, and the same was notified as the Constitution (One Hundred and First Amendment) Act, 2016.

As per Article 279A (1) of the amended Constitution, the GST Council was to be constituted by the President within 60 days of the commencement of Article 279A. The notification for bringing into force Article 279A with effect from September 12, 2016 was issued on September 10, 2016.

The Union Cabinet in its meeting held on September 12, 2016 approved the setting-up of GST Council and its Secretariat. The Cabinet, *inter alia*, took decisions for the following:

1. Creation of the GST Council as per Article 279A of the amended Constitution.
2. Creation of the GST Council Secretariat, with its office in New Delhi.
3. Appointment of the Secretary (Revenue) as the Ex-officio Secretary to the GST Council.
4. Inclusion of the Chairperson, Central Board of Excise and Customs (CBEC), as a permanent invitee (non-voting) to all proceedings of the GST Council.

The Cabinet also decided to provide adequate funds for meeting the recurring and non-recurring expenses of the GST Council Secretariat, the entire cost for which shall be borne by the Central Government. GST Council Secretariat shall be manned by officers taken on deputation from both the Central and State Governments.

GST Council is a joint forum of the Centre and the States. The Council consists of the following members:

1. Union Finance Minister—Chairperson.
2. Union Minister of State, in-charge of Revenue or Finance—Member.
3. Minister in-charge of finance or taxation or any other Minister nominated by each State Government—Members.

As per Article 279A (4), the Council will make recommendations to the Union and the States on important issues related to GST, like the goods and services that may be subjected or exempted from GST, model GST laws, principles that govern place of supply, threshold limits, GST rates including the floor rates with bands, special rates for raising additional resources during natural calamities/disasters, special provisions for certain States etc. [1]

8.2 Guiding Principle and Decision-making at GST Council

GST Council works on the basis of consensus. The guiding principle of GST Council is to ensure harmonization on different aspects of GST between the Centre and the States as well as among States. It has been provided in Article 279A that the GST Council, in its discharge of various functions, shall be guided by the need for a harmonized structure of GST and for the development of a harmonized national market for goods and services.

Article 279A of the Constitution provides that every decision of the GST Council shall be taken at a meeting by a majority of not less than 3/4th of the weighted votes of the Members present and voting, in accordance with the following principles:

- The vote of the Central Government shall have a weightage of one-third of the total votes cast, and
- The votes of all the State Governments taken together shall have a weightage of two-thirds of the total votes cast in that meeting.

One half of the total number of members of the GST Council shall constitute the quorum at its meetings.

The above arrangements are meant to protect the interests of each State and the Centre when the Council takes a decision and is in the spirit of co-operative federalism.

8.3 Functions of GST Council

GST Council is entrusted to make recommendations to the Union and the States on following matters pertaining to GST:

1. Taxes, cesses and surcharges levied by the Union, the States and the local bodies which may be subsumed in the goods and services tax.
2. Goods and services that may be subjected to, or exempted from the goods and services tax.
3. Model Goods and Services Tax Laws, principles of levy, apportionment of GST levied on supplies in the course of inter-State trade or commerce under Article 269A and the principles that govern the place of supply.
4. Threshold limit of turnover below which goods and services may be exempted from GST.
5. Rates (including floor rates with bands) of GST.
6. Any special rate or rates for a specified period, to raise additional resources during any natural calamity or disaster.
7. Special provision with respect to the States of Arunachal Pradesh, Assam, Jammu and Kashmir, Manipur, Meghalaya, Mizoram, Nagaland, Sikkim, Tripura, Himachal Pradesh and Uttarakhand.
8. Any other matter relating to GST as the Council may decide.

8.4 Meetings of GST Council

8.4.1 First Meeting of GST Council, September 22-23, 2016: The two-day inaugural meeting of the Council, consisting of Centre and State representatives, took the following decisions.

1. Businesses with an annual turnover of less than ₹ 20 lakh would be exempted from GST.
2. Threshold would be ₹ 10 lakh in the North-Eastern and hill States, which have been given a carve-out in the constitutional amendment that paved the way for GST.
3. State authorities would have jurisdiction over asseessees with annual turnover of less than ₹ 1.5 crore. For those with turnover of over ₹ 1.5 crore, there would be cross examination by officers from either State or the Centre to avoid dual control.
4. Power for assessment of 11 lakh service tax assesses, who are currently assessed by the Centre, would remain with it. New assesses would be divided between the Centre and the States.
5. Financial year 2015-16 would be the base year for compensating the States in case of any revenue loss to States following the implementation of GST.
6. All cesses would be subsumed under the new tax. The inclusion of cesses in the GST would significantly benefit all businesses and would increase the available pool of credits which could be used to offset the GST liability.
7. A cross-empowerment model was agreed upon which would allow taxpayers to restrict their interaction to a single tax authority for Central GST, State GST and Integrated GST (IGST). Central GST and State GST are two components of a single GST levied on intra-state sales, while IGST applies to inter-State sales.
8. A consensus on composition scheme was arrived at and it was decided that traders with gross annual turnover cut-off of ₹ 50 lakh (subsequently increased to ₹ 75 lakh in the sixteenth meeting of the Council held on June 11, 2017) can pay tax at specified rates which are lower that the GST rates. The composition scheme provides for an easier method of calculating tax liability and it allows option for GST registration for dealers with turnover below the compounding cut-off. The scheme has been introduced to reduce the administration cost associated with collection of tax from small traders.

8.4.2 Second Meeting, September 30, 2016: The Council approved two agenda items. First, five sets of draft rules governing payments, refunds, returns, invoices, debt and credit notes were approved. These were finalised in anticipation of the GST legislations under which the final rules were to be notified. The second decision was with regard to the exemptions from various tax laws and taxes in place currently with which the Centre and States incentivise a variety of industries to invest.

8.4.3 Third Meeting, October 18-20, 2016: The third meeting of the GST Council, which ended a day ahead of schedule, failed to reach a decision on the GST tax rates. The Council discussed possible GST rates, including a four-slab structure of 6, 12, 18 and 26 percent with lower rates for essential items and highest band for luxury goods.

Centre proposed the imposition of a cess over and above the GST on ultra luxury and demerit goods such as big cars, aerated beverages and tobacco products. The Centre had proposed the cess as a means to fund compensation to States for tax revenue loss during the first five years of GST. However, most States objected to the proposal to levy an additional cess on demerit goods.

8.4.4 Fourth Meeting, November 3-4, 2016: The GST Council agreed on a 4-slab GST rates of 5, 12, 18 and 28 percent on goods which it claimed would not be inflationary and yet protect revenues of Centre and State Governments. The broad objective was to maintain equivalence to the existing tax burden on various goods.

8.4.5 Fifth Meeting, December 2-3, 2016: In this two-day meeting of the GST Council consensus could not be reached on the issue of sharing of administrative powers between the Centre and the States. However, certain headway was made on finalization of the draft legislations, and the same were expected to be finalized in the next meeting of the Council. Due to the delay in building of consensus, GST implementation from April 1, 2016 became uncertain. The fifth meeting of the GST Council also deliberated on the impact of demonetisation on revenue.

8.4.6 Sixth Meeting, December 11-12, 2016: This two-day meeting was convened to sort out the vexed issue of *cross empowerment*, or dual control of assessees under the proposed pan-India indirect tax regime. The meeting was also expected to finalise three legislations—Central GST, Integrated GST and the Compensation Law—with the intent of placing these in Parliament during its ongoing Winter Session that ended on December 16, 2016. However, the deadlock continued on the issue of dual control between the Centre and the States in the December 11 meeting, and the December 12 meeting was cancelled.

8.4.7 Seventh Meeting, December 22-23, 2016: The GST Council in its seventh meeting decided to redraft the Compensation Bill to include *other receipts* apart from previously agreed cess on luxury and demerit goods as the source to fund compensation, with States voicing concerns about a likely decline in their revenues following the scrapping of high-denomination currency notes.

Even though the Council cleared most provisions of supporting draft Bills of compensation and Central GST (CGST), the Centre and the states failed to make a breakthrough over the vexed issue of division of control over tax assessees as it did not come up for discussion in the two-day long meeting. The pending issues of dual control and draft Integrated GST (IGST) Bill were left to be taken up in the next meeting.

8.4.8 Eighth Meeting, January 3-4, 2017: The issue of dual control remained unresolved. Some States raised a new issue of split in tax rate in ratio of 60:40 between States and the Centre instead of equally dividing GST between the Centre and the States. Issues relating to administrative powers were left to be deliberated in the next meeting.

8.4.9 Ninth Meeting, January 16, 2017: The possibility of implementing GST by the targeted deadline of April 1, 2017, receded with the ninth meeting of the GST Council failing to agree on the contentious issue of administrative control of GST.

Eight earlier meetings of the Council had failed to resolve the deadlock between the Centre and the States on the issue of *cross empowerment*, or dual control of assessees, and who would exercise control over them.

The States wanted exclusive control on businesses with turnover below ₹ 1.5 crore (the existing threshold for central excise), including the service taxpayers.

Consensus was almost reached on the territorial control issue of levying GST on the high seas. The Centre's proposal to tax transactions that take place within 12 nautical miles from coastal state borders was opposed by several States, which feared loss of substantial revenue in this way.

8.4.10 Tenth Meeting, February 18, 2017: The tenth meeting of the GST Council held in Udaipur managed to approve only one draft law pertaining to compensation to states, even as three crucial draft laws—Central GST (CGST), Integrated GST (IGST) and State GST (SGST)—got caught in a tussle between the States and the Centre. There were clashes between the Centre and the States over the drafting of minutes of the previous GST Council meeting, which held up the deliberations of the meeting. The dispute over the minutes related to the wordings over the division of new registrants, permission to States to tweak division of taxpayers after consultation with the Centre and referral of disputes relating to imports and exports to the Centre.

8.4.11 Eleventh Meeting, March 4, 2017: This meeting cleared the Central GST and Integrated GST Bills. It cleared the decks for the Central Government to take these two Bills to the Parliament for their passage.

The State GST and the UT-GST Bills were under the review of the Law Commission and were slated to be taken up in the next meeting of the Council.

Small restaurants and *dhabas* became eligible for composition scheme and they would pay GST of 5 percent, to be shared equally between the Central and the State Governments.

8.4.12 Twelfth Meeting, March 16, 2017: The Council approved the Draft Bills for implementing GST in States and Union Territories (UTs). The UT-GST Draft Law was for the Union Territories like Andaman and Nicobar Islands, Lakshadweep, Daman and Diu and Dadra and Nagar Haveli, which do not have legislative assemblies and thus not covered under the constitutional meaning of *state*.

The GST Council in its eleventh meeting had cleared the Central GST (CGST) and Integrated GST (IGST) Bills. The GST Council in its tenth meeting had also approved a Draft Bill to compensate States for any revenue loss arising out of GST for a period of five years.

Thus, the GST Council completed its formal approval to all five the legislations.

The GST Council also decided to levy cess on the following five categories of products to create a fund with a corpus of around ₹ 50,000 crore for meeting potential compensation liability.

1. Pan masala.
2. Chewing tobacco and cigarettes.
3. Luxury cars.
4. Aerated drinks and mineral water.
5. Coal and lignite.

The Council, however, kept the option of adding more items to the list later.

It also cleared a proposal to cap the cess on luxury cars and aerated drinks at 15 percent over the peak rate of 28 percent. However, the ceiling for the cess on *sin* goods would be much higher. It was said that for paan masala, the cap would be 135 percent. On tobacco and cigarettes, the cap would be 290 percent or ₹ 4,170 per 1,000 cigarette sticks. A call was yet to be taken on whether or not a cess would be imposed on *bidis*. The cess on coal and lignite (environment cess) would have an upper limit at ₹ 400 per tonne. The Council decided to levy cess on all cars and not only the luxury cars.

The actual cess on *demerit goods*, which would help create a corpus for compensating States for any loss of revenue from GST implementation in the first five years, may be lower than the approved caps as the Council has kept a *little* headroom for future exigencies. For example, if a luxury car under pre-GST system suffered a total tax of 40 percent, then under the GST a 28 percent tax plus 12 percent cess (instead of 15 percent) may be levied to keep the tax incidence at the same level, leaving a headroom of 3 percent for future exigencies.

What the GST Council cleared was the ceiling. The exact levy would be decided by it later. Table 8.1 shows the maximum rate of GST cess on various demerit goods.

Table 8.1: Maximum Rate of GST Cess on Various Demerit Goods

Commodity	Maximum rate at which GST cess can be collected (percent)
Pan masala	135
Sweetened mineral and aerated water	15
Motor cars and vehicles (with the exception of motor vehicles for transportation of 10 or more people)	15
Tobacco products	₹ 4,170 per 1,000 sticks or 290 percent or a combination of both
Coal and lignite*	₹ 400 per tonne

*clean energy cess.

The Council also cleared a proposal for the nil rate to be applied for goods and services going to special economic zones (SEZs). In other words, supplies made to SEZs would be zero-rated (a tax rate of zero) and considered as physical exports.

In the earlier draft, in case of procurement of supplies by SEZ, tax was to be paid and then refund claimed of such tax paid but as per the discussion in the Council meeting the same supplies were accepted as zero-rated.

It is noteworthy that GST regime has 9 sets of rules and regulations, out of which the Council had already approved 5—registration, payment, invoices, returns and refund. The Council decided to finalize Rules on the remaining four issues relating to composition scheme, valuation, input tax credit (ITC) and transitional provisions in the next (thirteenth) meeting on March 31, 2017.

8.4.13 Thirteenth Meeting, March 31, 2017: This meeting finalized five sets of rules relating to registration, refunds, returns, payment and invoice debit and credit. It also gave its tentative nod to four more sets of rules dealing with composition scheme, valuation, input tax credit (ITC), and transitional provisions. These sets of rules were left to be finalized after receiving industry feedback. These 9 sets of rules were to form the basis of the implementation of GST. After this, the Council was left with the vexatious and time-consuming work of fitting the various goods and services into the four tax slabs.

8.4.14 Fourteenth Meeting, May 18-19, 2017: At its fourteenth meting in Srinagar, the Council agreed on a four-tier tax structure for services. The four slabs of 5 percent, 12 percent, 18 percent and 28 percent mirrored the GST rates on goods.

The highest rate of 28 percent was made applicable, among other luxury services, on cinema tickets which was lower then the pre-GST entertainment tax which ranged from 45 percent to 100 percent in different States. [2]

The fitment of rates of goods was discussed during the Council meeting. The Council approved the rate structure on majority of the goods and services. In other words, the Council largely completed the exercise of fitment of various goods in different rate slabs.

The Council also approved seven sets of rules (out of nine), barring two sets of rules (related to transitional provisions and returns) which were still to be vetted.

8.4.15 Fifteenth Meeting, June 3, 2017: The main objective of the fifteenth meeting of the Council was to decide tax rates on certain remaining items which included gold, textiles and footwear.

The Council decided to tax gold, gems, and jewellery at 3 percent. A nominal rate of 0.25 percent was decided on rough diamond. GST on apparel below ₹ 1,000 was fixed at 5 percent. GST on all biscuits was fixed at 18 percent. GST on readymade garments was fixed at 12 percent and on yarn and fabric cotton at 5 percent. The Council decided to tax footwear priced below ₹ 500 at 5 percent and the rest at 18 percent. It decided to tax *bidis* at 28 percent without cess.

The Council cleared all the pending rules related to transitional provisions and returns. It decided to set up a committee to look into complaints regarding anti-profiteering clause.

All the States agreed to rollout GST from July 1, 2017.

8.4.16 Sixteenth Meeting, June 11, 2017: It may be recalled that the Council in its earlier meetings had decided a 4-slab GST rates of 5, 12, 18 and 28 percent for goods and services. It had fitted almost all goods and services into these 4 tax rates when it met in Srinagar on May 18-19, 2017 for its fourteenth meeting. GST rates for almost 1,211 goods and around 500 services were fixed.

However, representations were received from various stakeholders to reduce tax rates on a variety of items. Taking note of these representations, the Council lowered tax rates on 66 goods and services which included packaged food, insulin, school bags and movie tickets.

GST on cashew, *agarbattis* and insulin was reduced from 12 percent to 5 percent. It was reduced from 18 percent to 12 percent on packaged food, exercise books and cutlery. Similarly, it was reduced from 28 percent to 18 percent on plastic tarpaulin, school bags, computer printers and ball bearings. GST rate on children's colouring books was reduced from 12 percent to nil. Instead of a uniform rate of 28 percent on cinema tickets, it was made 28 percent on tickets above ₹ 100 and 18 percent for tickets up to ₹ 100.

The levy on job work for textiles, gems and jewellery, printing and leather was lowered from 18 percent to 5 percent.

The Council also widened the scope of a concessional tax payment scheme for small businesses and restaurants. It relaxed the turnover ceiling of ₹ 50 lakh to ₹ 75 lakh per annum for businesses to take part in the GST composition scheme. The scheme allows traders, manufacturers and restaurant owners to pay presumptive tax at the rate of 1, 2, and 5 percent respectively. This will allow more small businesses to avail a hassle-free compliance regime. It is noteworthy that these segments are large job creators and hence a priority area for the Government. It may also be noted that service providers (except restaurants) are outside the ambit of this scheme.

While a lot of small businesses such as shopkeepers and small eateries are expected to opt for the scheme, manufacturers who supply to large buyers may be forced to be part of the GST chain.

The Centre and all the States (except West Bengal) decided to rollout GST from July 1, 2017. [3]

Tax rate for lottery, rules for electronic way (e-way), bills to replace the challans and anti-profiteering rules were left to be decided in the subsequent meetings of the Council.

The Council decided to meet again on June 18, 2017 to take stock of the rollout preparedness and any new proposal from State Governments.

8.4.17 Seventeenth Meeting, June 18, 2018: The Council took the following decisions with respect to GST rates for services.

Transport of goods by a vessel shall attract GST rate of 5 percent with ITC in respect of input services and GST paid on ships, vessels including bulk carriers and tankers.

Accommodation in hotels, inns, guest houses, clubs, campsites or other commercial places meant for residential or lodging purposes where room tariff is ₹ 2,500 and above but less than ₹ 7,500 per room per day shall attract GST rate of 18 percent with full ITC.

Accommodation in hotels including 5 star and above rated hotels, inns, guest houses, clubs, campsites or other commercial places meant for residential or lodging purposes, where room rent is ₹ 7,500 and above per day per room shall attract GST rate of 28 percent with full ITC.

Supply of food/drinks in air-conditioned restaurant in 5-star or above rated hotels shall attract GST rate of 18 percent with full ITC.

It was decided that supply of lottery shall attract GST rates as under:

- Lottery run by State Governments: 12 percent of face value of lottery ticket.
- Lottery authorized by State Governments: 28 percent of face value of lottery ticket.

8.4.18 Eighteenth Meeting, June 30, 2017: This meeting of the Council was held hours before the final GST rollout on July 1, 2017. The Council reduced the tax on fertilizers from 12 percent to 5 percent. The decision was taken in view of apprehensions that the price of crop nutrient may increase following the implementation of GST. Another decision, which also brought relief to farmers, was to reduce the tax rate on exclusive parts of tractors from 28 percent to 18 percent. While issues relating to farmers were discussed, the meeting was originally called just to thank the Council members for helping in the implementation of GST.

8.4.19 Nineteenth Meeting, July 17, 2017: Over two weeks into the GST regime, the all-powerful GST Council met on July 17, 2017 to take stock of the implementation of the new indirect tax. This was the first meeting of the Council since the launch of the GST on July 1, 2017. However, unlike the earlier meetings, when the Centre and the States used to sit across the table and decide on a plethora of issues, this time the interaction was through video conferencing.

After the last Council meet on 30 June, 2017 it was decided that next meeting would take place on August 5, 2017. However, the date of the meeting was advanced as the Council wanted to take stock of the situation post-GST rollout and get a nation-wide report.

Showing its ability to take quick decisions, the Council increased the fixed cess on cigarettes by 48 paise to 79 paise per stick (or ₹ 485 to ₹ 792 per thousand sticks). The move was aimed to prevent cigarette manufacturers to reap windfall arising out of an anomaly that had crept in during fixing the rates. It is noteworthy that this fixed cess is over and above the GST rate of 28 percent plus 5 percent ad valorem cess on the commodity in question.

To sum up, GST Council was notified with effect from September 12, 2016. Including the first meeting of the Council on September 23, 2016, there have been 19 sessions so far on a range of issues including supporting legislations, GST rules, rates of taxes and fitment of a large number of goods and services into the four-tier structure of 5 percent, 12 percent, 18 percent and 28 percent.

The following major decisions have been taken by it in its various meetings:

1. The threshold exemption limit shall be ₹ 20 lakh. For special category States enumerated in Article 279A of the Constitution, threshold exemption limit is fixed at ₹ 10 lakh.
2. Composition scheme threshold shall be ₹ 75 lakh. Composition scheme shall not be available to inter-state suppliers, service providers (except restaurant service) and specified category of manufacturers.
3. Existing tax incentive schemes of Central or State Governments may be continued by respective governments by way of reimbursement through budgetary route. The schemes, in the present form, would not continue in GST.
4. There would be four tax rates, namely 5 percent, 12 percent, 18 percent and 28 percent. Besides, some goods and services would be under the list of exempt items. A cess over the peak rate of 28 percent on certain specified luxury and demerit goods would be imposed for a period of 5 years to compensate States for any revenue loss on account of implementation of GST.

5. The five laws, namely CGST Law, UT-GST Law, IGST Law, SGST Law and GST Compensation Law were recommended which were subsequently enacted.
6. Power to collect GST in territorial waters shall be delegated by Central Government to the States.
7. Formula and mechanism for GST compensation cess was finalised.
8. The following 9 sets of rules were recommended and subsequently approved, which form the backbone of GST:

- Registration.
- Invoice.
- Payments.
- Returns.
- Refunds
- Composition levy scheme
- Valuation.
- Input tax credit (ITC)
- Transitional provisions.

Endnotes

1. See also section 6.11 of chapter 6 of this book.
2. Prior to the Constitution (One Hundred and First Amendment) Act, 2016, States were empowered, under Entry 62 of List II (State List) in the Seventh Schedule of the Constitution, to levy 'taxes on luxuries, including taxes on entertainment, amusements, betting and gambling'. After the Constitution (One Hundred and First Amendment) Act, 2016, taxes on entertainments and amusements can be levied and collected by a Panchayat or a Municipality or a Regional Council or a District Council.
3. Taking the ordinance route, West Bengal passed the SGST Act on June, 2017.

9

Meaning, Justification and Components of GST

The basic objective of tax reform in any country should be to establish a tax system that is economically efficient, distributionally acceptable, and simple to administer.

GST is the most ambitious and remarkable indirect tax reform in India's post-Independence history. Its objective is to levy a single national uniform tax across India on all goods and services. GST has replaced a number of Central and State taxes, made India more of a national integrated market, and brought more producers into the tax net. By improving efficiency, it can add substantially to growth as well as government finances. Implementing a new tax, encompassing both goods and services, by the Centre and the States in a large and complex federal system, is perhaps unprecedented in modern global tax history.

9.1 What is GST?

GST was launched at the stroke of midnight hour of June 30-July 1, 2017 by Prime Minister Shri Narendra Modi, in the presence of President Shri Pranab Mukherjee from the Central Hall of Parliament.

GST is a tax on goods and services with comprehensive and continuous chain of set-off benefits up to the retailer level. It is essentially a tax only on value addition at each stage, and a supplier at each stage is permitted to set-off, through a tax credit mechanism, the GST paid on the purchase of goods and services. Ultimately, the burden of GST is borne by the end-user (i.e. final consumer) of the commodity/service.

According to clause 12A of Article 366 of the Constitution, *goods and services tax* means any tax on supply of goods, or services or both except taxes on the supply of the alcoholic liquor for human consumption. According to the same Article, *goods* includes all materials, commodities, and articles (clause 12), *services* means anything other than goods (clause 26A) and *State* with reference to Articles 246A, 268, 269, 269A and Article 279A includes a Union Territory with legislature (clause 26B). [1]

The power to levy GST is derived from Article 246A of the Constitution which confers concurrent powers to both Parliament and State Legislatures to make laws with respect to GST. However, clause 2 of Article 246A read with Article 269A provides exclusive power to the Parliament to legislate with respect to inter-state trade or commerce. The taxable event under GST is the supply of goods and/or services. CGST and SGST are levied on intra-state supplies while IGST is levied on inter-state supplies.

9.2 Justification for GST

9.2.1 Absence of Tax Cascading: With the introduction of GST, a continuous chain of set-off from the original producer's point and service provider's point up to the retailer's level has been established, eliminating the burden of all *cascading* or *pyramiding* effects of an indirect tax system. This is the essence of GST. GST taxes only the final consumer. Hence the cascading of taxes (*tax-on-tax*) is avoided and production costs are cut down.

Prior to the introduction of GST, the indirect tax system of India suffered from various disabilities. There was a burden of *tax-on-tax* in the pre-GST system of Central excise duty and the sales tax system of the States. The introduction of Central VAT (CENVAT) did remove the cascading burden of taxes to a good extent by providing a mechanism of set-offs for tax paid on inputs and services up to the stage of production, and was an improvement over the pre-CENVAT Central excise duty. Similarly, the introduction of VAT by the States removed the cascading effect by giving set-off for tax paid on inputs as well as tax paid on previous purchases and again was an improvement over the previous sales tax regime.

However, both the CENVAT and the State VAT had certain deficiencies. CENVAT was deficient because it did not extend to include chain of value additions in the distributive trade below the stage of production. Further, it did not include several Central taxes (such as additional excise duties, additional customs duties, surcharges etc.) in its overall framework. Hence, the benefits of a comprehensive input tax set-offs was not available to manufacturers/dealers under CENVAT.

Likewise, in the State-level VAT scheme, CENVAT load on the goods was not removed and the cascading effect of that part of tax burden had remained unrelieved. Moreover, there were several taxes in the States (such as luxury tax, entertainment tax, etc.) which had not been subsumed under the VAT. In addition, although the burden of Central sales tax (CST) on inter-State movement of goods had been lessened with reduction of CST rate from 4 percent to 2 percent, this burden had also not been fully phased out.

GST has taken under its wings a profusion of indirect taxes of the Centre and the States. It has integrated taxes on goods and services for set-off relief. Further, it has also captured certain value additions in the distributive trade. There is now a continuous chain of set-offs which would eliminate the burden of all cascading effects.

9.2.2 Inclusion of Services in the Tax Base: From equity point of view, services should be taxed in the same way as goods. Taxation of goods and exclusion of services distorts the relative prices of goods vis-à-vis services, encouraging artificially the demand for services. In the process, the allocation of resources is also distorted. If tax is imposed on goods and not on services, a relatively high rate of tax would be required on goods to generate a given amount of revenue. If tax is imposed both on goods and services, a moderate tax rate can yield the given revenue. Administratively, taxation of both goods and services is desirable because it would reduce disputes pertaining to distinction between goods and services.

The composition of national income in India has changed steadily over the years. While the share of agriculture and allied activities in the gross domestic product (GDP) has declined, that of the tertiary sector has increased. The expansion of services has not only been conducive for employment generation but also for better efficiency of the system and improved quality of life. The changes in relative shares of various sectors in GDP over the years are shown in Table 9.1.

The compositional shift in favour of the service sector, brought about by the rapid expansion of the service sector, is in line with the development experience of a number of countries. It is well-known that as an economy develops, the shares of industrial and service sectors in GDP increase at the cost of the agricultural sector.

Table 9.1: Changes in the Sectoral Composition of GDP: Selected Years

(percent)

Year	Agriculture	Industry	Services
1950-51	53.1	16.6	30.3
1960-61	48.7	20.5	30.8
1970-71	42.3	24.0	33.8
1980-81	36.1	25.9	38.0
1990-91	29.6	27.7	42.7
2000-01	22.3	27.3	50.4
2012-13	13.9	27.3	58.8
2013-14	13.9	26.1	59.9

Source: Government of India, *Economic Survey*, 2013-14, p. 6.

Tax revenue from the agricultural sector being negligible, the industrial sector continued to constitute the only principal tax base till the mid-1990s. Despite the fact that the services sector had shown substantial buoyancy, its contribution to the exchequer was nil. In this connection, the Finance Minister, in his 1994-95 budget speech, observed, "There is no sound reason for exempting services from taxation when goods are taxed and many countries treat goods and services alike for tax purpose". [2]

The Tax Reforms Committee (TRC) [Chairman: Raja Chelliah], 1991 also recommended imposition of tax on certain select services, viz. advertising, non-life insurance and telephone services and services of stock brokers.

Thus, in order to impart buoyancy to government revenues and to provide consistency and equity in the tax structure via-a-via the composition of income, a modest effort was made in the 1994-95 budget when a 5 percent tax was imposed on telephone and non-life insurance services and services of stock brokers with effect from July 1, 1994.

Presently, services sector in India constitutes a tax base with vast potential which has not been exploited as yet. It is in this context that GST is justified as it has subsumed under it almost all the services for the purpose of taxation.

9.2.3 Reduction in Operating Costs: Since major Central and State indirect taxes have got subsumed under GST, the multiplicity of taxes has been substantially reduced which, in turn, would decrease the operating costs of the country's tax system. [3] With GST in place, the burden of CST has also been removed. The uniformity in tax rates and procedures across the country will go a long way in reducing compliance costs.

In short, GST is a comprehensive indirect tax levy on manufacture, sale and consumption of goods as well as services at the national level. GST is an indirect tax for the whole of India to make it one unified common market. GST is designed to give India a world class tax system and improve tax collections. It would end the long-standing distortions of differential treatment of manufacturing sector and services sector. GST will facilitate seamless credit across the entire supply chain and across all States under a common tax base.

9.3 Components of GST

There are three categories of indirect taxes under GST, namely CGST, SGST and IGST.

9.3.1 Central Goods and Services Tax (CGST): GST levied by the Centre on intra-State supply of goods or services or both is called CGST. It is levied under Central Goods and Services Tax (CGST) Act, 2017 which makes provisions for the levy and collection of tax on intra-state supply of goods or services or both by the Central Government. The Act is divided into 21 chapters which deal with matters connected with the levy, collection and administration of GST.

9.3.2 State Goods and Services Tax (SGST): GST levied by the States on intra-state supply of goods or services or both under their respective SGST Acts is called SGST. Union territories with legislature (Delhi and Puducherry) are covered under the definition of *state*. However, Union territories without legislature are governed by Union Territory Goods and Services Tax (UT-GST), Act, 2017 which makes provisions for the levy and collection of tax on intra-UT supply of goods or services or both in the Union Territories without legislature. Thus, it extends to the Union territories of: (a) Andaman and Nicobar Islands, (b) Lakshadweep, (c) Dadra and Nagar Haveli, (d) Daman and Diu and (e) Chandigarh.

9.3.3 Integrated Goods and Service Tax (IGST): GST makes distinction between intra-state and inter-state supply of goods and services. Hence, IGST—as a part of GST regime—is levied on inter-State supply (including stock transfers) of goods and services. It is levied and collected by the Centre so that the credit chain is not disrupted. IGST also applies on imports.

The Centre levies and collects IGST on all inter-State supplies of goods and services under Article 269A (1) of the Constitution. The said Article reads, "269A. (1) Goods and services tax on supplies in the course of inter-State trade or commerce shall be levied and collected by the Government of India and such tax shall be apportioned between the Union and the States in the manner as may be provided by Parliament by law on the recommendations of the Goods and Services Tax Council.

Explanation—For the purposes of this clause, supply of goods, or of services, or both in the course of import into the territory of India shall be deemed to be supply of goods, or of services, or both in the course of inter-State trade or commerce".

The relevant enactment for this purpose is the Integrated Goods and Services Tax (IGST) Act, 2017 which makes provisions for the levy and collection of tax on inter-state supply of goods or services or both by the Central Government.

IGST is charged on *movement of goods and services* from one state to another. For example, if goods are moved from Maharashtra to Karnataka, IGST will be levied on such goods. The revenue from IGST is shared between the Central Government and the importing state (Karnataka) as per the manner prescribed by the authorities.

IGST is designed to ensure seamless flow of input tax credit from one State to another. One State has to deal only with the Central Government to settle the tax amounts and not with every other state, thus making the process easier.

Any IGST input tax credit is first applied to set-off IGST (this will happen if there are two or more inter-State transactions of the same commodity), then CGST. The balance can be set-off against SGST.

IGST is broadly CGST plus SGST. The inter-State seller will pay IGST on value addition after adjusting available credit of IGST, CGST, and SGST on his purchases. The exporting State will transfer to the Centre the credit of SGST used in payment of IGST. The importing dealer will claim credit of IGST while discharging his output tax liability in his own State. The Centre will transfer to the importing State the credit of IGST used in payment of SGST. The relevant information is also submitted to the Central Agency which will act as a clearing house mechanism, verify the claims and inform the respective governments to transfer the funds.

IGST is deposited into an IGST Account administered by the Central Government and is distributed between the Centre and the consuming State.

A. Imports of Goods and Services: Import of goods and services are treated as inter-State supplies and are subject to IGST in addition to the applicable customs duties.

B. Non-vatable Additional Tax: For an initial period of 2 years—or as further extended on the recommendation of the GST Council—a non-vatable additional tax not exceeding 1 percent on inter-State supply of goods would be levied and collected by the Centre and assigned to the originating State.

The major advantages of IGST model are as under:

1. Maintenance of uninterrupted input tax credit (ITC) chain on inter-State transactions.
2. No upfront payment of tax or substantial blockage of funds for the inter-State seller or buyer.
3. No refund claim in exporting State, as ITC is used up while paying the tax.
4. Self-monitoring mechanism.
5. Level of computerization is limited to inter-State dealers and Central and State Governments are able to computerize their processes expeditiously.
6. As all inter-State dealers are e-registered and correspondence with them is by e-mail, the compliance level is substantially high.
7. IGST can take into account *business-to-business* as well as *business-to-consumer* transactions.

What is the logic for CGST, SGST and IGST? India is a federal polity where both the Centre and the States have been assigned the powers to levy and collect taxes. Both the levels of Government have distinct responsibilities to perform, as per the Constitution, for which they need to raise resources. A dual GST is, therefore, in keeping with the constitutional requirement of fiscal federalism. The Centre and States simultaneously levy GST. The three taxes are implemented to help taxpayers to take input tax credit, thus ensuring one-country, one-tax and one-market.

It is noteworthy that CGST and IGST laws are the exclusive domain of the Centre. Central Board of Excise and Customs (CBEC) is responsible for administration of the CGST and IGST laws. In addition, excise duty regime would continue to be administered by the CBEC for levy and collection of Central excise duty on five specified petroleum products [4] as well as on tobacco products. [5] CBEC would also continue to handle the work relating to levy and collection of customs duties.

To sum up, GST is meant to evolve an efficient and harmonized consumption-based tax system in the country. GST is a consumption-based tax because the tax is received by the State in which the goods or services are consumed and not by the state in which such goods are manufactured. GST has replaced parallel systems of indirect taxation at the Central and State levels. The changeover to GST is a game-changing tax reform which will significantly contribute to the buoyancy of tax revenues, acceleration of growth, and generation of many positive externalities.

Endnotes

1. Clauses 12A, 26A and 26B in Article 366 were inserted by Section 14 of the Constitution (One Hundred and First Amendment) Act, 2016.
2. Government of India, Ministry of Finance, *Budget Speech of the Finance Minister, 1994-95, Part B*, p. 24.
3. Operating Costs of a Tax: These are made up of administrative costs plus compliance costs of a tax. See section 1.6 of chapter 1 of this book.
4. Petroleum and petroleum products have been constitutionally included as *goods* under GST. However, it has also been provided that petroleum and petroleum products shall not be subject to the levy of GST till notified at a future date on the recommendation of the GST Council. The present taxes levied by the Centre and the States on petroleum and petroleum products—excise duty/CENVAT by the Centre and sales tax/VAT by the States—will continue to be levied in the interim period. The five petroleum products which have been kept in abeyance for the purpose of GST are the following: (a) petroleum crude, (b) motor spirit (petrol), (c) high speed diesel, (d) natural gas, and (e) aviation turbine fuel.
5. Tobacco and tobacco products would be subject to GST. In addition, the Centre would have the power to levy Central excise duty on these products.

10

Salient Features of GST

After missing several deadlines and overcoming almost a decade of political differences—on how to replace a multi-layered set of Central and State taxes and levies with a uniform nationwide tax—GST was finally introduced from July 1, 2017. GST has subsumed a profusion of Central and State indirect taxes to create a single unified market. GST will make India a seamless national market, boosting trade and industry and hence growth rate.

10.1 Destination-based Consumption Tax

As against the erstwhile system of tax on the manufacture of goods or on sale of goods or on provision of services, GST is applicable on *supply* of goods or services or both.

GST is a destination-based consumption tax as against the erstwhile origin-based tax system. This implies that all SGST collected will ordinarily accrue to the State where the consumer of the goods and/or services sold resides. In other words, the tax would accrue to the taxing authority which has jurisdiction over the place of consumption which is also termed as place of supply.

In the case of inter-State trade, the inter-State seller pays IGST on the sale of his goods to the Central Government after adjusting credit of IGST, CGST and SGST on his purchases (in that order). The exporting State transfers to the Centre the credit of SGST used in payment of IGST. The importing dealer claims credit of IGST while discharging his output tax liability (both CGST and SGST) in his own State. The Centre transfers to the importing State the credit of IGST used in payment of SGST. Since GST is a destination-based tax, all SGST on the final product will ordinarily accrue to the consuming State.

10.2 Dual GST Model

It is a dual GST with the Centre and the States simultaneously levying it on a common base. GST levied by the Centre on intra-State supply of goods and services is called Central GST (CGST) and that levied by the States (including Union territories with legislature) is called State GST (SGST). Union territories without legislature levy Union Territory GST (UT-GST).

CGST and SGST are levied simultaneously on every transaction of supply of goods and services. Further, both CGST and SGST are levied on the same price or value unlike the erstwhile State VAT which was levied on the value of the goods inclusive of Central Value Added Tax (CENVAT).

While the location of the supplier and the recipient within the country is immaterial for the purpose of CGST, SGST is chargeable only when the supplier and the recipient are both located within the same State.

This dual GST model is implemented through multiple statutes (one for CGST and one each SGST statute for every State). To the extent feasible, uniform procedures for collection of both CGST and SGST are prescribed in the respective legislations for CGST and SGST. The basic features of law such as chargeability, definition of taxable event and taxable person, measure of levy including valuation provisions, basis of classification etc. are uniform across these statutes as far as practicable.

CGST and SGST are paid electronically into the accounts of the Centre and the States separately. Centre levies and administers CGST and IGST while respective States levy and administer SGST.

10.3 Integrated GST (IGST) on Inter-State Transactions and Imports

IGST mechanism has been designed to ensure seamless flow of input tax credit from one State to another. Centre levies IGST which is CGST plus SGST on all inter-State transactions of taxable goods and services. [1]

10.4 Input Tax Credit (ITC)

ITC is an important feature of GST. There are well-defined rules for availing ITC.

Credit of CGST paid on inputs may be used only for paying CGST on the output and the credit of SGST/UT-GST paid on inputs may be used only for paying only SGST/UT-GST. Since CGST and SGST are two parallel taxes, under the dual GST regime, levied simultaneously on goods and services therefore the cross utilisation of CGST input tax credit for payment of SGST output tax liability and vice versa is not permitted. In other words, the two streams of input tax credit (ITC) cannot be cross utilised, except in specified circumstances of inter-State supplies, for payment of IGST. In other words, the GST credit pool is fungible with CGST and SGST and the same can be used for payment of IGST, CGST and SGST and vice versa.

The order of utilisation of the IGST credit will be first towards IGST, then CGST and the balance towards SGST liability. Similarly an SGST credit can be utilised first towards SGST liability and then towards IGST, whereas a CGST credit will be used first toward CGST and then towards IGST.

More specifically, ITC is permitted to be utilized in the following manner:

- ITC of CGST is allowed for payment of CGST and IGST in that order.
- ITC of SGST is allowed for payment of SGST and IGST in that order.
- ITC of UT-GST is allowed for payment of UT-GST and IGST in that order.
- ITC of IGST is allowed for payment of IGST, CGST and SGST/U-TGST in that order.
- ITC of CGST cannot be used for payment of SGST/UTGST and vice versa.
- ITC of Additional Tax is not permitted.

ITC is broad-based because it is available in respect of taxes paid on any supply of goods or services or both used or intended to be used in the course or furtherance of business. The law allows an assessee to carry forward his input tax credit and ensures that no ITC is lost while migrating to the new regime. There are detailed guidelines in this regard.

Accounts are settled periodically between the Centre and the State to ensure that the credit of SGST used for payment of IGST is transferred by the originating State to the Centre. Similarly, the IGST used for payment of SGST is transferred by Centre to the destination State.

Further, the SGST portion of IGST (IGST may contain CGST, SGST and Cess on luxury items) collected on B2C supplies is also transferred by Centre to the destination State. The transfer of funds is carried out on the basis of information contained in the returns filed by the taxpayers.

Under GST there is a continuous chain of production and distribution. All entities under GST can pass on the tax burden except the end-user (i.e. the final consumer). The status of a trader differs from that of the consumer in the sense that the former can pass on the burden of GST to the latter, the latter cannot because the production-distribution process ends with him.

Those who can pass on the tax burden (called tax shifting) to succeeding entity suffer what the economists call *impact of the tax* (or initial tax burden). Those who cannot shift the tax burden (consumers) suffer *incidence of the tax*. Thus, the incidence of GST is on the consumer. Or, to put it differently, consumer is the final bearer of GST burden.

The illustration shown in Table 10.1 indicates, in terms of a hypothetical example, how GST works.

Table 10.1: Hypothetical Example of GST Calculation

Stage of supply chain	Purchase value of inputs	Value addition	Value at which supply of goods and services made to next stage	Rate of GST (percent)	GST on output	Input tax credit	Net GST = GST on output – input tax credit
Manufacturer	100	30	130	10	13	10	13 - 10 = 3
Whole seller	130	20	150	10	15	13	15 - 13 = 2
Retailer	150	10	160	10	16	15	16 - 15 = 1

Source: The Empowered Committee of State Finance Ministers, *First Discussion Paper on Goods and Services Tax in India,* New Delhi, November 10, 2009, p. xxxix.

10.5 GST and Foreign Trade

10.5.1 Exports: Exports are zero-rated supplies under GST law. In its twelfth meeting held on March 16, 2017, the GST Council cleared a proposal for the zero rate to be applied for goods and services going to special economic zones (SEZs). In other words, supplies made to SEZs are zero-rated and considered as physical exports. In the earlier decision—in case of procurement of supplies by SEZs—tax was to be paid and then refund claimed of such tax paid but as per the discussion in the said meeting the same supplies were accepted as zero-rated.

10.5.2: Imports: As per explanation to clause (1) of article 269A of the Constitution, IGST (CGST plus SGST) will be levied on all imports into the territory of India. Thus, import of goods is treated as inter-state supplies and hence subject to IGST in addition to the applicable customs duties. Import of services is treated as inter-state supplies and hence subject to IGST.

Though the additional duty of excise (or CVD) and the special additional duty (or SAD) on imports have been subsumed under GST, levy of basic customs duty (BCD) on import of goods is continuing.

While the full set-off is available of the IGST paid on import of goods and services, BCD paid on import is not eligible for set-off.

The incidence of tax follows the destination principle and the tax revenue in case of SGST accrues to the State where the imported goods and services are consumed. Unlike in the past, the States where imported goods are consumed now gain their share from the IGST paid on imported goods.

In short, following duties are levied on import of goods: Basic customs duty and cess as applicable + IGST+ GST compensation cess. IGST and GST compensation cess are paid after adding customs duty and customs cess to the value of imports.

Additional duty of customs continues to be levied on imports of petroleum and tobacco products. [2]

10.6 Implementation and Administration of GST

The administration of the Central GST is with the Centre and for State GST with the States. The taxpayer is required to submit periodical returns to both the Central GST authority and to the concerned State GST authorities.

Section 23 of the CGST Act specifies persons who are not required to be registered (e.g. a farmer, a person having wholly exempt turnover etc.). Section 24 of the CGST Act specifies persons who are required to take registration irrespective of the turnover (e.g. persons making inter-State supply, casual taxable persons, non-resident taxable persons etc.)

Accounts are settled periodically between the Centre and the States to ensure that the credit of SGST used for payment of IGST is transferred by the exporting State to the Centre. Similarly the IGST used for payment of SGST is transferred by the Centre to the importing State.

The laws, regulations and procedures for levy and collection of CGST and SGST have been harmonized to the extent possible.

Harmonised System of Nomenclature (HSN) code is used for classifying goods under the GST regime. Taxpayers whose turnover is above ₹ 1.5 crore but below ₹ 5 crore shall use 2 digit code and the taxpayers whose turnover is ₹ 5 crore and above shall use 4 digit code. Taxpayers whose turnover is below ₹ 1.5 crore are not required to mention HSN Code in their invoices. [3] Services are classified as per the services accounting code (SAC).

See also chapter 13 of this book.

In the light of the above discussion, Table 10.1 provides a comparison, in summarized form, of pre-GST and post-GST systems of taxation of goods and services in India.

Table 10.1: Pre-GST and Post-GST Systems of Taxation of Goods and Services in India: A Comparison

Pre-GST system	Post-GST system
Centre and the States enjoyed mutually exclusive powers of taxation. No concurrent powers of taxation and hence no joint occupancy of tax fields.	Centre and the States are concurrently empowered to levy GST on goods and services (i.e. common tax fields).
Centre levied excise duty on the *manufacture* of goods while States levied sales tax/VAT on the *sale* of goods.	GST is levied on the *supply* of goods or services or both.
Centre had the exclusive power to tax services.	Centre and the States both tax goods and services under GST.
Origin-based taxation.	GST is destination-based consumption tax.
Different exemption lists.	Uniform exemption list.
Different rates of taxes.	Uniform rates throughout the country.
Different procedures to collect taxes.	Uniform procedures to collect GST.

To sum up, the introduction of GST is a very significant step in the field of indirect tax reforms in India. By amalgamating a large number of Central and State taxes into a single tax, it would mitigate cascading or double taxation in a major way and pave the way for a common national market. From the viewpoint of consumers, the biggest advantage would be in terms of a reduction in the overall tax burden on goods. Introduction of GST would also make Indian products competitive in the domestic and international markets. Moreover, GST, because of its transparent character, would be easier to administer.

If the value added tax (VAT) was a major improvement over the pre-existing Central excise duty at the national level and the sales tax system at the State level, then GST is a further significant breakthrough towards a comprehensive indirect tax reform in the country.

Endnotes

1. For details, see section 9.3.3 of chapter 9 of this book.
2. See endnotes 4 and 5 of chapter 9 of this book.
3. Harmonized Commodity Description and Coding System generally referred to as Harmonized System of Nomenclature (or simply HSN) is a multi-purpose international product nomenclature developed by the World Customs Organization (WCO). It comprises about 5,000 commodity groups, each identified by a six digit code, arranged in a legal and logical structure and is supported by well-defined rules to achieve uniform classification.
   The system is used by more than 200 countries and economies as a basis for their customs tariffs and for the collection of international trade statistics.

HSN standardizes the classification of merchandise under sections, chapters, headings, and sub-headings. This results in a six-digit code for a commodity (two digits each representing the chapter, heading, and sub-heading).

HSN has 21 sections, 99 chapter, 1,244 headings, and 5,224 sub-headings.

Each Section is a collection of various chapters. Sections represent a broader class of goods, and chapters represent a particular class of goods.

Each chapter is further divided into various headings depending upon different types of goods belonging to the same class.

Each heading contains products, which are ultimately assigned an HSN code.

For better identification of goods, India and a few other countries use eight-digit codes for deeper classification.

India, a member of WCO since 1971, has been using HSN codes since 1986 to classify commodities for Customs and Central Excise. Customs and Central Excise added two more digits to make the codes more precise, resulting in an eight-digit classification.

Under GST, the majority of dealers will need to adopt two-, four-, or eight-digit HSN codes for their commodities, depending on their turnover the year prior.

- Dealers with turnover of less than ₹ 1.5 crore are not required to adopt HSN codes for their commodities.
- Dealers with turnover between ₹ 1.5 crore and ₹ 5 crore are required to use two-digit HSN codes for their commodities.
- Dealers with turnover equal to ₹ 5 crore and above are required to use four-digit HSN codes for their commodities.
- In the case of imports/exports, HSN codes of eight digits are compulsory, as GST has to be compatible with international standards and practices.

11

Working Mechanism of GST with Numerical Illustrations

In this chapter some hypothetical numerical examples are given to show the working of CGST, SGST and IGST. The commodity in question is computer (called X) which presently is subject to GST rate of 18 percent.

11.1 Intra-state Single Transaction

A in Mumbai sells X to B (end-user or final consumer) in Mumbai for ₹ 20,000. Both the seller and the buyer are located in the same state (Maharashtra). Being an intra-state transaction, GST is payable at the rate of 18 percent. Or, to put it differently, CGST and SGST are separately and simultaneously payable at the rate of 9 percent, and hence form part of the invoice of A to B as under (all figures in ₹):

Cost of X	20,000
CGST @ 9 percent	1,800
SGST @ 9 percent	1,800
Total	23,600

A collects ₹ 1,800 as CGST which he deposits in the account of the Central Government. Similarly, he collects ₹ 1,800 as SGST which he deposits in the account of Maharashtra Government. Table 11.1 depicts the transaction.

Table 11.1: Hypothetical Example Showing the Working of CGST and SGST (Dual GST) for Intra-state Single Transaction of Commodity X

GST rate = 18 percent (CGST rate = 9 percent; SGST rate = 9 percent)

Sale	Nature of sale	Sale price (₹)	Amount (₹) received as GST by			
			Centre		Maharashtra	
1.	Intra-state (Maharashtra) sale of X from A to B	20,000	CGST	1,800	SGST	1,800

It is noteworthy that GST is imposed on A but he shifts its burden to B. In the following illustrations also, GST is shifted by one entity to another except the end-user (i.e. the final consumer). This is a characteristic feature of an indirect tax.

11.2 Intra-state Double Transaction

To continue the example given in Table 11.1 (A in Mumbai sells X to B in Mumbai for ₹ 20,000), now B sells X to C (end-user) in Pune for ₹ 30,000. Again, being an intra-state transaction, CGST and SGST are payable and hence form part of the invoice of B to C as under (all figures in ₹):

Cost of X	30,000
CGST @ 9 percent	2,700
SGST @ 9 percent	2,700
Total	35,400

B collects ₹ 2,700 as CGST. After deducting CGST input tax credit of ₹ 1,800, he deposits ₹ 900 in the account of the Central Government. Similarly, he collects ₹ 2,700 as SGST.

After deducting SGST input tax credit of ₹ 1,800, he deposits ₹ 900 in the account of Maharashtra Government. Table 11.2 depicts the transactions.

Table 11.2: Hypothetical Example Showing the Working of CGST and SGST (Dual GST) for Intra-state Double Transactions of Commodity X

GST rate = 18 percent (CGST rate = 9 percent; SGST rate = 9 percent)

ITC = input tax credit

Sale	Nature of sale	Sale price (₹)	Amount (₹) received as GST by			
			Centre		Maharashtra	
1.	Intra-state (Maharashtra) sale of X from A to B	20,000	CGST	1,800	SGST	1,800
2	Intra-state (Maharashtra) sale of X from B to C	30,000	CGST (-) CGST ITC CGST (net)	2,700 1,800 900	SGST (-) SGST ITC SGST (net)	2,700 1,800 900
Total GST revenue				2,700		2,700

11.3 Inter-state Single Transaction

A in Mumbai (Maharashtra) sells X to B in Bengaluru (Karnataka) for ₹ 20,000. Being an inter-state transaction, IGST is payable at the rate of 18 percent and hence forms part of the invoice of A to B as under (all figures in ₹):

Cost of X	20,000
IGST @ 18 percent	3,600
Total	23,600

IGST so collected by A from B is deposited by the former in the account of the Central Government. The apportionment of the deposited amount between the Centre and the importing State is governed by Section 17 of the Integrated Goods and Services Tax Act, 2017 which reads as follows, "Out of the integrated tax paid to the Central Government…the amount of tax calculated at the rate equivalent to the central tax on similar intra-State supply shall be apportioned to the Central Government. The balance amount of integrated tax remaining in the integrated tax account in respect of the supply for which an apportionment to the Central Government has been done…shall be apportioned to the State where such supply takes place".

Broadly speaking, IGST (being the sum total of CGST and SGST) is apportioned between the Centre and the importing State in the ratio of 50:50. Table 11.3 depicts the transaction.

Table 11.3: Hypothetical Example Showing the Working of IGST for Inter-state Single Transaction of Commodity X

IGST = 18 percent

Sale	Nature of sale	Sale price (₹)	Amount (₹) received as GST by					
			Centre		Maharashtra		Karnataka	
1.	Inter-state sale of X from A (Maharashtra) to B (Karnataka)	20,000	IGST	3,600	...	...		
Total GST revenue				3,600		...		
Adjustments of IGST between Centre and Karnataka								
			Transferred to Karnataka	1,800			Received from Centre	1,800
Final GST revenue				1,800				1,800

11.4 Inter-state Double Transaction

To continue the example given in Table 11.3 [A in Mumbai (Maharashtra) sells X to B in Bengaluru (Karnataka) for ₹ 20,000], now B in Bengaluru (Karnataka) sells X to C in Chennai (Tamil Nadu) for ₹ 30,000. Again, being an inter-state transaction, IGST is payable at the rate of 18 percent and hence forms part of the invoice of B to C as under (all figures in ₹):

Cost of X	30,000
IGST @ 18 percent	5,400
Total	35,400

B collects ₹ 5,400 as IGST. After deducting IGST input tax credit of ₹ 3,600, he deposits ₹ 1,800 in the account of the Central Government. Table 11.4 depicts the transactions.

11.5 Intra-state and Inter-state Transactions

A in Mumbai sells X to B in Mumbai for ₹ 20,000. Both the seller and the buyer are located in the same state (Maharashtra). Being an intra-state transaction, CGST and SGST are payable and hence part of the invoice of A to B as under (all figures in ₹):

Cost of X	20,000
CGST @ 9 percent	1,800
SGST @ 9 percent	1,800
Total	23,600

A collects ₹ 3,600 as GST out of which he deposits ₹ 1,800 in the account of the Central Government and the remaining ₹ 1,800 in the account of Maharashtra Government.

Now B sells the same X to C in Bengaluru (Karnataka) for ₹ 40,000. Being an inter-State transaction, IGST at the rate of 18 percent is payable and hence part of the invoice of B to C as under (all figures in ₹):

Cost of X	40,000
IGST @ 18 percent	7,200
Total	47,200

Table 11.4: Hypothetical Example Showing the Working of IGST for Inter-state Double Transaction of Commodity X

IGST = 18 percent; ITC = input tax credit

Sale	Nature of sale	Sale price (₹)	Amount (₹) received as GST by					
			Centre		Maharashtra		Karnataka	
1.	Inter-state sale of X from A (Maharashtra) to B (Karnataka)	20,000	IGST	3,600	...	...		
2.	Inter-state sale of X from B (Karnataka) to C (Tamil Nadu)	30,000	IGST (-) IGST ITC IGST (net)	5,400 3,600 1,800				
Total GST revenue				5,400		...		
Adjustments of IGST between Centre and Karnataka								
			Transferred to Karnataka	2,700			Received from Centre	2,700
Final GST revenue				2,700				2,700

IGST of ₹ 7,200 is collected by B from C. After deducting CGST input tax credit of ₹ 1,800 and SGST input tax credit of ₹ 1,800, B deposits IGST (net) of ₹ 3,600 into the account of Central Government.

Further, C sells the same X to D (end-user or final consumer) in Bengaluru (Karnataka) for ₹ 60,000. Once again it is a case of intra-State transaction and hence subject to both CGST at the rate of 9 percent (₹ 5,400) and SGST at the rate of 9 percent (₹ 5,400) which also form part of the invoice of C to D as under (all figures in ₹):

Cost of X	60,000
CGST @ 9 percent	5,400
SGST @ 9 percent	5,400
Total	70,800

IGST input tax credit to the extent of ₹ 5,400 is set-off against the CGST of ₹ 5,400 by C and hence there is zero CGST (net) from C to Central Government. The remaining IGST input tax credit of ₹ 1,800 (₹ 7,200 - ₹ 5,400) is set-off against the SGST of ₹ 5,400 payable to Karnataka Government by C. Thus, C deposits ₹ 3,600 as SGST (net) into the account of Karnataka Government.

The work of the taxpayers stops here.

11.5.1 Adjustments of CGST, SGST and IGST among Centre, Maharashtra and Karnataka (Table 11.5a): As is known, GST is a consumption-based tax, i.e. the

State where the goods are finally consumed will collect the tax. Thus, Maharashtra, where X was sold will not get any GST revenue. Central Government and Karnataka both, therefore, will get ₹ 5,400 each. Maharashtra (exporting state) will transfer to the Centre the credit of SGST of ₹ 1,800 used in payment of IGST. The Centre will transfer to Karnataka (importing state) ₹ 1,800 IGST credit used.

The above example shows the need for CGST, SGST and IGST. All 3 together will serve the purposes of GST, viz

- One-country, one-tax and one-market.
- Both the Centre and the States earn revenue.

Table 11.5a depicts the various transactions.

Table 11.5a: Hypothetical Example of CGST, SGST and IGST on Intra-state and Inter-state Transactions of Commodity X

GST rate = 18 percent (CGST rate = 9 percent and SGST rate = 9 percent)
IGST rate = 18 percent; ITC = Input tax credit

Sale	Nature of sale	Sale price (₹)	Amount (₹) received as GST by					
			Centre		Maharashtra		Karnataka	
1.	Intra-state (Maharashtra) sale of X from A to B	20,000	CGST	1,800	SGST	1,800	...	...
2.	Inter-state (Maharashtra and Karnataka) sale of X from B to C	40,000	IGST (-) CGST ITC (-) SGST ITC IGST (net)	7,200 1,800 1,800 3,600	...	...	...	...
3.	Intra-state (Karnataka) sale of X from C to D	60,000	CGST (-) IGST ITC* CGST (net)	5,400 5,400 0	...	...	SGST (-) IGST ITC (7,200 – 5,400) SGST (net)	5,400 1,800 3,600
Total GST revenue				5,400		1,800		3,600
Adjustments of CGST, SGST and IGST among Centre, Maharashtra and Karnataka								
			Received from Maharashtra (-) Transferred to Karnataka Net	1,800 1,800 0	Trans-ferred to Centre	1,800	Received from Centre	1,800
Final GST revenue				5,400		0		5,400

*Although IGST ITC is ₹ 7,200, CGST can set it off only to the extent of ₹ 5,400. The remaining IGST ITC of ₹ 1,800 will be set-off against SGST of Karnataka Government.

It is noteworthy that according to Table 11.5a, the entire transfer received by the Centre from Maharashtra (₹ 1,800) is passed on to Karnataka.

We take another example to show that the transfer from Maharashtra to Centre is first used to compensate Karnataka for the IGST input tax credit deducted from SGST. The remaining amount is retained by the Centre. In other words, the transfer from Maharashtra to Centre is apportioned between the Karnataka and the Centre.

A in Mumbai sells X to B in Mumbai for ₹ 15,000. Both the seller and the buyer are located in the same state (Maharashtra). Being an intra-state transaction, CGST and SGST are payable and hence part of the invoice of A to B as under (all figures in ₹):

Cost of X	15,000
CGST @ 9 percent	1,350
SGST @ 9 percent	1,350
Total	17,700

A collects ₹ 2,700 as GST out of which he deposits ₹ 1,350 in the account of the Central Government and the remaining ₹ 1,350 in the account of Maharashtra Government.

Now B sells the same X to C in Bengaluru (Karnataka) for ₹ 26,250. Being an inter-state transaction, IGST at the rate of 18 percent is payable and hence part of the invoice of B to C as under (all figures in ₹):

Cost of X	26,250
IGST @ 18 percent	4,725
Total	30,975

IGST of ₹ 4,725 is collected by B from C. After deducting CGST input tax credit of ₹ 1,350 and SGST input tax credit of ₹ 1,350, B deposits IGST (net) of ₹ 2,025 into the account of Central Government.

Further, C sells the same X to D (end-user or final consumer) in Bengaluru (Karnataka) for ₹ 45,000. Once again it is a case of intra-state transaction and hence subject to both CGST at the rate of 9 percent (₹ 4,050) and SGST at the rate of 9 percent (₹ 4,050) which also form part of the invoice of C to D as under (all figures in ₹):

Cost of X	45,000
CGST @ 9 percent	4,050
SGST @ 9 percent	4,050
Total	53,100

IGST input tax credit to the extent of ₹ 4,050 is set-off against the CGST of ₹ 4,725 by C and hence there is zero CGST (net) from C to Central Government. The remaining IGST input tax credit of ₹ 675 (₹ 4,725 - ₹ 4,050) is set-off against the SGST of ₹ 4,050 payable to Karnataka Government by C. Thus, C deposits ₹ 3,375 as SGST (net) into the account of Karnataka Government.

The work of the taxpayers stops here.

11.5.2 Adjustments of CGST, SGST and IGST among Centre, Maharashtra and Karnataka (Table 11.5b): As is known, GST is a consumption-based tax, i.e. the State where the goods are finally consumed will collect the tax. Thus, Maharashtra, where X was sold will not get any GST revenue. Central Government and Karnataka both, therefore, will get ₹ 4,050 each instead of only ₹ 3,375 each. Maharashtra (exporting state) will transfer to the Centre the credit of SGST of ₹ 1,350 used in payment of IGST. The Centre will transfer to Karnataka (importing state) ₹ 675 IGST credit used. The remaining amount of ₹ 675 will be retained by the Centre.

Table 11.5b depicts the various transactions.

Table 11.5b: Hypothetical Example of CGST, SGST and IGST on Intra-state and Inter-state Transactions of Commodity X

GST rate = 18 percent (CGST rate = 9 percent and SGST rate = 9 percent)
IGST rate = 18 percent; ITC = input tax credit

Sale	Nature of sale	Sale price (₹)	Amount (₹) received as GST by					
			Centre		Maharashtra		Karnataka	
1.	Intra-state (Maharashtra) sale of X from A to B	15,000	CGST	1,350	SGST	1,350	...	...
2.	Inter-state (Maharashtra and Karnataka) sale of X from B to C	26,250	IGST (-) CGST ITC (-) SGST ITC IGST (net)	4,725 1,350 1,350 2,025	...	...	...	...
3.	Intra-state (Karnataka) sale of X from C to D	45,000	CGST (-) IGST ITC* CGST (net)	4,050 4,050 0	...	...	SGST (-) IGST ITC (4,725 - 4,050) SGST (net)	4,050 675 3,375
Total GST revenue				3,375		1,350		3,375
Adjustments of CGST, SGST and IGST among Centre, Maharashtra and Karnataka								
			Received from Maharashtra (-) Transferred to Karnataka Net	1,350 675 675	Transferred to Centre	1,350	Received from Centre	675
Final GST revenue				4,050		0		4,050

*Although IGST ITC is ₹ 4,725, CGST can set it off only to the extent of ₹ 4,050. The remaining IGST ITC of ₹ 675 will be set off against SGST of Karnataka Government.

Just like exports from India are generally exempt from tax/duty, so also exports from one State to another are exempt from GST. Exporting State should be satisfied that goods produced by it are being consumed in other States. Apparently, production activities in the exporting state lead to enhanced employment opportunities for its residents and profit earning by its entrepreneurs, apart from other benefits of higher production.

12

Exemptions, Threshold Limits, Rate Structure and Composition Scheme under GST

Besides being the main source of revenue, both for the Central and State Governments, GST is an effective instrument to realise various socio-economic objectives of national policies. Exemptions/lenient tax treatment of essential goods and services of mass consumption serve the objective of tax equity. [1] Threshold limits benefit the small traders. GST rates influence the relative prices of different goods and services and hence the allocation of resources among various sectors of the economy. Rate structure also determines the investment climate in the country and the aggregate demand and thus the scale of operations in the economy.

12.1 Scope of GST

GST is leviable on all goods and services except the following:

1. Goods outside the purview of GST.
2. Goods within the purview of GST but currently kept in abeyance.
3. Goods exempted from GST.
4. GST threshold limits

12.1.1 Goods outside the Purview of GST: Alcohol for human consumption [2] and electricity [3] are outside the purview of GST. In the case of alcoholic liquor for human consumption, States continue to levy the taxes presently being levied, i.e. State excise duty and sales tax/VAT.

12.1.2 Goods within the Purview of GST but Currently Kept in Abeyance: Petroleum and petroleum products have been constitutionally included as *goods* under GST. However, it has also been provided that petroleum and petroleum products shall not be subject to the levy of GST till notified at a future date on the recommendation of the GST Council. The present taxes levied by the Centre and the States on petroleum and petroleum products—excise duty/CENVAT by the Centre and sales tax/VAT by the States—will continue to be levied in the interim period. The five petroleum products which have been kept in abeyance for the purpose of GST are the following: (a) petroleum crude, (b) motor spirit (petrol), (c) high speed diesel, (d) natural gas, and (e) aviation turbine fuel.

Domestic LGP and PDS kerosene are already under rate category of 5 percent GST.

Tobacco and tobacco products are subject to GST. In addition, the Centre is continuing to levy excise duty on these products.

Continuance of excise duties on petroleum and tobacco for the Centre, and petroleum and alcohol for the States provides some degree of fiscal autonomy to the two levels of government.

12.1.3 Goods Exempted from GST (Zero-rated): Under GST law, the Central or the State Government, on the recommendation of the GST Council can exempt the supplies from the levy of GST either generally or subject to conditions. Like goods, services can also be classified into two broad categories: essential services (e.g. health and education) and luxury services (e.g. entertainment and tourism). The rationale for exemption/lenient tax treatment of essential services is the same as for essential goods. Similarly, luxury services are taxed at a high rate like luxury goods.

There is a list of exempted goods and services which is harmonized for the Centre and the States as well as across States as far as possible.

Choices which the GST Council makes regarding exemptions will be critical. The more the exemptions that are retained/granted, the higher will be the average GST rate. There is no getting away from a simple and powerful reality: the broader the scope of exemptions, the less effective the GST will be.

See Table 12.1 of this chapter for an illustrative list of goods exempted from GST.

12.1.4 GST Threshold Limits: Prior to the introduction of GST, thresholds prescribed in different VAT Acts of States varied from State to State. Acknowledging the desirability of a uniform threshold across States, GST Council, in its First Meeting held on September 22-23, 2016 decided that businesses with an annual turnover of less than ₹ 20 lakh would be exempted from GST. Also, the threshold would be ₹ 10 lakh in the North-Eastern and hill states, which have been given a carve-out in the constitutional amendment that paved the way for GST.

Presently, a common threshold exemption applies to both CGST and SGST. Taxpayers with a turnover below it are exempt from GST. Thus, businesses with an annual turnover of less than ₹ 20 lakh are exempted from GST. The threshold is ₹ 10 lakh in the case of businesses in 11 North-Eastern and hill states, namely Assam, Arunachal Pradesh, Manipur, Meghalaya, Mizoram, Nagaland, Tripura, Sikkim, Uttrakhand, Himachal Pradesh and Jammu and Kashmir. It is noteworthy that a lower threshold had prevailed in these States during the VAT regime.

Threshold exemption is built into a tax regime to keep small traders out of tax net. This has three-fold objectives:

1. It is difficult to administer small traders and the cost of administering such traders is very high in comparison to the tax paid by them.
2. Compliance costs and efforts are saved for such small traders.
3. Small traders get relative advantage over large enterprises on account of lower tax incidence.

Many small entrepreneurs feel that they can bypass GST if their turnover is less than ₹ 20 lakh. However, this exemption has its own flip side. If a business is not under GST, the businesses it supplies to cannot get the benefit of input tax credit. They may eventually switch to vendors who are registered under GST and can issue invoices which include GST. Thus, even if a business is small with a turnover of less than ₹ 20 lakh, it may be desirable for it, particularly a manufacturer supplying components to a large firm, to get itself registered under GST. The threshold exemption scheme is optional.

12.2 Rate Structure of GST

To get the design of the GST right, it is necessary to aim at tax rates that protect revenue, simplify administration, encourage compliance, avoid adding to inflationary pressures, and keep India in the range of countries with reasonable levels of indirect taxes.

CGST and SGST are levied at rates jointly decided by the Centre and the States. The rates are notified on the recommendations of the GST Council.

At its fourth meeting held on November 3-4, 2016 in New Delhi, the GST Council agreed on a 4-slab GST rates of 5, 12, 18 and 28 percent which it claimed would not be inflationary and yet protect revenues of Centre and State Governments. [4]

CGST, IGST and SGST provide for a maximum tax of 20 percent each. Taken any of the two taxes together, the maximum tax burden in the GST regime at 40 percent (20 percent Centre and 20 percent States) is an enabling provision for financial emergencies. The actual rates in the four-slab structure are 5 percent, 12 percent, 18 percent and 28 percent.

There is a zero tax rate on several items, including foodgrains. The second category subject to 5 percent contains items of mass consumption used by common people. There are two standard rates of 12 and 18 percent. The 28 percent rate applies to luxury items (cars, aerated drinks, cigarettes), dubbed as *demerit goods*.

GST rates on various goods were approved by GST Council in its Fourteenth meeting held on May 18, 2017 in Srinagar (Jammu and Kashmir). The Council broadly approved the GST rates for goods at 0 percent (or exempt), 5 percent, 12 percent, 18 percent and 28 percent (Table 12.1).

Table12.1: Rate Structure of GST on Goods

GST rate (percent)	Illustrative list of goods
0*	Majority of the goods in the consumer price index (CPI) including milk, eggs, curd, fresh vegetables, unpacked foodgrains, unpacked *paneer*, *gur*, unbranded natural honey, unbranded *atta*, unbranded *besan*, unbranded *maida*, common salt, silk and jute, contraceptives, exports and supplies to special economic zone (SEZ) units/SEZ developers, children's colouring books.
0.25	Rough diamonds.
3	Gold, gems and jewellery.
5	Essential food items and mass consumption goods including sugar, tea, roasted coffee beans, edible oils, skimmed milk powder, milk food for babies, packed food, packed *paneer*, newsprint, PDS kerosene, domestic LPG, coal, building bricks, renewable energy devices, cotton and natural fibre, apparel costing below ₹ 1,000, footwear costing below ₹ 500, cashew, *agarbattis*, insulin.
12	Mobiles, medicines, telephones, LED lights, butter, *ghee,* almonds, sausages, pickles, chutney, morabba, toppings, instant food mix, packed coconut water, umbrellas, fertilizers, exercise books, cutlery.

Contd...

18	Computers, capital goods, industrial intermediates, hair oil, soap, toothpaste, toilet and facial tissues, iron and steel fountain pens, man-made fibres, footwear costing ₹ 500 and above, insecticides, refractory bricks, computer printers, ball bearings, school bags, plastic tarpaulin.
28	Consumer durables, motor cars, auto components, wrist watches, cement, chewing gum, custard powder, perfumes, shampoos, cosmetics, fireworks, motorcycles, furniture, bidis and bidis leafs.
Compensation cess over and above 28 percent	Pan masala, tobacco and tobacco products (60 to 204 percent), cigarettes (5 to 21 percent plus fixed rate per 1,000 sticks based on category and length), aerated waters (12 percent), motor cars (small cars: 1 to 3 percent; mid segment/large cars/SUVs: 15 percent), motorcycles with engine capacity greater than 350cc (3 percent), coal and lignite** (₹ 400 per tonne).

*Zero-rated, nil-rated and exempt goods are interchangeable terms under GST law. However, in fiscal literature there is a distinction between zero-rated and exempted goods. See endnote 13 of chapter 1 of this book.

**Clean environmental cess on coal has been replaced by compensation cess.

Source: Government of India, Central Board of Excise and Customs (website).

As in the case of goods, services are also taxable in all the tax rate slabs. It is noteworthy that health and educational services are exempt from GST [5] GST rates on various services were approved by GST Council in its fourteenth meeting held on May 19, 2017 in Srinagar (Jammu and Kashmir). The Council broadly approved the GST rates for services at Nil, 5 percent, 12 percent, 18 percent and 28 percent. Subsequently, some changes were made in the rate structure in the Council's seventeenth meeting held on June 18, 2017 (Table 12.2).

Table12.2: Rate Structure of GST on Services

GST rate (percent)	Illustrative list of services*
0 (exempted)**	Healthcare services by a clinical establishment, an authorised medical practitioner or para-medics • Services provided by an educational institution to its students, faculty and staff • Services by government or a local authority Services by the Reserve Bank of India • Services by a foreign diplomatic mission located in India • Services relating to cultivation of plants and rearing of all life forms of animals • Services provided by an arbitral tribunal • Services by way of admission to a museum, national park, wildlife sanctuary, tiger reserve or zoo • Services by way of training or coaching in recreational activities relating to arts or culture • Services by way of sponsorship of sporting events • Services provided by the Goods and Services Tax Network (GSTN).
5	Transport of goods by rail • Transport of goods in a vessel • Renting of motorcab • Transport of passengers by air in economy class • Selling of space for advertisement in print media • Services by way of job work in relation to printing of newspapers • Leasing of aircrafts • Supply of tour operators' services.

Contd...

12	Transport of passengers by air in other than economy class • Transport of goods in containers by rail by any person other than Indian Railways • Supply of food/drinks in restaurant not having facility of air-conditioning or central heating at any time during the year and not having licence to serve liquor • Renting of hotels, inns, guest houses, clubs, campsites or other commercial places meant for residential or lodging purposes having room tariff ₹ 1,000 and above but less than ₹ 2,500 per room per day • Construction of a complex, building, civil structure or a part thereof, intended for sale to a buyer, wholly or partly.
18	Supply of food/drinks in restaurant having licence to serve liquor • Supply of food/drinks in outdoor catering • Renting of hotels, inns, guest houses, clubs, campsites or other commercial places meant for residential or lodging purposes where room tariff of ₹ 2,500 and above but less than ₹ 7,500 per room per day • Services by way of admission or access to circus, Indian classical dance including folk dance, theatrical performance, drama • Composite supply of works contract.
28	Services by way of admission to entertainment events or access to amusement facilities • Services provided by a race club by way of totalisator or a licensed bookmaker in such club • Gambling • Accommodation in hotels including 5 star and above rated hotels, inns, guest houses, clubs, campsites or other commercial places meant for residential or lodging purposes, where room rent is ₹ 7,500 and above per night per room.

*For a complete list of GST rates on various services, see Appendix 3 of this book.
**For a complete list of services exempted from GST, see Appendix 4 of this book.
Source: Government of India, Central Board of Excise and Customs (website).

12.3 Composition Scheme under GST

The composition scheme is an important feature of GST to protect the interests of small traders and small-scale industries. A composition option (i.e. to pay tax at a flat rate without credits) is available to small taxpayers below a certain threshold. It is a kind of presumptive tax [6]

The objective of composition scheme is to bring simplicity and to reduce the compliance cost for the small taxpayers. Moreover, it is optional and the eligible person opting to pay tax under this scheme can pay tax at a prescribed percentage of his turnover every quarter, instead of paying tax at normal rate.

The scheme is available to small taxpayers whose aggregate turnover in the preceding financial year did not cross ₹ 75 lakh. In the case of following States, the limit of turnover is ₹ 50 lakh: Arunachal Pradesh, Assam, Manipur, Meghalaya, Mizoram, Nagaland, Sikkim, Tripura and Himachal Pradesh.

Composition scheme allows small businesses to avail a hassle-free compliance regime. It is noteworthy that these segments are large job creators and hence a priority area for the government.

Rates of composition levy for different categories of registered persons are given in Table 12.3.

Table 12.3: Rates of Composition Levy for Different Categories of Registered Persons

S. No.	Category of registered person	Rate of tax
1.	Manufactures, other than manufacturers of such goods as may be notified by the Government	2 percent (1 percent Central tax plus 1 percent State tax) of the turnover
2.	Restaurant services	5 percent (2.5 percent Central tax plus 2.5 percent State tax) of the turnover
3.	Traders or any other supplier eligible for composition levy	1 percent (0.5 percent Central tax plus 0.5 percent State tax) of the turnover

The scheme allows option for GST registration for dealers with turnover below the compounding cut-off.

12.3.1 Persons Not Eligible for Composition Scheme: Following persons are not allowed to opt for the composition scheme.

1. A Casual taxable person or a non-resident taxable person.
2. Suppliers whose aggregate turnover in the preceding financial year crossed ₹ 75 lakh.
3. Supplier who has purchased any goods or services from unregistered supplier unless he has paid GST on such goods or services on reverse charge basis.
4. Suppliers of services other than restaurant services.
5. Persons supplying goods which are not taxable under GST law.
6. Persons making any inter-State outward supplies of goods.
7. Suppliers making any supply of goods through an electronic commerce operator who is required to collect tax at source.
8. A manufacture of following goods: (a) ice cream and other edible ice, whether or not containing cocoa, (b) pan masala and (c) tobacco and manufactured tobacco substitutes.

The methodology to compute *aggregate turnover* is given in Section 2(6) of MGL. Accordingly, aggregate turnover means the aggregate value of all taxable and non-taxable supplies, exempt supplies and export of goods/and/or services of a person having the same PAN, to be computed on all-India basis and excludes taxes, if any, charged under the CGST Act, SGST Act, and the IGST Act, as the case may be. Explanation: Aggregate turnover does not include the value of supplies on which tax is levied on reverse charge basis and the value of inward supplies.

Taxable person who was not eligible for the composition scheme would be liable to pay tax, interest and in addition he shall also be liable to a penalty equivalent to the amount of tax payable.

Though the composition scheme requires lesser GST compliance, it has several drawbacks, particularly for the manufacturers. Firstly, only businesses which operate within a particular state can opt for this scheme. Secondly, opting for composition scheme breaks the chain of seamless input tax credit. A composition scheme dealer cannot collect any tax from its buyers. Hence, those who buy from a composition scheme dealer are not able to take credit of any input tax. Likewise, if a composition scheme dealer purchases from a registered dealer, the former cannot avail credit of tax paid on his inputs. To opt or not for the composition scheme, depends upon the judgement and business circumstances of an individual.

The composition scheme is optional.

Endnotes

1. Tax equity refers to *fair* or *just* or *equitable* distribution of tax burden among taxpayers. Though fairness and justness in taxation are universally accepted, these terms are rarely defined rigorously and can be interpreted in various ways. Hence, there is no unanimity of opinion as to the type of tax system which results in the most equitable distribution of tax burden.
   Tax equity is the prime characteristic of a good tax system. It is the basic criterion for evaluating a tax system. This classical canon of taxation is based on the natural desire among people for justice.
   An inequitable tax system may hinder the establishment of a stable political, social, and economic order. The French and American Revolutions were partly the result of perceived inequity in the tax systems. In India, the duty on salt which hit the poor the most symbolised national protest against the British rulers during the freedom struggle. Tax equity ensures better tax compliance because unjust tax systems induce people to evade taxes. If properly defined and effectively implemented, an equitable tax system can prevent concentration of economic power in a few hands.
2. Under Entry 51 of List II (State List) in the Seventh Schedule of the Constitution, the States are empowered to levy, "duties of excise on: (a) alcoholic liquors for human consumption; (b) opium, Indian hemp and other narcotic drugs and narcotics; but not including medicinal and toilet preparations containing alcohol or any substance included in sub-paragraph (b) of this entry". The revenues accrue to the states in the form of licence duties from the vendors as well as the tax, which can be specific or ad valorem.
   State excise duties (on liquors and other narcotics) are an important source of States' own tax revenues. Their relative revenue significance has declined over the years because of the policy of prohibition adopted in some States from time to time (notably Gujarat and Bihar). However, it is difficult to totally prohibit the consumption of alcohol in the States. Attempts at full prohibition lead to illegal production and export of the tax base to the neighbouring States.
   It is noteworthy that while in Western countries the main objective of duties on intoxicants is revenue collection, in India the overriding consideration in imposing these duties is to discourage consumption of intoxicants as a matter of public policy. Since demand for alcoholic beverages is generally price-inelastic, this tax provides a case for keeping high tax rates for controlling the level of consumption. In fact, high tax rates yield both high revenues and greater control on consumption.
3. Under Entry 53 of List II (State List) in the Seventh Schedule of the Constitution, the electricity duty is charged to consumers along with the electricity consumption rates. The rates are meant for the providers of electricity (electricity boards) while the electricity duty is meant for the state treasury.

4. Earlier, the Centre had proposed a 4-slab structure of 6, 12, 16 and 26 percent.
5. Improvement in the health status of the population has been one of the major thrust areas in social development programmes of India since Independence. Over the past seven decades, India has built up a vast health infrastructure and manpower at primary, secondary and tertiary care levels in the government, voluntary and private sectors manned by professionals and para-medicals. India has invested massive amounts under the successive Five Year Plans in medical education, training and research which has ensured large manpower from the super-specialists to the auxiliary midwives.

   Education has been a thrust sector ever since India attained Independence in 1947. Right from the inception of planning, the crucial role of education in economic and social development has been recognised and emphasised. Efforts to increase people's participation in education and to diversify educational programmes in order to promote knowledge and skills required for nation-building have characterised successive Five Year Plans. Despite a series of problems that the country faced soon after Independence, it has been possible to create a vast educational infrastructure in terms of large enrolments and teaching force and massive capabilities for management, research and development.
6. Presumptive tax relates to the use of appropriate indicators of income, wealth, sales etc. instead of the actual records of these tax bases. The chief advantage of presumptive taxation is its simplicity, both for the tax collectors and the taxpayers. It is, therefore, cost-effective for the administration. The simplicity attribute may also encourage tax compliance. Presumptive taxation particularly suits the developing countries with a large unorganised business sector consisting of small retail establishments, and self-employed professionals. It is easy to administer this tax which can become an effective source of revenue.

13

Administration of GST

13.1 Point of Levy of GST

13.1.1 Point of Levy of GST on the Supply of Goods: In the pre-GST period, India followed an origin-based tax system and therefore the point of taxation was at the origin of sale and the originating State kept the tax so collected, irrespective of where the consumer was located. Under GST, which is a multi-point levy (i.e. levy at each successive value addition in the value chain), the tax moves with goods and is credited to the account of the destination State based on the place of supply as determined under the IGST Act, 2017. GST is charged on supply and point of levy is determined as per time of supply under section 12 of the CGST Act, 2017. [1]

13.1.2 Point of Levy of GST on the Supply of Services: GST on services is a tax on supply and the point of levy is as determined in terms of section 13 of the CGST Act, 2017. The revenue is remitted to the State where the service is consumed based on the place of supply as determined under the IGST Act, 2017. By default, the place of supply of services is the place where the service recipient is located in the case of business-to-business (B2B) transactions and place of the service provider in the case of business-to-consumer (B2C) transactions. However, there are exceptions to this rule.

13.2 Registration of Businesses

A person is liable to register if the aggregate turnover (all India) is more than ₹ 20 lakh (₹ 10 lakh in the case of Special Category States) or if he is engaged in inter-state supplies.

A person dealing exclusively in zero-rated (or exempted) goods is not liable to register irrespective of turnover.

13.2.1 Registration for Existing Businesses/Applicants: Earlier, tax payers were separately registered with the state and/or with central tax administrations or with both based on their business activity. In the GST regime, a taxpayer will have to obtain state-wise registration. Even within a state, the taxpayer will have an option to obtain multiple registrations for different business verticals.

13.2.2 Registration for New Businesses/Applicants: Each taxpayer will be allotted a state-wise Permanent Account Number (PAN) based on 15-digit Goods and Services Taxpayer Identification Number (GSTIN). Those tax payers who are already registered under the current state or central tax regime, are migrated to the common portal and granted GST registration suo motu with a request to provide additional information where required.

A new applicant is allowed to apply for registration on the common portal without prior enrolment.

13.3 Contents of Invoice Issued under GST

A registered assessee supplying taxable goods/services shall issue at the time of supply, a tax invoice showing complete details of the transaction as under:

- Name, address and GSTIN of the assessee.
- Name, address and GSTIN of the buyer/service recipient.
- Date of invoice.
- Value of goods/services.
- Description of goods/services.
- Rate and value of CGST, SGST or IGST.
- Signature of taxpayer.

13.4 Modes of Tax Payment

Under the GST regime, tax is payable by the taxable person on the supply of goods and services. Liability to pay tax arises when the taxable person crosses the threshold exemption, i.e. ₹ 20 lakh (₹ 10 lakh for Special Category States) except in certain specified cases where the taxable person is liable to pay GST even though he has not crossed the threshold limit. The CGST and SGST are payable on all intra-State supply of goods and services and IGST is payable on all inter-State supply of goods and services.

Payment of GST can be made electronically with a common *challan* (i.e. document for payment of taxes) for all the taxes. Various modes of GST payment are available to the taxpayer including the following:

- Internet banking.
- Debit/credit cards.
- National Electronic Funds Transfer (NEFT). [2]
- Real Time Gross Settlement (RTGS). [3]
- Over the counter payments (for payments up to ₹ 10,000 per tax period) in cash cheque or demand draft (DD).

13.5 Tax Deduction and Tax Collection at Source

There is obligation on certain persons including government departments, local authorities and government agencies, who are recipients of supply, to deduct tax at the rate of 1 percent from the payment made or credited to the supplier where total value of supply, under a contract, exceeds ₹ 2.5 lakh.

There is obligation on electronic commerce operators to collect *tax at source*, at such rate not exceeding 2 percent of net value of taxable supplies, out of payments to suppliers supplying goods or services through their portals.

13.6 Filing of Returns

There is a provision for electronic filing of returns by different class of persons at different cut-off dates. Returns, that allow the auto-population of data from the vendors and automated matching of invoices, shall be filed online by a normal/casual taxpayer in a sequential manner within different cut-off dates.

It may be noted that most of the returns are auto generated by the GSTN system and the dealer is expected to validate the data and also fill in the missing data. The payment of tax due is a must for filing valid returns under the GST regime. Details of return filing are given in Table 13.1.

13.6.1 Self-assessment of Tax Payable: There is a system of self-assessment of the taxes payable by the registered person.

13.6.2 Audit of Registered Persons: Audit of registered persons is conducted in order to verify compliance with the provisions of Act.

13.7 Remission of Tax/Duty

Model GST Law permits remission of tax on supply of goods.

Remission of tax/duty means relieving the taxpayer from the obligation to pay tax on goods when they are lost or destroyed due to any natural causes. Remission is subject to conditions stipulated under the law and rules made thereunder.

Remission of tax applies only when tax is payable as per law, i.e. taxable event should have happened and tax is required to be paid as per law. Under GST Law, levy is applicable upon supply of goods. Where goods are lost or destroyed before supply, taxable event does not occur in order to pay tax. Accordingly, question of remission of tax does not rise.

In simple terms, remission is allowed only for those cases where supply of goods is found to be deficient in quantity due to natural causes.

13.8 Refund of Tax

Refund of tax can be sought by taxpayer or by any other person who has borne the incidence of tax within 2 years from the relevant date. The refund regime is expected to be simple under GST as opposed to the pre-GST manual verification system. The refund can be obtained in the following scenarios:

- Refunds on exports.
- Refunds of carry forward input tax credit granted only in case of an inverted duty structure.

13.8.1 Limitation Periods: Limitation period for raising demand is 3 years from the due date of filing of annual return or from the date of erroneous refund for raising demand for short-payment or non-payment of tax or erroneous refund and its adjudication in normal cases.

Limitation period for raising demand is 5 years from the due date of filing of annual return or from the date of erroneous refund for raising demand for short-payment or non-payment of tax or erroneous refund and its adjudication in case of fraud, suppression or wilful misstatement.

13.10 Other Administrative Provisions

- **Arrears of Tax:** Arrears of tax are recovered using various modes including detaining and sale of goods, movable and immovable property of defaulting taxable person. Officers have restrictive powers of inspection, search, seizure and arrest.

Table 13.1: Details of Return Filing

Category of taxpayer	Details to be given	Periodicity/last date	Form to be used
Aggregate turnover less than ₹ 20 lakh	Nil	Nil	Nil
Aggregate turnover up to ₹ 75 lakh and availing the composition scheme	•Consolidated details of outward supplies made by the assessee during the quarter including that of advances received. •Details of supplies received (auto-populated from the GSTR-1 of the supplier)	Quarterly/18th of the month following the quarter	GSTR-4
Aggregate turnover more than ₹ 20 lakh and not availing composition scheme but supplying to consumers (only B2C supplies)	Tax-rate-wise summary of all intra-state supplies made.	Monthly/10th of the following month.	GSTR-1
	Supplies received.	Auto-populated by the computer and only needs to be verified and submitted by 15th of the following month	GSTR-2
	Final return	Auto-populated by the computer and only needs to be verified and submitted by 20th of the following month.	GSTR-3
All other suppliers including suppliers to re-sellers and/or consumers (both B2B and/or B2C suppliers)	•Invoice-wise details of all B2B supplies and inter-state B2C supplies of value above ₹ 2.5 lakh •Tax-wise summary of B2C intra-state supplies. •State-wise and tax-rate-wise summary of B2C inter-state supplies of value below ₹ 2.5 lakh.	Monthly/10th of the following month	GSTR-1
	Supplies received	Auto-populated by the computer and only needs to be verified and submitted by the 15th of the following month	GSTR-2
	Final return	Auto-populated by the computer and only needs to be verified and submitted by the 20th of the following month.	GSTR-3

Source: Website of the Central Board of Excise and Customs.

- **Dispute Resolution Mechanism:** An elaborate adjudication and appellate procedure is prescribed under the GST law. There is a separate appellate tribunal called the Goods and Services Tax Appellate Tribunal (GST Appellate Tribunal) to deal with disputes. The Tribunal hears appeals against the orders passed by the Appellate Authority or the Revisional Authority. States would adopt the provisions relating to Tribunal in respective SGST Act.
- **Penalties:** There are provisions for penalties for contravention of the law.
- **Advance Ruling:** Advance Ruling Authority would be constituted by States in order to enable the taxpayer to seek a binding clarity on taxation matters from the department. Centre would adopt such authority under CGST Act.
- **Anti-profiteering Provisions:** As per section 171 of the CGST Act, 2017 any reduction in rate of tax on any supply of goods or services or the benefit of input tax credit shall be passed on to the recipient by way of *commensurate* reduction in prices.
- **Reverse Charge Mechanism:** Reverse charge mechanism applies to supplies of both goods and services. In the case of purchase of goods from unregistered dealers, the receiver of goods is not entitled to get input tax credit. Further, the recipients who are registered under composition schemes are liable to pay tax under reverse charge.
- **Exemptions Granted in the Pre-GST System:** Minimal exemptions and concessions are available under the GST regime. However, the tenure of certain exemptions, such as the area-based tax exemptions, granted by the governments would extend to the GST regime and the governments may have to honour the commitments. Since tax exemption may not be possible under the GST regime, these exemptions may still be granted in the form of post-tax cash refund schemes after the collection of tax, so that the GST chain is not disturbed.
- **Transitional Provisions:** Elaborate transitional provisions have been provided for smooth transition of existing taxpayers to GST regime.

Endnotes

1. For various definitions related to supply, see section A2.1 of Appendix 2 of this book.
2. National Electronic Funds Transfer (NEFT): Electronic Funds Transfer (EFT) system was introduced in the mid-1990s. EFT facilitates transfer of funds from one bank account to another. In the beginning EFT system was permitted only for government transactions and RBI-initiated payments. NEFT is an electronic message-based payment system, and was introduced by the Reserve Bank of India in November 2005 to replace the EFT system which was public key infrastructure (PKI)-enabled and the settlements were effected on a decentralized mode.
3. Real Time Gross Settlement (RTGS) System: The Indian RTGS system was operationalised in March 2004. The system started operations with four banks and settled only inter-bank transactions. Subsequently, the system was opened for settlement of customer transactions. It was operationalised for settlement of multilateral net settlement batch (MNSB) files from September 2006.

14

Technological Infrastructure and Institutional Set-up for Implementing GST

An important objective of tax reform is simplification of tax administration and compliance, which is dependent on three factors. The first determining factor for simplicity is the tax design itself. Generally, the more rational and neutral the tax design, the simpler it would be to administer and encourage compliance. If the tax is levied on a broad base at a single rate, there would be few classification disputes and the tax-specific record keeping requirements for vendors would be minimal. It would simplify enforcement, and encourage voluntary compliance.

The second factor is the infrastructure for tax administration, including the design of tax forms, data requirements, system of tax rulings and interpretations, and the procedures for registration, filing and processing of tax returns, tax payments and refunds, audits, and appeals. A modern tax administration focuses on providing services to taxpayers to facilitate compliance. It harnesses information technology to enhance the quality of services, and to ensure greater transparency in administration and enforcement.

The third factor in a federation (such as India) is the degree of harmonization among the taxes levied by the Centre and the States. Thus, under the dual GST—consisting of a Centre GST and a State GST—harmonization of the Centre and State GSTs would be critical to keep the overall compliance burden low. Equally important is harmonization of GSTs across the states.

14.1 Goods and Services Tax Network (GSTN)

Among the various steps that have been taken for the introduction of GST is the establishment of a strong information technology (IT) infrastructure. For this purpose the Government has set up an Empowered Group (Chairman: Nandan Nilekani). Significant progress has been made in the conceptualization and design of the GSTN—a common portal for the Centre and States that will enable electronic processing of the key business processes of registration, returns, and payments.

For the implementation of GST in the country, the Central and State Governments have jointly registered GSTN as a not-for-profit, non-government company under erstwhile section 25 of the Companies Act, 1956. It will provide shared IT infrastructure and services to Central and State Governments, tax payers and other stakeholders. GSTN is a special purpose vehicle (SPV) which aims to provide a standard and uniform interface to the taxpayers, and shared infrastructure and services to Central and State/UT Governments. It will be the interface between the government and the taxpayers.

GSTN is working on developing a state-of-the-art comprehensive IT infrastructure including the common GST portal providing front-end services of registration, payments and returns to taxpayers. It will also assist some States with back-end IT modules that include processing of returns, registrations, audits, assessments, appeals etc. All States, accounting authorities, Reserve Bank of India (RBI) and banks are also preparing their IT infrastructure for the administration of GST. There would be no manual filing of returns. All taxes can also be paid online. All mis-matched returns would be auto-generated, and there would be no need for manual interventions. Most returns would be self-assessed.

The functions of the GSTN, inter alia, include the following:

1. Facilitating registration.
2. Forwarding the returns to Central and State authorities.
3. Computation and settlement of IGST.
4. Matching of tax payment details with banking network.
5. Providing various MIS reports to the Central and the State Governments based on the tax payer return information.
6. Providing analysis of tax payers' profile.
7. Running the matching engine for matching, reversal and reclaim of input tax credit.

GSTN would also be integrating the common GST portal with the existing tax administration IT systems and would be building interfaces for taxpayers.

GSTN is a unique and complex IT initiative. It is unique as it seeks, for the first time, to establish a uniform interface for the taxpayer and a common and shared IT infrastructure between the Centre and States.

GSTN will render the following services through the common GST Portal:

1. Registration (including existing taxpayer master migration and issue of PAN-based registration number).
2. Payment management including payment gateways and integration with banking systems.
3. Return filing and processing.
4. Taxpayer management, including account management, notifications, information, and status tracking.
5. Tax authority account and ledger management.
6. Computation of settlement (including IGST settlement) between the Centre and States; clearing house for IGST.
7. Processing and reconciliation of GST on imports and integration with EDI systems of customs.
8. MIS including need-based information and business intelligence.
9. Maintenance of interfaces between the Common GST Portal and tax administration systems.
10. Providing training to stakeholders.
11. Providing analytics and business intelligence to tax authorities.
12. Carrying out research, study best practices and provide training to stakeholders.

The structure of GSTN was approved by the Empowered Committee (EC). GSTN will be set up as a National Information Utility. GSTN will implement common PAN-based registration, returns filing and payments processing for all States on a shared platform. The use of PAN as a common identifier in both direct and indirect taxes, will enhance transparency and check tax evasion.

National Securities Depository Limited (NSDL) is the technology partner for incubating the National Information Utility that will establish and operate the IT backbone for the GST. In this regard, NSDL set up a pilot project in collaboration with 11 States prior to GST roll-out across the country. Three Joint Working Groups of officials have also been constituted comprising officials from the Central Government, State Governments, and the Empowered Committee (EC) of State Finance Ministers to work on legislation, business procedures and IT infrastructure respectively.

GSTN has appointed M/s Infosys as managed service provider (MSP) at a total project cost of around ₹ 1,380 crore for a period of 5 years.

14.2 Ministry of Finance

14.2.1 Department of Revenue: It exercises control in respect of matters relating to all the Direct and Indirect Union Taxes through two statutory Boards namely, the Central Board of Direct Taxes (CBDT) and the Central Board of Excise and Customs (CBEC). Each Board is headed by a Chairman who is also ex-officio Special Secretary to the Government of India. Matters relating to the levy and collection of all Direct taxes are looked after by the CBDT whereas those relating to levy and collection of Customs and Central Excise duties and other Indirect taxes fall within the purview of the CBEC. The two Boards were constituted under the Central Board of Revenue Act, 1963.

14.2.2 Central Economic Intelligence Bureau (CEIB): The CEIB functioning under the Ministry of Finance is responsible for coordination, intelligence sharing, and investigations at national as well as regional levels amongst various law enforcement agencies. The existing coordination mechanism in the CEIB consists of Regional Economic Intelligence Councils (REICs) at regional level and the Group on Economic Intelligence and meetings of the heads of investigating agencies under the Department of Revenue at the centre. While the Group on Economic Intelligence is focused on matters relating to intelligence sharing, the REICs and heads of agencies meetings cover both intelligence and investigations.

14.2.3 Economic Intelligence Council (EIC): It came into existence in 2003 and is chaired by the Finance Minister and comprises senior functionaries of various ministries and intelligence agencies, including the Governor of RBI and the Chairman of the Securities and Exchange Board of India (SEBI). The EIC meets at least once a year to discuss and take decisions regarding trends in economic offences and strategies on intelligence sharing, coordination etc. Implementation of decisions taken by the EIC is monitored by the Working Group on Intelligence Apparatus, set up for this purpose within the EIC.

14.3 Central Board of Excise and Customs (CBEC)

The CBEC is a part of the Department of Revenue under the Ministry of Finance,

Government of India. It deals with the tasks of formulation of policy concerning levy and collection of customs and central excise duties, prevention of smuggling, and administration of matters relating to customs, central excise and narcotics to the extent under the CBEC's purview. The Board is the administrative authority for its subordinate organizations, including Custom Houses, Central Excise Commissionerates, and the Central Revenues Control Laboratory.

The Directorate General of Central Excise Intelligence (DGCEI) is the apex intelligence organization functioning under the CBEC. It is entrusted with the responsibility of detecting cases of evasion of central excise and service tax. The Directorate develops intelligence, especially in new areas of tax evasion through its intelligence network across the country and disseminates information in this respect by issuing modus operandi circulars and alert circulars to apprise field formations of the latest trends in duty evasion. Wherever found necessary, DGCEI on its own, or in coordination with field formations, organises operations to unearth evasion of central excise duty and service tax.

14.4 National Academy of Customs, Excise and Narcotics (NACEN)

One of the biggest challenges is to train the indirect tax officials of both the Central and State Governments about the concepts, processes and procedures of GST. NACEN—the apex training institution for capacity building in indirect taxation under the Central Board of Excise and Customs—has been mandated to impart training on GST to Central and State Government officers. NACEN is conducting a mammoth capacity building exercise to train about 60,000 indirect tax officers of the Centre and the States so that officers are well-equipped to implement GST. NACEN has already created a team of almost 2,000 trainers across the country to train the field officers. Considering the limited time available, NACEN, apart from classroom training, is also planning to use advanced information technology tools such as Virtual Classrooms and E-Learning modules, to ensure larger coverage.

As part of this capacity building exercise, the NACEN has prepared a compilation of frequently asked questions (FAQs)—based on inputs gathered while conducting training and interactive sessions—as a training tool for helping the officers as well as public, to get acquainted with the Model GST Law and its nuances.

14.5 Serious Frauds Investigation Office (SFIO)

It functions under the Ministry of Corporate Affairs and takes up for investigation complex cases having inter-departmental and multidisciplinary ramifications and substantial involvement of public interest, either in terms of monetary misappropriation or in terms of persons affected. It also takes up cases where investigation has the potential of contributing towards a clear improvement in systems, laws, or procedures.

14.5 Financial Intelligence Unit (FIU)

The FIU-IND was established by the Government of India on November 18, 2004 for coordinating and strengthening efforts for national and international intelligence by investigation and enforcement agencies in combating money laundering and terrorist financing. FIU-IND is the national agency responsible for receiving, processing, analysing, and disseminating information relating to suspect financial transactions. It is an independent body reporting to the Economic Intelligence Council headed by the Finance Minister. For administrative purposes, the FIU-IND is under the control of the Department of Revenue, Ministry of Finance.

15

Implications of GST for Various Sectors of the Indian Economy

As the world economy slows, and increasing financial volatility and turbulence become the *newest normal*, only a few economies have the resilience to be a refuge of stability and the potential to be an outpost of opportunity. India is one of those few. As oil and commodity prices continue to be soft, macroeconomic stability seems reasonably assured for India. This bedrock of stability coupled with reforms can propel the economy to a high growth trajectory. Key amongst these reforms is the national level GST.

The GST has been an initiative that has commanded broad consensus across the political spectrum. It has also been a model of co-operative federalism in practice with the Centre and States coming together as partners in embracing growth and employment-enhancing reforms. It was a long-awaited reform and its implementation has validated expectations of important government actions and effective political will to modernize the economy. Given the historic opportunity afforded by the GST, the aim should be to clean up the Indian tax system that had effectively become an *exemptions raj* with serious consequences for revenues and governance.

15.1 GST and the Economy

Many benefits of GST are claimed for the Indian economy.

15.1.1 Higher Investment and Growth: An oft-cited study by the National Council of Applied Economic Research (NCAER) suggested that growth would increase by 0.9-1.7 percent of GDP, purely based on the elimination of the cascading of taxes on exports. [1]

Under the pre-GST system, Union excise duties/CENVAT and States' sales tax/ VAT applied to all capital goods, but the input tax credits were generally limited to manufacturing plant and equipment. For example, no input tax credits were allowed for the Union excise duties on capital equipment acquired for use in transportation, infrastructure, distribution, or construction sectors because these sectors were all outside the scope of excise duties which were applicable to manufacturing only. Similarly, no credit was allowed for the State VAT on capital goods acquired by the service sector (e.g. telecommunications, transportation, finance, insurance, and IT services).

GST is expected to provide a more seamless and efficient crediting of taxes paid on capital goods. If this happens, prices of capital goods would come down, thereby increasing their demand, boosting investment and hence growth.

In fact, investment was discouraged under the earlier system through the application of excise duties and VAT to capital goods, for which no set-off or input tax credit was provided. This increased the cost of capital goods and reduced investment, which in turn led to lower employment and output.

15.1.2 Curbing Black Money: The government of Prime Minister Shri Narendra

Modi has placed a great deal of emphasis on controlling black money. This has been reflected in a series of measures taken recently. [2] These measures can be significantly complemented by GST which can be less intrusive, more self-policing, and hence more effective way of reducing corruption and rent-seeking. The complementary role of GST in curbing black money has, at least, two aspects.

The first relates to the self-policing incentive inherent in GST. To claim input tax credit, each dealer has an incentive to request documentation from the dealer behind him in the value-added/tax chain. Provided the chain is not broken through wide ranging exemptions, especially on intermediate goods, this self-policing feature of GST can work very powerfully.

According to Pomeranz, "Value added tax (VAT) is a stark example of a tax believed to facilitate enforcement through a built-in incentive structure that generates a third party reported paper trail on transactions between firms, which makes it harder to hide the transaction from the government". [3]

Second, the GST will in effect have a dual monitoring structure—one by the States and one by the Centre. Hence, there will be a greater probability that evasion will be detected. Even if one tax authority overlooks and/or fails to detect evasion, there is the possibility that the other overseeing authority may not.

15.1.3 One-country, One-tax, and One-market: Pre-GST tax structure unmade India by fragmenting markets along state lines. This had the collateral consequence of favouring imports and disfavouring domestic production. These distortions were caused mainly by the following three features of the then existing tax system:

1. Central sales tax (CST) on inter-state sales of goods.
2. Other numerous inter-state taxes like entry tax.
3. Extensive nature of exemptions from additional duties of customs [commonly known as countervailing duty (CVD)] [4] and special additional duty of customs (SAD). [5]

A. Abolition of Central Sales Tax (CST): CST on inter-state sales of goods led to inefficiencies in the supply chain of goods. Goods produced locally within the jurisdiction of consumption attracted lower tax than those produced outside. This tax encouraged geographic fragmentation of production. The tax could be avoided partially through branch/stock transfers by manufacturers. However, the tax savings from branch transfers got substantially offset by the incremental costs of logistics and warehousing of goods in multiple locations.

B. Elimination of other Inter-state Taxes: Prior to the introduction of GST, there were inter-state taxes that were levied by the States in addition to the CST. These included entry tax not in lieu of octroi and entry tax in lieu of octroi. These taxes caused horrible difficulties for transporters. Highlighting the problems of transporters, *Economic Survey, 2016-17* remarked, "Images of queues of trucks in India, idling at state borders with their drivers haggling for official clearances or being subject to extortion are legion. The consequent damages to trade and economic activity too have been extensively catalogued". [6] All these taxes have now been folded into the GST with enormous benefits.

There is ample evidence to suggest that logistical costs within India are high. One study suggests that in one day, trucks in India drive 280 kilometres while the figure for US is 800 kilometres. This raises direct costs (wages to drivers, passed on to firms), indirect costs (firms keeping larger inventory), and location choices (locating closer to suppliers/customers instead of lowest-cost location in terms of wages, rent etc.). Further, only about 40 percent of the total travel time is spent driving, check points and other official stoppages take up almost one-quarter of total travel time. Eliminating check point delays could keep trucks moving almost 6 hours more per day, equivalent to additional 164 kilometres per day, thus, pulling India above global average and to the level of Brazil. [7]

All of these barriers to inter-state trade become even more important in India because the share of roads in freight traffic is high (about 72 percent). The implication is that it is especially important for India to reduce costs to inter-state trade because of the excessive reliance on roads for movement of goods.

C. CVD and SAD Exemptions: It is a well-accepted proposition in tax theory that achieving neutrality of incentives between domestic production and imports requires that all domestic indirect taxes should also be levied on imports. So, if a country levies excise duty/sales tax/GST on domestic production/sales, it should also levy them on imports. In India, this was achieved through CVD and SAD which were levied on imports to offset the impact of the excise duty and sales tax/VAT levied on domestically manufactured goods.

However, in some cases there were CVD and SAD exemptions which acted perversely to favour foreign production over domestically produced goods, i.e. they provided negative protection for Indian manufacturing. Moreover, CVD and SAD were not applied on the whole range of imports.

Two arguments in favour of CVD and SAD exemptions were typically given. First, that CVD and SAD exemptions on inputs helped manufacturers by reducing their input costs. The second rationale advanced for exempting many imported goods from CVD and SAD was that there was no competing domestic production. This argument was faulty because the absence of competing domestic production was by itself the result of not having the neutrality of incentives that the CVD created. In other words, domestic producers might have chosen not to enter because the playing field was not level.

Now if an exemptions-free GST is levied on imports, as seems to be the case, it would ensure neutrality of incentives. In effect, India would be promoting domestic manufacturing without becoming protectionist and without violating any of its international trade obligations under the World Trade Organization (WTO) or under India's free trade agreements (FTAs).

15.2 GST and Business/Industry

Following can be the potential benefits of GST for business and industry:

15.2.1 Simplification, Rationalization and Harmonization of Tax System: GST has taken under its wings 17 indirect taxes (8 Central and 9 State taxes). Central Government levied excise duty/CENVAT on various commodities and the same set of commodities was subjected to sales tax/VAT by the States. In fact, there was no national policy as regards the burden of taxes on different goods. The scenario has changed with the introduction of GST. Instead of multiple taxes at different levels of the government, there is one tax with common base, exemption list, rate structure and administrative procedures. There is now no multiple-record-keeping for a variety of taxes. This will reduce investment of resources and manpower in maintaining records. GST will improve the ease-of-doing-business and transportation of goods across the country.

Apart from reducing compliance costs, common tax rates and procedures across the country would make business tax neutral, irrespective of the choice of place of doing business.

15.2.2 Mitigation of Tax Cascading: By amalgamating a large number of Central and State taxes into a single tax and allowing set-off of prior-stage taxes, GST would mitigate the ill effects of cascading and pave the way for a common national market. A system of seamless tax credits throughout the value-chain, and across boundaries of States, would ensure that there is minimal cascading of taxes. This would reduce hidden costs of doing business.

Complete and comprehensive input tax set-off and phasing out of CST would reduce the cost of locally manufactured goods and services. These may lead to lowering of tax burden on an average dealer in industry and trade. This will increase the competitiveness of Indian goods and services in the international market and give boost to Indian exports.

15.2.3 Easy Compliance: A robust and comprehensive IT system would be the foundation of GST regime in India. Therefore, all taxpayer services such as registrations, returns, payments, refunds etc. would be available to the taxpayers online, which would make compliance easy and transparent. Electronic matching of input tax credits across India will make the process more transparent and accountable. Improved environment of compliance would encourage more paper trail of transactions. [8]

15.2.4 Hassles-free Movement of Goods: Soon after the introduction of GST from July 1, 2017, most of the States dismantled border check posts for commercial taxes. It may be recalled that during pre-GST period truck drivers often had to queue up for hours to pay octroi/entry tax and get their consignments and papers checked, causing delays and adding to costs. Many State Governments, through advisories to their field staff, are ensuring that truckers are not harassed.

15.2.5 Reduced Interface between Taxpayer and Tax Collector: All interactions under GST are through the common GSTN portal and hence there will be less public interface between the taxpayer and the tax administration. Timelines have been provided for important activities like obtaining registration, refunds etc.

15.3 GST and Small-scale Businesses

Small-scale enterprises have emerged as a highly vibrant and dynamic sector of the Indian economy over the years. This sector not only plays crucial role in providing large employment opportunities, at comparatively lower capital cost than large industries, but also helps in industrialization of rural and backward areas, thereby reducing regional imbalances, and assuring more equitable distribution of national income and wealth. Small industries are complementary to large industries as ancillary units and contribute enormously to the socio-economic development of the country. The sector contributes significantly to manufacturing output, employment and exports of the country.

GST takes care of the small-scale businesses through: (a) threshold limits, (b) composition scheme and (c) relatively simpler procedures for GST compliance.

15.3.1 Threshold Limits: Threshold limit means the limit below which tax is not applicable. Prior to the introduction of GST, the threshold prescribed in different VAT Acts of States varied from State to State. The threshold of goods under State VAT was ₹ 5 lakh for a majority of bigger States and a lower threshold for North Eastern States and Special Category States.

Under GST, a common threshold exemption applies to both CGST and SGST. Taxpayers with a turnover below it are exempt from GST. Thus, businesses with an annual turnover of less than ₹ 20 lakh are exempted from GST. The threshold is ₹ 10 lakh in the case of businesses in North-Eastern and hill states. It is noteworthy that a lower threshold had prevailed in these States during the VAT regime.

15.3.2 Composition Scheme: A composition scheme for small traders, businesses and industries has also been envisaged under GST to adequately protect their interests. The composition scheme for the purpose of GST has an upper ceiling of ₹ 75 lakh on gross annual turnover. For businesses below this ceiling, the scheme allows traders, manufacturers and restaurant owners to pay presumptive tax at the rate of 1, 2, and 5 percent respectively. This will allow small businesses to avail a hassle-free compliance regime.

15.3.3 Simpler Procedures: Small retailers doing a large number of small transactions for up to a value of ₹ 200 per transaction to unregistered customers are not required to issue invoice for every such transaction. They can issue one consolidated invoice at the end of each day for all transactions done during the day. However, they should issue the invoice where the customer so demands. Similarly, in order to keep compliance burden low for small taxpayers, GST law provides that taxpayers with annual turnover of up to ₹ 1.5 crore need not mention the HSN Code of the goods in the invoices. [9]

15.4 GST and Consumers

Consumers may benefit from GST as under:

15.4.1 Single and Transparent Tax Proportionate to the Value of Goods and Services: In the pre-GST regime, cost of most goods and services in the country was laden with a host of many hidden taxes due to multiple indirect taxes being levied by the Centre and the States, with incomplete or no input tax credits available at progressive stages of value addition. Under GST, there is only one tax from the manufacturer to the consumer, leading to transparency of taxes paid by the final consumer.

15.4.2 Relief in Overall Tax Burden: For the consumers, the biggest gain would be in terms of a reduction in the overall tax burden on goods. Due to efficiency gains and prevention of leakages, GST is expected to reduce overall tax burden on most commodities, which will benefit consumers. Many essential items of mass consumption are either exempt from GST or bear 5 percent rate of tax.

Table 15.1 lists the items on which tax incidence under GST is lower than pre-GST incidence of indirect taxes.

Table 15.1: Items on which Tax Incidence under GST is Lower than Pre-GST Incidence of Indirect Taxes

(percent)

S. No.	Description of item	Pre-GST incidence*	GST rate
1.	Wheat	2.5	0
2.	Rice	2.75	0
3.	Unbranded flour	3.5	0
4.	Curd, lassi, butter milk	4	0
5.	Unbranded natural honey	6	0
6.	Ultra high temperature (UHT) milk	6	5
7.	Tea	6	5
8.	Milk powder	6	5
9.	Sugar	6	5
10.	Sweatmeats	7	5
11.	Vegetable edible oils	6	5
12.	Spices	6	5
13.	Ketchup and sauces	12	12
14.	Mustard sauce	12	12
15.	Toppings, spreads and sauces	12	12
16.	Mineral water	27	18
17.	Sugar confectionery	21	18
18.	Children's drawing/colouring books etc.	7	0
19.	Footwear up to ₹ 500 per pair	10	5
20.	Kerosene pressure lanterns	8	5
21.	Coal	9	5
22.	Toothpowder	17	12
23.	LED	15	12
24.	X-ray films for medical use	23	12
25.	Diagnostic kits and reagents	16	12
26.	Fixed speed diesel engines	16	12
27.	Fly ash bricks and fly ash blocks	16	12
28.	Sewing machines	16	12
29.	Hair oil	27	18
30.	Toothpaste	27	18
31.	Soap	27	18
32.	Other footwear	21	18

Contd...

33.	LGP stove	21	18
34.	Aluminium foils	19	18
35.	School bags	22	18
36.	Printers	19	18
37.	Staplers	27	18
38.	Tractor rear tyres and tubes	20	18
39.	Helmets	20	18
40.	CCTV	19	18
41.	Baby carriages	27	18
42.	Plastic tarpaulin	19	18
43.	Bamboo furniture	23	18
44.	Headgears and parts thereof	27	18
45.	Cement	29	28

*Pre-GST tax incidence would be higher if the tax incidence on account of Central sales tax (CST), octroi, entry tax etc. (which was more than 2 percent) is also included.
Source: Government of India, Central Board of Excise and Customs (website).

15.5 GST and Government Revenues

Central and State Governments stand to gain from GST in the following manner:

15.5.1 Simple and Easy to Administer: Multiple indirect taxes at the Central and State levels have been replaced by GST. Backed with a robust end-to-end IT system, GST would be simpler and easier to administer than all the erstwhile indirect taxes of the Centre and the States. GST with a common base and common rates (across goods and services and across States and between the Centre and States) will facilitate administration and improve compliance while also rendering manageable the collection of taxes on inter-State sales.

15.5.2 Better Controls on Leakages: GST will broaden the tax base and result in better tax compliance due to a robust IT infrastructure. Due to the seamless transfer of input tax credit from one stage to another in the chain of value additions, there is an in-built mechanism in the design of GST that would incentivize tax compliance by traders.

Uniform GST rates will reduce the incentive for evasion by eliminating rate arbitrage between neighbouring States and that between intra- and inter-State sales. [10]

15.5.3 Higher Revenue Efficiency: GST is expected to decrease the cost of collecting taxes and will, therefore, lead to higher revenue efficiency. [11] There may also be revenue gain for the Centre and the States due to widening of the tax base, increase in trade volumes and improved tax compliance. Also, because of its transparent character, GST would be easier to administer.

15.5.4 States' Share in IGST on Imports: Additional duties of customs [commonly known as countervailing duty (CVD)] and special additional duty of customs (SAD) levied on imports have been subsumed under GST. As per explanation to clause (1) of Article 269A of the Constitution, IGST will be levied on all imports into the territory of India. Unlike during the pre-GST period, States—where imported goods are consumed—

will now gain their share from this IGST paid on imported goods.

15.5.5 Compensation Provisions: Due to a shift from origin-based to destination-based indirect tax structure, some States might face drop in revenue in the initial years. To help the States during this transitional phase, the Centre has committed to compensate loss of revenue to any State for a period of 5 years. Section 18 of Constitution (One Hundred First Amendment) Act, 2016 provides for compensation to States by law, on the recommendation of the GST Council, for loss of revenue arising on account of implementation of GST for a period of 5 years. Thus, it is a constitutional obligation on the part of the Centre to compensate a State if it suffers loss of revenue on account of switch over to GST.

15.6 GST and Foreign Trade

Under GST, imports of goods and services are treated as inter-state supplies and IGST is levied on import of goods and services into the country. The incidence of tax follows the destination principle and the revenue in case of SGST accrues to the State where the imported goods and services are consumed. Full and complete set-off is available on the IGST paid on import of goods and services.

Exports are treated as zero-rated supplies. No tax is payable on exports of goods or services. However, input tax credit is available and the same is available as refund to the exporters.

To sum up, GST is a major milestone in reforming India's indirect tax system. Replacement of Central excise duties/CENVAT, service tax, States' sales tax/VAT, entry tax and a host of other indirect taxes by the GST would: (a) eliminate cascading effects of commodity taxes, (b) create a national market, and (c) align taxation of imports and exports correctly. It would also improve the competitiveness of production and exports from India.

GST is a historic and game-changing tax reform. Domestically, it will help improve governance, strengthen tax institutions, facilitate *make-in-India by making-one-India*, and impart buoyancy to the tax base. It will also set the global standard for a value-added tax (VAT) in large federal systems in the years to come.

Endnotes

1. National Council for Applied Economic Research, "Moving to Goods and Services Tax in India: Impact on India's Growth and International Trade", 2009.
2. In recent years, the issue of corruption and black money has come to the forefront after a series of financial scandals. Generation of black money—and its stashing abroad in tax havens and offshore financial centres—has dominated discussions and debates in public fora during the recent past. Members of the Parliament, the Supreme Court of India and the public at large have unequivocally expressed concern on the issue, particularly after some reports suggested enormous estimates of such unaccounted wealth being held abroad.

   After uproar in the Parliament, the Government of India came out with a *White Paper* on Black Money in May 2012. The *White Paper* presented the different facets of black money and its complex relationship with policy and administrative regime in the country. It also reflected upon the policy options and strategies that the Government had been pursuing to address the issue of black money and corruption in public life.

3. Pomeranz, Dina, "No Taxation without Information: Deterrence and Self-Enforcement in the Value Added Tax," Harvard University and NBER, 2013.
4. Under Section 3(1) of the Customs Tariff Act, 1975, an additional duty on goods imported into the country was leviable. The rate of this duty was equal to the excise duty on like articles if produced or manufactured in India. The underlying philosophy of a countervailing duty is to ensure that the protection provided by the import duty to domestic industry is not reduced.
5. This duty was also known as special CVD and was levied under Section 3(5) of the Customs Tariff Act, 1975. This duty was in addition to basic customs duty and CVD levied under Sections 3(1) and 3(3) respectively of the said Act. It was equal to sales tax/VAT, local tax or any other charge on a like article on its sale, purchase or transportation in India.
6. Government of India, *Economic Survey, 2016-17*, p. 233.
7. JPS Associates (2011), "Economic Cost of Inter-State Barriers in Goods Traffic".
8. For various types of compliance costs, see section 1.6.2 of chapter 1 of this book.
9. See endnote 3 of chapter 10 of this book.
10. During the pre-GST period, differential rates of sales tax on the same set of commodities in different States often led to uneconomic diversion of trade as well as production centres. It was not uncommon for people of one State making purchases in other States to avoid or reduce sales tax liability.
11. Every tax involves some revenue yield and a corresponding cost of collection. The main items comprising the latter are wages of the officials and costs of materials. Cost of collection when expressed as a proportion of tax revenue is called cost-yield ratio. It is indicative of the overall efficiency of tax administration. Thus, the lower the cost of collection, the more productive is the tax and vice versa. Unusually high cost-yield ratios prove drag on public exchequer. Cost-yield ratios may be used to evaluate administration of competing taxes. Administrative costs are generally high in developing economies which are in the process of evolving tax system and tax administration. Widespread illiteracy and lack of accounting practices make assessment procedures extremely difficult in these countries.

16

GST and Fiscal Federalism

According to the traditional classification followed by political scientists, constitutions are either unitary or federal in nature. A federation means a union of several states brought about by the instrument of a treaty or agreement. The modern concept of federalism is associated with the establishment of American federation in 1787. Since there is no agreed definition of a federal state, the model of the US is often taken as the reference point.

A federal set up creates a multiple polity based on divided functions and powers among central, state and local governments. Fiscal federalism, as a branch of public finance, deals with financial arrangements and their working in a federal polity. Fiscal federalism is a subject of topical interest in India in view of some recent developments of historical importance, including the introduction of GST.

16.1 Nature of India's Federal Polity

The Constitution of India adopted on November 26, 1949, became operative on January 26, 1950. It provides for two layers of Government, one at the Central level, and the other at the level of the States. A federal polity of this kind requires division of powers and responsibilities between the Centre and the States and generally brings in its wake problems and conflicts in Centre-State relations. Other important countries of the world with federal set up of government are: US, Canada, Australia, Brazil, and Nigeria.

Why did the framers of the Constitution opt for a federal set up? Answering this question, the Commission on Centre-State Relations, 1988, observed, "In a country too large and diverse for a unitary form of Government, they envisaged a system which would be worked in co-operation by the two levels of government—national and regional—as a common endeavour to serve the people. Such a system, it was conceived, would be most suited to Indian conditions as it would at once have the advantages of a strong unified central power, and the essential values of federalism". [1]

The very first Article of the Constitution defines India as a Union of States. Though the word federation has been deliberately avoided in the Indian Constitution, the fiscal structure created under it is essentially federal in nature. The political system introduced by India's constitution possesses all the essentials of a federal polity.

India's constitution is the supreme organic law of our land. Both the Centre and State Governments derive their authority from the constitution. The States are not allowed to secede from the union.

There is a division of legislative, administrative and financial powers and functions between the Union and the State Governments. Under Article 246 read with Seventh Schedule of the Constitution, these powers and functions have been defined through precise entries in the three lists in the Schedule. Thus, the Centre has exclusive powers to legislate in respect of matters contained in List I (Union List) such as defence, foreign affairs, citizenship, railways, posts and telegraph, telephones, broadcasting, airways, banking, coinage and currency. Similarly, the States enjoy the power to legislate on matters mentioned in List II (State List) such as public order, police, public health, local government, agriculture and fisheries. The Parliament and the State Legislatures have concurrent powers to make laws on any matters in List III (Concurrent List). The framers of the Constitution recognised that there was a category of subjects of common interest which could not be allocated exclusively either to the Union or the States. Some of the items included in the Concurrent List are: marriage and divorce, forests, economic and social planning, population control and family planning, legal, medical, and other professions. This list does not contain any head of taxation which means the Centre and the States have no concurrent powers of taxation. Residuary powers of legislation including taxation belong to the Centre as per Entry 97 of List I.

The foregoing three-fold division of subjects of legislation rests on the ground that matters of national concern are placed in the Union List and those of purely State or local significance in the State List. Matters of common Centre-State interest are included in the Concurrent List.

The Supreme Court stands at the head of India's judiciary to guard this distribution of powers and to invalidate any action which violates the limitations imposed by the Constitution.

According to Article 254 of the Constitution of India, if any provision of a State law is repugnant to any provision of a Central law, then the Central law shall prevail and the law made by the State shall be void to the extent of repugnancy.

The most common application of Article 254 arises when both the Central and State Governments enact legislation on the same matter contained in List III (Concurrent List) of the Seventh Schedule of the Constitution. In such a situation, if there is repugnancy then Central law prevails over the State law.

It is, of course, true that the Indian constitution has a strong Central bias. The financial powers of the Central Government are overwhelming. According to some scholars the constitution of India is neither purely federal nor purely unitary but is a combination of both. India's constitution is sometimes described as federal in times of peace and unitary in times of war.

16.2 Post-Independence Evolution of Fiscal Federalism

Constitutional provisions regarding taxation and borrowing powers of the Centre and the States, place the former in a commanding position. Not only the major sources of tax revenue belong to the Centre, its borrowing (internal and external) powers are also unlimited. Moreover, the Central Government enjoys the exclusive right to print currency.

It was in the 1950-51 budget speech that the Finance Minister announced the constitution of the First Finance Commission, an epoch-making arrangement for the evolution of sound fiscal federalism in India. The First Finance Commission was set up in November 1951 and it submitted its report in December 1952 for the period 1952-57. Since then thirteen more Finance Commissions have submitted their reports, the last being the Fourteenth Finance Commission which submitted its report in December 2014 for the period 2015-16 to 2019-20.

Recommendations of the Finance Commission constitute the core of fiscal federalism in India. Finance Commission is a unique feature of the Indian Constitution without parallel in the existing federal constitutions of the world. Reports of the Finance Commissions provide glimpses of the events, challenges, problems and their solutions in the highly complex area of federal finance. These Reports highlight contemporary issues in Centre-State relations and record measures suggested by the Finance Commissions, from time to time, to solve them.

16.2.1 Inter-governmental Transfers: Though the Constitution creates a dual polity based on divided governmental powers and functions, this division is not watertight. As the Administrative Reforms Commission, 1968, observed, "Exact correspondence of resources and functions is not possible to secure in any federal situation but in India the balance is tilted rather heavily in favour of the Centre and the outstanding feature of the financial relationship between the Centre and the States consequently is that the former is always the giver and the latter the receivers. The favourable position given to the Centre in regard to financial resources reflects the strong-centre theme running through the Constitution and many feel that this has been an important factor in keeping the country united". [2]

Emergence of imbalances between functional responsibilities and financial resources of different tiers of government is a characteristic feature of all federations, particularly of those whose economies are more dynamic. Even in older federations (like the United States and Canada), financial conflicts between the national and sub-national governments persist and their once-for-all solution is difficult to find. The mismatch between functions and taxation powers occurs partly because of changing responsibilities of governments at different levels and partly because of the dominant position of federal government in regard to taxation powers, which is often by design. Therefore, vertical imbalances in terms of resources and expenditure responsibilities emerge between different levels of government calling for transfer of resources from the Centre to the States. This is the familiar problem of federal finance.

Since the commencement of the Constitution in 1950, various problems and conflicts have arisen in Centre-State financial relations in India. Such problems are endemic of all federal governments in the world. States have often complained that there is a perceptible trend of centralisation of resources, in addition to centralisation of certain State functions.

Federalism is not only a unifying but also a levelling up force. Considerable economic inequalities exist among different States of India and their reduction is an argument in favour of centralisation of resources.

16.2.2 Fiscal Decentralisation Initiatives: The Constitution of India, operative since 1950, has shown flexibility towards changing needs and aspirations of the people. The passage of the Constitution (Seventy-third Amendment) Act, 1992 marked a milestone in the history of modern India. With this amendment, a uniform structure of *panchayats* emerged throughout the country. Similarly, the passage of the Constitution (Seventy-fourth Amendment) Act, 1992 was a landmark in the history of municipal administration in India. As a result of these amendments, *panchayats* and municipalities are now constitutional bodies forming the third tier of the federal polity of India.

Article 243G read with Eleventh Schedule of the Constitution explicitly requires the States to devolve powers and authority on *panchayats* which may be necessary to enable them to function as institutions of self-government. Similarly, Article 243W read with Twelfth Schedule of the Constitution provides the illustrative list for the devolution of functions to the municipalities. Many States have amended their municipal laws to ensure conformity with the new constitutional provisions.

Every state is required to set up a State Finance Commission under Article 243-I read with Article 243-Y of the Constitution. The Commission, in turn, is required to review the financial position of the municipalities and make recommendations as to: (a) the principles which should govern: (i) the distribution between the State and the Municipalities of the net proceeds of taxes, duties, tolls and fees leviable by the State, which may be divided between them, and the allocations between the Municipalities of their respective shares of such proceeds, (ii) the determination of the taxes, duties, tolls and fees which may be assigned to, or appropriated by, the Municipalities, (iii) the grants-in-aid to Municipalities from the Consolidated Fund of the State, (b) the measures needed to improve the financial position of the Municipalities and (c) any other matter referred to the Finance Commission in the interest of sound finance of the Municipalities.

16.2.3 Fiscal Responsibility and Budget Management (FRBM) Act, 2003: The Fiscal Responsibility and Budget Management Act, 2003 and the Fiscal Responsibility and Budget Management Rules, 2004 made under Section 8 of the Act came into force on July 5, 2004. The salient features of the Act are as under:

1. Rules to be made under the Act to specify the annual targets for reduction of fiscal deficit and revenue deficit, contingent liabilities and total liabilities.
2. The revenue deficit and fiscal deficit may exceed the targets specified in the rules only on grounds of national security or national calamity or such other exceptional grounds as the Central Government may specify.
3. Central Government shall not borrow from the Reserve Bank of India except by way of advances to meet temporary excess of cash disbursements over cash receipts.
4. Reserve Bank of India not to subscribe to the primary issues of the Central Government securities from the year 2006-07.
5. Central Government to take suitable measures to ensure greater transparency in its fiscal operations.
6. Central Government to lay in each financial year before both Houses of Parliament three statements, viz. Medium-Term Fiscal Policy Statement, Fiscal Policy Strategy

Statement and Macroeconomic Framework Statement along with the Annual Financial Statement and Demands for Grants.

7. Finance Minister to make a quarterly review of trends in receipts and expenditure in relation to the Budget and place the review before both Houses of Parliament.

The process of fiscal consolidation under FRBMA has been continuous. It has yielded rich dividends in terms of creating fiscal space for increased spending on infrastructure and social sectors. The traditional annual budgeting has moved to a more meaningful medium-term fiscal planning framework. FRBMA provides the basic structure around which many fiscal measures have been implemented. Some of the important amongst these include: (a) reducing peak rates of customs duties, (b) rectifying anomalies like inverted duty structure, (c) rationalizing excise duties, (d) relying on voluntary tax compliance, (e) introduction of State level VAT, (f) increasing productivity of expenditure through an outcome budget framework and (g) innovative financing mechanisms like creation of special purpose vehicles for infrastructure projects.

Twelfth Finance Commission award contained incentives to promote fiscal reforms. Consequently, many States have undertaken fiscal measures to reform their tax systems and expenditure management practices. 26 States have enacted their own FRBM laws.

16.3 GST and Fiscal Federalism

The introduction of GST has marked a clear departure from the scheme of distribution of fiscal powers envisaged in the Constitution. The dual GST imposes tax on the same taxable event—supply of goods and services—simultaneously by both the Centre and the States. Both the Centre and the States are empowered to levy GST across the value chain from the stage of manufacture to consumption. The credit of GST paid on inputs at every stage of value addition is available for the discharge of GST liability on the output, thereby ensuring GST is charged only on the component of value addition at each stage. This would ensure that there is no *tax-on-tax* in the country.

Prior to the introduction of GST, fiscal powers between the Centre and the States were clearly demarcated in the Constitution with no overlap between the respective domains. In other words, there were no concurrent powers of taxation (or joint occupancy of tax fields) by the two levels of government. The Centre had the powers to levy tax on the manufacture of goods (except alcoholic liquor for human consumption, opium, narcotics etc.) while the States had the powers to levy tax on the sale of goods. In the case of inter-State sales, the Centre had the power to levy Central Sales Tax (CST), but the tax was collected and retained entirely by the originating States.

Taxes with inter-state base and those in the case of which all-India uniformity in rates was desirable, to facilitate industry and trade, were vested in the Central Government. Taxes which were location-specific and related to subjects of local consumption were with the States. As for services, it was the Centre alone that was empowered to levy service tax. Broadly speaking, taxes on production were levied by the Centre and taxes on sale and purchase by the State Governments. The absence of joint occupancy of tax fields had successfully minimised double taxation, tax rivalry between the Centre and the States, and duplicate tax administration.

Since the States were not empowered to levy any tax on the sale or purchase of goods in the course of their importation into or exportation from India, the Centre levied and collected this tax as additional duties of customs, which were in addition to the basic customs duty. These additional duties of customs—additional duties of customs (commonly known as CVD) and special additional duty of customs (SAD)—counter balanced excise duties, sales tax, State VAT and other taxes levied on the like domestic product.

Introduction of the GST has concurrently empowered the Centre and the States to levy and collect it. The assignment of concurrent jurisdiction to the Centre and the States for the levy of GST requires a unique institutional mechanism that would ensure that decisions about the structure, design and operation of GST are taken jointly by the two. GST Council is the institutional mechanism for this purpose.

16.4 Towards Co-operative Federalism

Tax revenue is generally the main source of financing public expenditure at different levels of the government. In most democratic countries, taxation powers of central, state and local governments are mentioned in the constitution itself. Taxation powers of the government at different levels may be mutually exclusive or overlapping. The joint occupancy of tax fields often causes friction not only between the federal and provincial governments but also among the provinces themselves. This conflict concerns the manner in which the tax capacity of a particular tax base is shared between the two levels; or, to use the common jargon, the way in which tax room is apportioned.

In this connection, it is pertinent to note the relevance of co-operative federalism. To quote, "The essence of a co-operative federalism is that the Centre and the State Governments should be guided by the broader national concerns of using the available resources for the benefit of the people. Co-operative federalism encourages the Government at different levels to take advantage of a large national market, diverse and rich natural resources and the potential of human capabilities in all parts of the country and from all sections of the society for building a prosperous nation. Co-operative federalism makes it possible to raise all the available resources by the Government at different levels in a co-ordinated way and channel them for use for the common good of the people. This requires a harmonious relationship and co-operative spirit between the Centre and the States and among the States themselves. While a healthy competition among the States for evolving efficient and socially desirable policies and programmes is welcome, any competition which nullifies each other's advantages in development and erodes the resource base of the States should be avoided. Co-operative federalism is intended to ensure a minimum bundle of basic services and a nationally acceptable level of living for all the people of the country". [3]

It is noteworthy that economic reforms initiated in 1991 did not seek to consult the states. In contrast, every state was taken on board at every stage of the implementation of GST.

Endnotes

1. Government of India, *Report of the Commission on Centre-State Relations* (Chairman: Justice R.S. Sarkaria) Part I, 1988, p. 8.
2. Administrative Reforms Commission, *Report of the Study Team on Centre-State Relationships*, Vol. I, 1968, p. 15.
3. Government of India, Planning Commission, *Ninth Five Year Plan* (1997-2002), Volume. I, p. 241.

17

Future Challenges Facing GST

Implementation of GST is undoubtedly the most significant tax reform, unparalleled in the fiscal history of India, may be the world. It not only signifies the spirit of co-operative federalism but also an achievement by a developing country, worth emulating by similar economies around the world. It also reaffirms India's desire to play an effective role in global economy.

GST is a completely new tax with new concepts like *place of supply* and new tax structures. GST is one indirect tax for the whole nation, which will make India one unified common market.

17.1 Implementation Challenges

Central Board of Excise and Customs (CBEC) would need to prepare for meeting the implementation challenges, which are quite formidable. The number of taxpayers is likely to go up significantly. The existing IT infrastructure of CBEC would also need to be suitably scaled up to handle such large volumes of data. Organizational structure and deployment of human resources needs review for smooth and effective implementation of GST.

Augmentation of human resources would be necessary to handle large taxpayers' base in GST scattered across the length and breadth of the country. Capacity building, particularly in the field of accountancy and information technology for the departmental officers has to be taken up in a big way. A massive four-tier training programme is being conducted under the leadership of NACEN. This training project is aimed at imparting training on GST law and procedures to more than 60,000 officers of CBEC and Commercial Tax officers of State Governments.

In the past, the Centre and State indirect tax administrations worked under different laws, regulations, procedures and formats and consequently the IT systems worked as independent sites. Integrating them for GST implementation would be complex since it would involve integrating the entire indirect tax ecosystem so as to bring all the tax administrations (Centre, State and Union Territories) to the same level of IT maturity with uniform formats and interfaces for taxpayers and other external stakeholders. Besides, GST being a destination-based tax, the inter-state trade of goods and services would need a robust settlement mechanism amongst the States and the Centre. This is possible only when there is a strong IT infrastructure and service backbone which enables to capture, process and exchange information amongst the stakeholders.

17.2 Public Outreach and Knowledge Sharing

It is expected that a momentous reform like GST is popularized and familiarized to the trade and industry who are the vital stakeholders in successful implementation of this reform. Massive public outreach and knowledge sharing programmes are being conducted by various formations of CBEC. GST is not merely a tax reform. It is also a reform that will revolutionize the way business is conducted in India.

GST requires a very high level of compliance. The age of hand-written ledgers, account books, balance sheets and manual record-keeping is gone. Everything will now be online and need to be updated regularly.

17.3 Anti-profiteering Action

As per Section 171 of the CGST Act, 2017 any reduction in rate of tax on any supply of goods or services or the benefit of input tax credit shall be passed on to the recipient by way of *commensurate* reduction in prices. An authority may be constituted by the government to examine whether input tax credits availed by any registered person or the reduction in the tax rate have actually resulted in a commensurate reduction in the price of the goods or services or both supplied by him.

Government has warned the industry time and again that it should pass on the benefit of lower taxes to consumers or face anti-profiteering action provided under the GST law.

The problem of *unjust profiteering* is akin to the problem of *unjust enrichment* under the erstwhile excise duty system. [1]

However, industry circles maintain that rules in this regard are vaguely worded, which makes them prone to misuse. In a complex production system where a variety of inputs go into manufacturing of a product, reaching a definitive conclusion on *commensurate* is difficult. The best way to check profiteering, and hence protect consumer welfare, is to ensure competition.

17.4 Possibilities of GST Evasion

The proponents of GST claim that evasion under it is difficult and minimal. The tax credit method ensures cross-checking of the records of taxpayers through invoices. Buyer firms insist on supplier firms to furnish invoices which help the former to claim tax credit. Since tax liability of a single taxpayer under GST is only a fraction of the total amount of tax, the incentive for evasion is relatively weak. Even a successful evasion would mean less revenue loss as compared to the one suffered under a system of turnover tax on gross value (excise duty or sales tax).

Despite the self-policing nature of GST, opportunities do exist under it for evasion and fraud. Unscrupulous elements may adopt the following methods to defraud tax authorities under GST:

1. Use of fake invoices to claim tax credit.
2. Tax credit claims on purchases for personal use.
3. Over-reporting of sales of zero-rated goods.
4. Secret deals between buyers and sellers as regards issuance of receipts.
5. Formation of fake companies which sell receipts to traders to enable them to claim tax credit on inputs.

Thus, GST is as susceptible to evasion and fraud as any other tax. An efficient tax machinery capable of cross-checking a large number of invoices through an elaborate computer system is a pre-requisite for the successful implementation of GST.

17.5 Consumer Protection in India

At the root of consumer protection is the recognition of an unequal relationship between consumers and producers. Protection of consumers is accomplished by setting minimum quality specifications and safety standards for both goods and services and establishing mechanisms to redress their grievances.

The consumer movement in India is as old as trade and commerce. In Kautilya's Arthashastra, there are references to the concept of consumer protection against exploitation by the trade and retailer with respect to quality, short weight, measurement and adulteration of goods.

Yet until the late 1970s, there was no systematic movement in the country for safeguarding the interest of consumers. However, now it is widely acknowledged that the level of consumer awareness and protection is a true indicator of development of the country and progressiveness of civil society.

The main reason for this is the rapidly increasing variety of goods and services which modern technology has made available. In addition, the growing size and complexity of production and distribution systems, the high level of sophistication in marketing and selling practices and in advertising and other forms of promotion, mass marketing methods and consumers' increased mobility resulting in reduction of personal interaction between buyers and sellers, have contributed to the increased need for consumer protection.

17.5.1 Consumer Protection Act, 1986: This Act was enacted with the objective to provide better protection of the interests of the consumers. The Act provides for effective safeguards to consumers against various types of exploitations and unfair dealings, relying on mainly compensatory rather than punitive or preventive approach. The Act applies to all goods and services unless specifically exempted and covers private, public and co-operative sectors and provides for speedy and inexpensive adjudication. The consumer rights under the Act are the following:

1. Right to be protected against marketing of goods and services, which are hazardous to life and property.
2. Right to be informed about quality, quantity, potency, purity, standard and price of goods and services, as the case may be, to protect consumer against unfair trade practices.
3. Right to be assured of access to a variety of goods and services at competitive prices.
4. Right to be heard and assured that consumer interest will receive due consideration at appropriate fora.
5. Right to seek redressal against unfair trade practices or restrictive trade practices or unscrupulous exploitation of consumers.
6. Right to consumer education.

17.5.2 Central Consumer Protection Council (CCPC): The objective of CCPC, established under the Consumer Protection Act, 1986, is to promote and protect consumer rights that include the right to be informed and the right to consumer education.

17.6 Competition Policy in India

The objective of competition is met by ensuring that there are sufficient numbers of producers so that no producer can attain a position of dominance. If the nature of the industry is such that dominance in terms of market share cannot be avoided, it seeks to ensure that there is no abuse on account of this dominance. Competition policy also seeks to forestall other forms of market failure, such as formation of cartels, leading to collusive pricing, division of markets and joint decisions to reduce supply. Mergers and acquisitions also need to be regulated as they reduce competition.

To strengthen the forces of competition in the market, both competition law and competition policy are required. The two complement each other. The competition law prohibits and penalizes anti-competitive practices by enterprises functioning in the market, i.e. it addresses market failures. Sector regulatory laws mimic competition in the areas of natural monopolies. Other regulatory laws, such as those for intellectual property or anti-dumping or even capital markets, too have an important interface with competition.

17.6.1 Competition Act, 2002: The Act is designed "to provide, keeping in view the economic development of the country, for the establishment of a Commission to prevent practices having adverse effect on competition; to promote and sustain competition in markets; to protect the interest of consumers; and to ensure freedom of trade carried on by other participants in markets, in India".

To put it differently, the main objectives of the Act are the following:

1. To provide for the establishment of a Commission to prevent practices having adverse effect on competition.
2. To promote and sustain competition in markets in India.
3. To protect the interests of consumers.
4. To ensure freedom of trade carried on by participants in markets in India and for related matters.

17.6.2 Competition Commission of India (CCI): Competition Act, 2002 provided for the establishment of a Competition Commission of India which was established on October 14, 2003. CCI is entrusted with the task to: (a) eliminate practices having adverse effect on competition, (b) promote and sustain competition in markets, (c) protect the interest of consumers and (d) ensure freedom of trade carried on by other participants.

CCI has been given, under the Act, the mandate to generate public awareness about competition issues. Its efforts in this area may be further strengthened. CCI should formulate, publish and post in the public domain guidelines covering various dimensions related to competition law for enhancing public awareness. Such guidelines will help enterprises by bringing greater clarity about the provisions of the competition law and the manner of its enforcement.

To sum up, the Indian GST is 21st century standard for VAT in federal systems.

GST will simplify tax administration and eliminate cascading of taxes. It will lead to reduction in the distortions in the structure of production, consumption and exports and further to a more efficient allocation of resources.

Some critics consider GST to be a regressive tax, meaning the poor pay more, as a percentage of their income, than the rich. However, defenders contend that GST can be considered a proportional tax if tax payments are expressed as a percentage not of income, but of lifetime consumption; savings and investments are tax-deferred, and when converted to consumption are subjected to GST. Others point out that the more important question to ask is not whether GST is regressive, but whether GST is more regressive than the alternative indirect taxes, namely, sales, excise and turnover tax (not income tax because that is a direct tax). In addition, they argue that what affects poverty and fairness is not the impact of any particular tax, but the impact of the tax structure as a whole, and how tax revenues are redistributed. When GST is combined with progressive taxes, and the revenues distributed to the poor, the total fiscal structure can be progressive.

Implementation of GST leaves behind an inefficient, complicated and fragmented indirect tax system. Switch over to GST is fraught with many problems—administrative and technical. However, such problems are endemic of any change of revolutionary proportions. Many of the problems will be transitory in nature. No one should expect a foolproof GST from day one. GST Council has successfully sorted out political, administrative and implementation differences among the stakeholders and it is competent enough to grapple with any future challenges and rectifications.

Endnote

1. The term *unjust enrichment* was used to describe a situation when a person undeservedly got enriched. In the context of refund of Union excise duty, the principle of unjust enrichment was the first and foremost principle which was kept in mind by the sanctioning authorities. If the manufacturer had charged excise duty to his buyer, it was clear that he had passed on the burden to the buyer and had already recovered duty from his customer. In such cases, refund of excess duty paid to the manufacturer would amount to excess and undeserved profit to him. It would not be equitable to refund the duty to him as he would get double benefit—first from the customer and again from the Excise Department. This is called unjust enrichment. Refund of duty should, ideally, be paid to the customer who had borne the burden of duty. Since it is practically not feasible to identify such customers on individual basis, the amount of refund was credited to Consumer Welfare Fund in accordance with section 12C of the Central Excise Act, 1944. The principle of unjust enrichment was held valid and constitutional by the Supreme Court in the famous case of Mafatlal Industries Ltd. (1997).

18

GST in Select Countries of the World

18.1 Canada

GST was introduced in Canada on January 1, 1991. It replaced a hidden 13.5 percent manufacturers' sales tax (MST) because the MST was hindering the manufacturing sector's ability to export competitively. The introduction of the GST was very controversial. The GST rate is 5 percent, effective January 1, 2008.

GST is levied on supplies of goods or services purchased in Canada and includes most products, except certain politically sensitive essentials such as groceries, residential rent, and medical services, and services such as financial services. Businesses that purchase goods and services that are consumed, used or supplied in the course of their *commercial activities* can claim "input tax credits" subject to prescribed documentation requirements. This avoids *cascading* (i.e. the application of the GST on the same good or service several times as it passes from business-to-business on its way to the final consumer). In this way, the tax is essentially borne by the final consumer. This system is not completely effective, as shown by criminals who defrauded the system by claiming GST input credits for non-existent sales by a fictional company. Exported goods are exempt (zero-rated), while individuals with low incomes can receive a GST rebate calculated in conjunction with their income tax.

In 1997, the provinces of Nova Scotia, New Brunswick and Newfoundland (now Newfoundland and Labrador) and the Government of Canada merged their respective sales taxes into the harmonized sales tax (HST). In New Brunswick, and Newfoundland and Labrador, the current HST rate is 13 percent, while in Nova Scotia it was raised from 13 percent to 15 percent, effective July 1, 2010. HST is administered by the Canada Revenue Agency, with revenues divided among participating governments according to a formula. Ontario and British Columbia both harmonized the GST with their provincial sales tax (PST) effective July 1, 2010.

The three territories of Canada (Yukon, Northwest Territories and Nunavut) do not have territorial sales taxes. The government of Quebec administers both the federal GST and the provincial Quebec Sales Tax (QST). It is the only province to administer the federal tax.

The tax is imposed at the rate of 5 percent on the supply of goods and services that are purchased in Canada, except certain items that are either *exempt* or *zero-rated.*

For tax-exempt supplies, the supply is not subject to GST and suppliers do not charge tax on their exempt supplies. Furthermore, suppliers that make exempt supplies are not entitled to recover GST paid on inputs acquired for the purposes of making the exempt good or service. Tax-exempt items include long-term residential rents, health and dental care, educational services, day-care services, music lessons, legal aid services, and financial services.

For tax-free (i.e. zero-rated) sales, GST is charged by suppliers at a rate of 0 percent so effectively there is no GST collected. However, when a supplier makes a zero-rated supply, it is eligible to recover any GST paid on purchases used in producing the particular supply or service. This effectively removes the cascading tax from these particular goods and services. Common zero-rated items include basic groceries, prescription drugs, inward/outbound transportation and medical devices. Certain exports of goods and services are also zero-rated.

18.2 Australia

Australia is the most recent example of an industrialized country replacing a tax at the manufacturing or wholesale level by the GST extending to the retail level. The previous tax was found to be unworkable, in spite of the high degree of sophistication in administration in Australia. It simply could not deal with the variety of supply chain arrangements in a satisfactory manner.

GST in Australia is a value added tax of 10 percent on the sales of most goods and services. GST is levied on most transactions in the production process, but is refunded to all parties in the chain of production other than the final consumer.

The tax was introduced on July 1, 2000, replacing the previous federal wholesale sales tax system and designed to phase out a number of various State and Territory Government taxes, duties and levies such as banking taxes and stamp duty.

All Australian businesses whose turnover is above the minimum threshold are required to register for GST. Businesses whose turnover is below the threshold may register if they wish to.

A GST-registered business must charge its customers GST on taxable goods and services it provides, but is entitled to a credit for any GST it has paid for its expenditures on these goods and services as well as capital purchases (called input tax credits). A registered business must periodically lodge business activity statements (monthly, quarterly or annually), and at the same time pay the net amount of GST owed to the tax office (if more GST is paid than collected, a refund is paid by the tax office instead).

Some goods and services (notably salaries, wages, fresh food, and real estate) are exempt from GST. Other goods and services (rental income and financial services) are *input-taxed*, which means that GST is not charged on the sale, but GST paid by that part of the business is not eligible to be claimed as an input tax credit.

GST is applicable to a supply of goods, services and transactions related to real property, obligations or rights. The supply must be for consideration to a relevant entity registered for GST in the course of enterprise. This does not include employment or hobby income.

Taxable supplies include goods wholly within Australia or from or to Australia. Certain types of supplies are free of GST as, for example, fresh unprocessed food, medical services, education courses, childcare, exports, pre-owned real estate and going concerns. When an enterprise purchases goods or services to be consumed or used for re-supply to an end customer they may receive a refund (input tax credit) on the amount of GST contained in the price, which means in effect no GST is paid on those supplies.

New residential and commercial properties are subject to GST but re-sale of existing properties is not. All real estate agent fees on either new or second-hand property are subject to GST. Processed foods such as biscuits, soft drinks, restaurant meals and take-away foods are also subject to GST.

Registered enterprises for GST must complete a business activity statement (BAS) for reporting to the Australian Taxation Office (ATO) for each quarter ending March, June, September and December. Businesses must lodge their Statements with the ATO within twenty working days of the end of each quarter.

Critics have argued that the GST is a regressive tax, which has a more pronounced effect on lower income earners, meaning that the tax consumes a higher proportion of their income, compared to those earning large incomes. However, due to the corresponding reductions in personal income taxes, state banking taxes, federal wholesale taxes and some fuel taxes that were implemented when the GST was introduced, it is claimed by some that people were effectively paying no extra tax.

18.3 Malaysia

GST is a value added tax in Malaysia. GST is levied on most transactions in the production process, but is refunded with exception of Blocked Input Tax, to all parties in the chain of production other than the final consumer.

The existing standard rate for GST effective from 1 April 2015 is 6 percent.

GST was scheduled to be implemented by the government during the third quarter of 2011, but the implementation was delayed until April 1, 2015. Its purpose is to replace the sales and service tax which has been used in the country for several decades. The government is seeking additional revenue to offset its budget deficit and reduce its dependence on revenue from Petronas, Malaysia's state-owned oil company. The 6 percent tax will replace a sales-and-service tax of between 5–15 percent.

The Goods and Services Tax Bill 2009 was tabled for its first reading at the Dewan Rakyat (the lower house of the Malaysian Parliament) on December 16, 2009. It was delayed amid mounting criticism. The government responded by asserting that the tax on oil income will not be sustainable in the future.

During the government reading of the 2014 budget, Malaysian Prime Minister Najib Razak announced a GST tax of 6 percent starting on April 1, 2015. Implementing GST tax is a part of the Government's tax reform programme to enhance the capability, effectiveness and transparency of tax administration and management.

During the unveiling of the national budget, it was announced that the following goods and services would be exempted from GST:

1. Agricultural products—paddy, fresh or chilled vegetables, certain provisionally preserved vegetables.
2. Essential foodstuff—oils, salt, flour etc.
3. Livestocks and livestock supplies or poultry—live animals and unprocessed meat.
4. Eggs.
5. Fish—live, fresh, frozen and dried.

6. First 300 kwh of electricity for domestic use.
7. Water for domestic users.
8. Goods supplied to designated areas from Malaysia—Labuan, Langkawi and Tioman.
9. Exported goods.
10. Exported services—such as architecture services in connection with land outside Malaysia.
11. Selected services in Malaysia—such as pilotage, salvage or towage services.
12. International services—such as transport of passengers or goods from a place in Malaysia to a place outside Malaysia.
13. Petrol, diesel and LPG.
14. Sale of residential property.
15. Services provided by government which are not considered commercial services, such as permits, licences etc. Services considered commercial are TV advertisement, rental of equipments, rental of multifunction halls etc.

18.4 New Zealand

GST is a value added tax in New Zealand. GST in New Zealand is designed to be a broad-based system with few exemptions. Exceptions that do exist include rents collected on residential rental properties, donations, precious metals and financial services. End-users pay this tax on all liable goods and services indirectly, in that the purchase price of goods and services includes GST.

The existing rate for GST effective from October 1, 2010 is 15 percent.

GST was introduced by the Fourth Labour Government of New Zealand on October 1, 1986 at a rate of 10 percent on most goods and services. It replaced existing sales taxes for some goods and services. GST was a part of the economic reforms initiated by Labour Finance Minister Roger Douglas. GST was introduced in conjunction with compensating changes to personal income tax rates.

Since its introduction it has had two increases, on July 1, 1989 the rate increased to 12.5 percent and on October 1, 2010 it increased again to 15 percent.

GST-registered organisations and individuals pay GST only on the difference between GST-liable sales and GST-liable supplies (i.e. they pay GST on the difference between what they sell and what they buy: income less expenditure). This is accomplished by reconciling GST received (through sales) and GST paid (through purchases) at regular periods (typically every two months, with some qualifying companies opting for one-month or six-month periods), then either paying the difference to the Inland Revenue (IR) if the GST collected on sales is higher or receiving a refund from IR if the GST paid on purchases is higher.

Businesses exporting goods and services from New Zealand are entitled to zero-rate their products: effectively, they charge GST at 0 percent. This permits the business to claim back the input GST, but the eventual, non-New Zealand based consumer does not pay the tax (businesses that produce GST-exempt supplies are not able to claim back input GST).

Because businesses claim back their input GST, the GST inclusive price is usually irrelevant for business purchasing decisions, other than in relation to cash flow issues. Consequently, wholesalers often state prices exclusive of GST, but must collect the full, GST-inclusive price when they make the sale and account to the IR for the GST so collected.

18.5 Singapore

GST in Singapore is a broad-based value added tax levied on import of goods, as well as nearly all supplies of goods and services. The only exemptions are for the sales and leases of residential properties and most financial services. Export of goods and international services are zero-rated.

Before 1986, Singapore's corporate income tax rate and top marginal personal income tax rate both stood at 40 percent. Such high rates were deemed to be uncompetitive. On the recommendation of the 1986 Economic Committee, Singapore's government decided that it needed to shift from direct to indirect taxes, to maintain its international competitiveness in attracting investments, and to sustain its economic growth to create well-paying jobs for Singaporeans.

GST was part of a larger tax restructuring exercise to enable Singapore to shift its reliance from direct taxes to indirect taxes. The government argued that tax reform was necessary to maintain Singapore's competitiveness, to sustain long-term growth and job creation. The government also argued that with an ageing population, Singapore's income tax base was expected to decline. With a broad-based GST, the taxation burden would be more evenly spread among the population.

GST was implemented at a single rate of 3 percent on April 1, 1994, with an assurance that it would not be raised for at least 5 years. To cushion the impact of GST on Singaporean households, an offset package was also introduced. Simultaneously, corporate tax rate was cut by 3 percent to 27 percent, and the top marginal personal income tax rate was cut by 3 percent to 30 percent. The initial GST rate of 3 percent was among the lowest in the world, as the focus was not to generate substantial revenue, but to allow people to get adjusted to the tax.

In 2002, the Economic Review Committee reviewed Singapore's tax policy, and recommended that further tax reform was necessary to bring in new investments. The Committee noted that other countries were aggressively cutting their direct tax rates to attract internationally mobile capital and labour, and recommended that the government rely more on GST for its tax revenues, while again cushioning the impact on Singaporean households through an offset package.

The government accepted the Committee's recommendations. The GST rate was increased from 3 percent to 4 percent in 2003, and to 5 percent in 2004. Each increase was accompanied by an offset package that was designed to make the average Singaporean household overall better off, even after accounting for the additional costs imposed by the increase in GST rates. Direct tax rates were also reduced correspondingly.

On February 15, 2007, Finance Minister Tharman Shanmugaratnam announced that the GST rate would be increased to 7 percent with effect from July 1, 2007.

To maintain the progressive nature of total taxes and transfers on individuals, Singapore reduced income tax on lower-income earners, as well as instituted direct transfer payments to lower-income groups, resulting in an overall lower tax burden for most Singaporean households. These offsets included lower income taxes, lower property taxes, rebates on rental and service and conservancy charges for public housing, and additional subsidies for health, education and community services. As a result of the income tax cuts, additional tax reliefs and rebates in 1994, about 70 percent of individuals that used to pay income taxes no longer needed to do so.

The Singapore government has argued that the GST on its own is a flat tax, but that it is part of an overall fiscal system that is highly progressive: higher-income earners pay the highest fraction of their income in taxes, and also spend more. When all taxes were taken into account (income tax, property tax, GST and other indirect taxes), the top 10 percent of households accounted for 38 percent of the taxes paid, while the top 20 percent contributed 53 percent of all taxes. In contrast, lower-income earners receive substantially more transfers than the taxes they pay. Low- and middle-income households effectively pay *negative* tax.

From 2006 to 2010, the second bottom decile of Singaporean households (ranked by income from work) received transfers (net of all taxes paid) amounting to 23 percent of their income, the 5th decile received transfers that netted off taxes paid, while the effective tax rate for the top decile was 11 percent . In particular, when the GST rate was raised from 5 percent to 7 percent in July 2007, a household in the bottom 20 percent had to pay additional GST of $ 370 per year, but received an offset package of $ 910 per year, in addition to permanent benefits of $ 1,000 per year.

Some critics contend that basic essentials such as food and healthcare should be made exempt from GST, to help lower-income households. The government argued that having such exemptions would actually help the higher-income more than poorer Singaporeans, because well-off households usually spend much more on essentials (whether food or healthcare or other basic necessities) than a lower-income household. In addition, lower-income households would not benefit much from such an exemption, as spending on essentials constitutes a small proportion of lower-income household expenditures. For example, for the bottom 20 percent of households, essential food items comprised only 6 percent of their total household expenditures; after including all other food items, the total was only 15 percent of their expenditures.

If essentials were to be exempted from GST, there would be a need to make up for the revenue shortfall through a higher GST rate on other goods and services, which lower-income households would also have to bear. The government argued that the experience of other countries demonstrated that granting exemptions would distort production and consumption decisions and cause a contentious and highly complex process of determining the goods and services that merit exemption. This would increase compliance and administration costs for businesses, and these costs would be passed on to consumers.

In addition, the experience of other countries have shown that exempting or reducing

GST on certain items did not mean that tax savings would be passed on to consumers. Therefore, the GST should be kept broad-based to keep the GST low and the GST system simple, while help is directly provided to the lower-income through transfers and subsidies.

Appendices

Appendix 1

Constitution (One Hundred and First Amendment) Act, 2016

Note: Prior to this amendment, the fiscal powers between the Centre and the States were clearly demarcated in the Constitution with no overlap between the respective domains. The Centre had the powers to levy tax on the manufacture of goods (except alcoholic liquor for human consumption, opium, narcotics etc.) while the States had the powers to levy tax on the sale of goods. In the case of inter-State sales, the Centre had the power to levy a tax (the Central Sales Tax) but the tax was collected and retained entirely by the States. As for services, it was the Centre alone that was empowered to levy service tax.

Introduction of the GST required amendments in the Constitution so as to simultaneously empower the Centre and the States to levy and collect this tax. The Constitution of India was amended by the Constitution (One Hundred and First Amendment) Act, 2016 for this purpose. Article 246A of the amended Constitution empowers the Centre and the States to levy and collect the GST.

This Act of Parliament received the assent of the President on September 8, 2016 and was subsequently notified.

An Act further to amend the Constitution of India.

Be it enacted by Parliament in the Sixty-seventh Year of the Republic of India as follows:

Short Title and Commencement:

1. (1) This Act may be called the Constitution (One Hundred and First Amendment) Act, 2016. (2) It shall come into force on such date as the Central Government may, by notification in the Official Gazette, appoint, and different dates may be appointed for different provisions of this Act and any reference in any such provision to the commencement of this Act shall be construed as a reference to the commencement of that provision.

Insertion of New Article 246A and Special Provision with Respect to Goods and Services Tax:

2. After Article 246 of the Constitution, the following article shall be inserted, namely: "246A. (1) Notwithstanding anything contained in Articles 246 and 254, Parliament, and, subject to clause (2), the Legislature of every State, have power to make laws with respect to goods and services tax imposed by the Union or by such State. (2) Parliament has exclusive power to make laws with respect to goods and services tax where the supply of goods, or of services, or both takes place in the course of inter-State trade or commerce.

Explanation: The provisions of this article, shall, in respect of goods and services tax referred to in clause (5) of Article 279A, take effect from the date recommended by the Goods and Services Tax Council".

Amendment of Article 248:

3. In Article 248 of the Constitution, in clause (1), for the word "Parliament", the words, figures and letter "Subject to Article 246A, Parliament" shall be substituted.

Amendment of Article 249:

4. In Article 249 of the Constitution, in clause (1), after the words "with respect to", the words, figures and letter "goods and services tax provided under Article 246A or" shall be inserted.

Amendment of Article 250:

5. In Article 250 of the Constitution, in clause (1), after the words "with respect to", the words, figures and letter "goods and services tax provided under Article 246A or" shall be inserted.

Amendment of Article 268:

6. In Article 268 of the Constitution, in clause (1), the words "and such duties of excise on medicinal and toilet preparations" shall be omitted.

Omission of Article 268A:

7. Article 268A of the Constitution, as inserted by Section 2 of the Constitution (Eighty-eighth Amendment) Act, 2003 shall be omitted.

Amendment of Article 269:

8. In Article 269 of the Constitution, in clause (1), after the words "consignment of goods", the words, figures and letter "except as provided in Article 269A" shall be inserted.

Insertion of New Article 269A and the Levy and Collection of Goods and Services Tax in the Course of Inter-State Trade or Commerce:

9. After Article 269 of the Constitution, the following article shall be inserted, namely: "269A. (1) Goods and services tax on supplies in the course of inter-State trade or commerce shall be levied and collected by the Government of India and such tax shall be apportioned between the Union and the States in the manner as may be provided by Parliament by law on the recommendations of the Goods and Services Tax Council. Explanation: For the purposes of this clause, supply of goods, or of services, or both in the course of import into the territory of India shall be deemed to be supply of goods, or of services, or both in the course of inter-State trade or commerce. (2) The amount apportioned to a State under clause (1) shall not form part of the Consolidated Fund of India. (3) Where an amount collected as tax levied under clause (1) has been used for payment of the tax levied by a State under Article 246A, such amount shall not form part of the Consolidated Fund of India. (4) Where an amount collected as tax levied by a State under Article 246A has been used for payment of the tax levied under clause (1), such amount shall not form part of the Consolidated Fund of the State. (5) Parliament may, by law, formulate the principles for determining the place of supply, and when a supply of goods, or of services, or both takes place in the course of inter-State trade or commerce".

Amendment of Article 270:

10. In Article 270 of the Constitution—(i) in clause (1), for the words, figures and letter "Articles 268, 268A and 269", the words, figures and letter "Articles 268, 269 and 269A" shall be substituted; (ii) after clause (1), the following clauses shall be inserted, namely—"(1A) The tax collected by the Union under clause (1) of Article 246A shall also be distributed between the Union and the States in the manner provided in clause (2). (1B) The tax levied and collected by the Union under clause (2) of Article 246A and Article 269A, which has been used for payment of the tax levied by the Union under clause (1) of Article 246A, and the amount apportioned to the Union under clause (1) of Article 269A, shall also be distributed between the Union and the States in the manner provided in clause (2)".

Amendment of Article 271:

11. In Article 271 of the Constitution, after the words "in those articles", the words, figures and letter "except the goods and services tax under Article 246A", shall be inserted.

Insertion of New Article 279A—Goods and Services Tax Council:

12. After Article 279 of the Constitution, the following article shall be inserted, namely—"279A. (1) The President shall, within sixty days from the date of commencement of the Constitution (One Hundred and First Amendment) Act, 2016, by order, constitute a Council to be called the Goods and Services Tax Council. (2) The Goods and Services Tax Council shall consist of the following members, namely: (a) the Union Finance Minister...Chairperson; (b) the Union Minister of State in charge of Revenue or Finance....Member; (c) the Minister in charge of Finance or Taxation or any other Minister nominated by each State Government....Members. (3) The Members of the Goods and Services Tax Council referred to in sub-clause (c) of clause (2) shall, as soon as may be, choose one amongst themselves to be the Vice-Chairperson of the Council for such period as they may decide. (4) The Goods and Services Tax Council shall make recommendations to the Union and the States on: (a) the taxes, cesses and surcharges levied by the Union, the States and the local bodies which may be subsumed in the goods and services tax; (b) the goods and services that may be subjected to, or exempted from the goods and services tax; (c) model Goods and Services Tax Laws, principles of levy, apportionment of Goods and Services Tax levied on supplies in the course of inter-State trade or commerce under article 269A and the principles that govern the place of supply; (d) the threshold limit of turnover below which goods and services may be exempted from goods and services tax; (e) the rates including floor rates with bands of goods and services tax; (f) any special rate or rates for a specified period, to raise additional resources during any natural calamity or disaster; (g) special provision with respect to the States of Arunachal Pradesh, Assam, Jammu and Kashmir, Manipur, Meghalaya, Mizoram, Nagaland, Sikkim, Tripura, Himachal Pradesh and Uttarakhand; and (h) any other matter relating to the goods and services tax, as the Council may decide. (5) The Goods and Services Tax Council shall recommend the date on which the goods and services tax be levied on petroleum crude, high speed diesel, motor spirit (commonly known as petrol), natural gas and aviation turbine fuel. (6) While discharging

the functions conferred by this article, the Goods and Services Tax Council shall be guided by the need for a harmonised structure of goods and services tax and for the development of a harmonised national market for goods and services. (7) One-half of the total number of Members of the Goods and Services Tax Council shall constitute the quorum at its meetings. (8) The Goods and Services Tax Council shall determine the procedure in the performance of its functions. (9) Every decision of the Goods and Services Tax Council shall be taken at a meeting, by a majority of not less than three-fourths of the weighted votes of the members present and voting, in accordance with the following principles, namely: (a) the vote of the Central Government shall have a weightage of onethird of the total votes cast, and (b) the votes of all the State Governments taken together shall have a weightage of two-thirds of the total votes cast, in that meeting. (10) No act or proceedings of the Goods and Services Tax Council shall be invalid merely by reason of: (a) any vacancy in, or any defect in, the constitution of the Council; or (b) any defect in the appointment of a person as a Member of the Council; or (c) any procedural irregularity of the Council not affecting the merits of the case. (11) The Goods and Services Tax Council shall establish a mechanism to adjudicate any dispute: (a) between the Government of India and one or more States; or (b) between the Government of India and any State or States on one side and one or more other States on the other side; or (c) between two or more States, arising out of the recommendations of the Council or implementation thereof".

Amendment of Article 286:

13. In Article 286 of the Constitution—(i) in clause (1): (A) for the words "the sale or purchase of goods where such sale or purchase takes place", the words "the supply of goods or of services or both, where such supply takes place" shall be substituted; (B) in sub-clause (b), for the word "goods", at both the places where it occurs, the words "goods or services or both" shall be substituted; (ii) in clause (2), for the words "sale or purchase of goods takes place", the words "supply of goods or of services or both" shall be substituted; (iii) clause (3) shall be omitted.

Amendment of Article 366:

14. In Article 366 of the Constitution—(i) after clause (12), the following clause shall be inserted, namely: '(12A) "goods and services tax" means any tax on supply of goods, or services or both except taxes on the supply of the alcoholic liquor for human consumption;'; (ii) after clause (26), the following clauses shall be inserted, namely: '(26A) "Services" means anything other than goods; (26B) "State" with reference to Articles 246A, 268, 269, 269A and Article 279A includes a Union territory with Legislature'.

Amendment of Article 368:

15. In Article 368 of the Constitution, in clause (2), in the proviso, in clause (a), for the words and figures "Article 162 or Article 241", the words, figures and letter "Article 162, Article 241 or Article 279A" shall be substituted.

Amendment of Sixth Schedule:

16. In the Sixth Schedule to the Constitution, in paragraph 8, in sub-paragraph (3): (i) in clause (c), the word "and" occurring at the end shall be omitted; (ii) in clause (d),

the word "and" shall be inserted at the end; (iii) after clause (d), the following clause shall be inserted, namely: "(e) taxes on entertainment and amusements".

Amendment of Seventh Schedule:

17. In the Seventh Schedule to the Constitution—(a) in List I—Union List: (i) for entry 84, the following entry shall be substituted, namely—"84. Duties of excise on the following goods manufactured or produced in India, namely: (a) petroleum crude; (b) high speed diesel; (c) motor spirit (commonly known as petrol); (d) natural gas; (e) aviation turbine fuel; and (f) tobacco and tobacco products"; (ii) Entries 92 and 92C shall be omitted; (b) in List II—State List: (i) Entry 52 shall be omitted; (ii) for Entry 54, the following entry shall be substituted, namely: "54. Taxes on the sale of petroleum crude, high speed diesel, motor spirit (commonly known as petrol), natural gas, aviation turbine fuel and alcoholic liquor for human consumption, but not including sale in the course of inter-State trade or commerce or sale in the course of international trade or commerce of such goods"; (iii) Entry 55 shall be omitted; (iv) for Entry 62, the following entry shall be substituted, namely: "62. Taxes on entertainments and amusements to the extent levied and collected by a Panchayat or a Municipality or a Regional Council or a District Council".

Compensation to States for Loss of Revenue on Account of Introduction of Goods and Services Tax:

18. Parliament shall, by law, on the recommendation of the Goods and Services Tax Council, provide for compensation to the States for loss of revenue arising on account of implementation of the goods and services tax for a period of five years.

Transitional Provisions:

19. Notwithstanding anything in this Act, any provision of any law relating to tax on goods or services or on both in force in any State immediately before the commencement of this Act, which is inconsistent with the provisions of the Constitution as amended by this Act shall continue to be in force until amended or repealed by a competent Legislature or other competent authority or until expiration of one year from such commencement, whichever is earlier.

Power of the President to Remove Difficulties:

20. (1) If any difficulty arises in giving effect to the provisions of the Constitution as amended by this Act (including any difficulty in relation to the transition from the provisions of the Constitution as they stood immediately before the date of assent of the President to this Act to the provisions of the Constitution as amended by this Act), the President may, by order, make such provisions, including any adaptation or modification of any provision of the Constitution as amended by this Act or law, as appear to the President to be necessary or expedient for the purpose of removing the difficulty: Provided that no such order shall be made after the expiry of three years from the date of such assent. (2) Every order made under sub-section (1) shall, as soon as may be after it is made, be laid before each House of Parliament.

Source: Government of India, Ministry of Law and Justice (Legislative Department), New Delhi, September 8, 2016.

Appendix 2

Model GST Law (MGL): Main Provisions

The Secretariat of the GST Council released the Model GST Law (MGL) in November 2016. The MGL provides a common draft of Central GST (CGST) Act and State GST (SGST) Act. MGL also includes the draft of Integrated GST (IGST) Act as well as draft GST Valuation Rules.

The law covers entire India, including Jammu and Kashmir. It may be recalled that service tax—during pre-GST period—was not extended to Jammu and Kashmir.

Following are the main provisions of MGL.

A2.1 Meaning, Scope, Time, Place and Value of Supply

A2.1.1 Meaning and Scope: Section 3 of the MGL deals with the meaning and scope of supply. The taxable event under GST is the supply of goods and/or services made for consideration in the course or furtherance of business. The taxable events under the indirect tax laws prior to GST (such as manufacture, sale, or provision of services) were subsumed in the taxable event known as *supply*.

The term *supply* is wide in its import and includes all forms of supply of goods and/or services such as sale, transfer, barter, exchange, license, rental, lease or disposal made or agreed to be made for a consideration by a person in the course or furtherance of business. It also includes import of services. Schedule I of MGL also provides for inclusion of certain transactions made without consideration within the scope of supply.

A *taxable supply* means a supply of goods and/or services which is chargeable to GST. In order to constitute a *supply*, the following elements are required to be satisfied:

1. Supply of goods and/or services.
2. Supply is for a consideration.
3. Supply is made in the course or furtherance of business.
4. Supply is made in the taxable territory.
5. Supply is a taxable supply.
6. Supply is made by a taxable person.

A2.1.2 Time of Supply: The time of supply fixes the point when the liability to charge GST arises. It also indicates when a supply is deemed to have been made. MGL provides separate time of supply for goods and services.

Section 12 of the MGL provides for time of supply of goods. The time of supply of goods shall be the earliest of the following:

1. Date on which the goods are removed by the supplier, where the supply of goods require removal; or
2. Date on which the goods are made available where the supply does not require removal; or

3. Date on which the supplier issues invoices with respect to the supply where the above two situations do not apply; or
4. Date on which the recipient shows the receipt of the goods in his books of accounts.

Unlike goods, in the case of services, the time of supply is determined by the fact whether the invoice for supply of services has been issued within the prescribed period or beyond such prescribed period (Section 13 of MGL).

A2.1.3 Place of Supply: One of the most important aspects of GST is determination of place of supply. Detailed provisions to determine the place of supply, separately for goods and services, are laid down in the IGST Act (Sections 7 to 10). The place of supply of goods is the place where the goods are delivered, except in few cases. The place of supply of services to a registered person is the location of such registered person.

The basic principle of GST is that it should effectively tax the consumption of such supplies at the destination thereof or as the case may at the point of consumption. So place of supply provision determine the place, i.e. taxable jurisdiction where the tax should reach. The place of supply determines whether a transaction is intra-state or inter-state. In other words, the place of supply of goods is required to determine whether a supply is subject to SGST plus CGST in a given State or else would attract IGST if it is an inter-state supply.

Place of supply provisions are different in respect of goods and services. Goods being tangible do not pose any significant problems for determination of their place of consumption. Services being intangible pose problems with regard to determination of place of supply mainly due to following factors:

1. The manner of delivery of service could be altered easily. For example telecom service could change from mostly post-paid to mostly pre-paid; billing address could be changed, billers address could be changed, repair or maintenance of software could be changed from onsite to online. Similarly, banking services earlier required customer to go to the bank, but now the customer can avail service from anywhere.
2. Service provider, service receiver and the service provided may not be ascertainable or may easily be suppressed as nothing tangible moves and there would hardly be a trail.
3. For supplying a service, a fixed location of service provider is not mandatory and even the service recipient may receive service while on the move. The location of billing could be changed overnight.
4. Sometime the same element may flow to more than one location. For example, construction or other services in respect of a railway line, a national highway or a bridge on a river may originate in one state and end in the other state. Similarly, a copyright for distribution and exhibition of film could be assigned for many states in single transaction or an advertisement or a programme is broadcaste across the country at the same time. An airline may issue seasonal tickets, containing say 10 leafs which could be used for travel between any two location in the country. The card issued by Delhi Metro could be used by a person located in Noida, or Delhi or Faridabad, without the Delhi Metro being able to distinguish the location or journeys

at the time of receipt of payment.

5. Services are continuously evolving and would thus continue to pose newer challenges. A couple of decades back no one could have thought of online booking of railway tickets, online shopping and mobile banking.

A2.1.4 Valuation of Supply: The value of taxable supply of goods and services shall ordinarily be *the transaction value* which is actually the price paid or payable, when the parties are not related and price is the sole consideration. It includes any amount which the supplier is liable to pay but which has been incurred by the recipient of the supply. MGL further elaborates various inclusions and exclusions from the ambit of transaction value. For example, the transaction value shall not include refundable deposit, discount allowed before or at the time of supply.

There are no separate valuation provisions for CGST, SGST and IGST and goods and services. Section 15 of MGL is common for all three taxes and also common for goods and services.

A2.2 Input Tax and Input Tax Credit

Input tax has been defined in Section 2(55) of the MGL and Section 2(15) of the IGST Act. Input tax, in relation to a taxable person, means the IGST, CGST and SGST, charged on any supply of goods and/or services to him which are used, or are intended to be used, in the course or furtherance of his business.

Input tax credit [Section 2(56) of MGL] and [Section 2(16) of IGST Act] means credit of input tax as defined above.

Thus, GST law provides for credit of GST paid on all the inputs, barring some exceptions. The following procedural conditions need to be fulfilled for claiming credit:

1. Possession of tax invoice.
2. Receipt of the underlying supply of goods/service.
3. Payment of tax charged in invoice by supplier.
4. Filing of GST return.

In addition, the credits claimed need to be matched with the tax liability of the supplier, and in case of any discrepancies, the amount of excess credit claimed will be added in the tax liability of the recipient.

The time limit for claim of credit is 1 year from the date of the invoice. However, no credit pertaining to a financial year is allowed to be claimed post-filing of the return for September of the next financial year, or the filing of the annual return for the year to which the credit pertains, whichever is earlier. Effectively, for the purchases made post-September month in a financial year, the time period for claiming credit is curtailed.

A2.3 Registration of Taxable Persons

Section 23 of MGL deals with registration of taxable persons. Any supplier who carries on any business at any place in India and whose aggregate turnover exceeds threshold limit as prescribed in a year is liable to get himself registered.

A person without GST registration can neither collect GST from his customers nor claim any input tax credit of GST paid by him.

A2.3.1 Compulsory Registration: As per paragraph 6 in Schedule V of MGL, the following categories of persons are required to be registered compulsorily irrespective of the threshold limit:

1. Persons making any inter-State taxable supply.
2. Casual taxable persons.
3. Persons who are required to pay tax under reverse charge.
4. Non-resident taxable persons.
5. Persons who are required to deduct tax.
6. Persons who are required to collect tax.
7. Persons who supply goods and/or services on behalf of other registered taxable persons whether as an agent or otherwise.
8. Input service distributors.
9. Persons who supply goods and/or services, other than branded services, through electronic commerce operators.
10. Every electronic commerce operator.
11. Such other person or class of persons as may be notified by the Central Government or a State Government on the recommendations of the GST Council.

A2.3.2 Advantages of Registration: Registration under GST regime confers the following advantages to the business:

1. Legally recognized as supplier of goods or services.
2. Proper accounting of taxes paid on the input goods or services which can be utilized for payment of GST due on supply of goods or services or both by the business.
3. Legally authorized to collect tax from his purchasers and pass on the credit of the taxes paid on the goods or services supplied to purchasers or recipients.

A2.4 Filing of Returns and Matching of Input Tax Credit

Every registered taxable person—who crosses the threshold limit for payment of taxes—needs to file return under GST. There are some other classes of persons who need to be registered and therefore will have to file returns like inter-state suppliers, TDS deductors, e-commerce operators, suppliers supplying goods through e-commerce operators etc.

For each month, a person who has not opted for composition scheme is required to file the returns, separately for outward supplies made, inward supplies received, and monthly return. In addition to these returns, separate returns are required to be filed by input service distributors and by a person deducting tax at source. An annual return is also required to be filed. The taxpayers having turnover exceeding the prescribed limit will also be required to get their accounts audited by a chartered accountant or a cost accountant, and submit a copy of the audited annual accounts with the annual return. In addition, they would also be required to submit a reconciliation statement, reconciling the value of supplies declared in the return furnished for the year with the audited annual financial statement, and any other documents as may be prescribed.

Returns filed by taxpayers serve the following purposes:

1. Mode for transfer of information to tax administration.
2. Compliance verification programme of tax administration.
3. Finalization of the tax liabilities of the taxpayer within stipulated period of limitation; to declare tax liability for a given period.
4. Providing necessary inputs for taking policy decision.
5. Management of audit and anti-evasion programmes of tax administration.

A2.5 Payment of GST

Section 44 of MGL deals with payment of GST. Under the GST regime, for any intra-state supply, taxes to be paid are the CGST, going into the account of the Central Government and the SGST, going into the account of the concerned State Government. For any inter-state supply, tax to be paid is IGST which will have components of both CGST and SGST. In addition, certain categories of registered persons are required to pay to the government account tax deducted at source (TDS) and tax collected at source (TCS). In addition, wherever applicable, interest, penalty, fees and any other payment will also be required to be made.

In general, the supplier of goods and/or service is liable to pay GST. However in specified cases like imports and other notified supplies, the liability may be cast on the recipient under the reverse charge mechanism. Further, in some cases, the liability to pay is on the third person (e.g. e-commerce operators are responsible for TCS and government department are responsible for TDS).

GST payment is to be made by the taxable person at the time of supply of goods as explained in section 12 of MGL and at the time of supply of services as explained in Section 13 of the MGL. The time is generally the earliest of one of the three events, namely receiving payment, issuance of invoice or completion of supply. Different situations envisaged and different tax points have been explained in the aforesaid sections.

A2.5.1 Features of GST Payment: The payment processes under GST regime have the following features:

1. Electronically-generated challan from GSTN Common Portal in all modes of payment and no use of manually prepared challan.
2. Hassle free, anytime, anywhere mode of payment of tax.
3. Convenience of making payment online.
4. Logical tax collection data in electronic format.
5. Faster remittance of tax revenue to the government account.
6. Paperless transactions.
7. Speedy accounting and reporting.
8. Electronic reconciliation of all receipts.
9. Simplified procedure for banks.
10. Warehousing of digital challan.

A2.5.2: Methods of GST Payment: Payment can be made by the following methods:

1. Through debit of credit ledger of the taxpayer maintained on the Common Portal of GSTN. Only tax can be paid. Interest, penalty and fees cannot be paid by debit in the credit ledger. Taxpayers are allowed to take credit of taxes paid on inputs (input tax credit) and utilize the same for payment of output tax. However, no input tax credit on account of CGST shall be utilized towards payment of SGST and vice versa. The credit of IGST would be permitted to be utilized for payment of IGST, CGST and SGST in that order.
2. In cash by debit in the cash ledger of the taxpayer maintained on the Common Portal of GSTN. Money can be deposited in the cash ledger by different modes, namely e-payment (internet banking, credit card, debit card); real time gross settlement (RTGS)/national electronic funds transfer (NEFT); over the counter payment in branches of banks authorized to accept deposit of GST.

Payment of taxes by the normal taxpayer is to be made on monthly basis by the 20th of the succeeding month. Cash payments are first deposited in the cash ledger and the taxpayer shall debit the ledger while making payment in the monthly returns and shall reflect the relevant debit entry number in his return. As mentioned earlier, payment can also be debited from the credit ledger. Payment of taxes for the month of March shall be paid by April 20. Composition taxpayers pay tax on quarterly basis. Timing of payment is from 0000 hrs. to 2000 hrs.

A2.6 Refunds

Sections 48 to 52 of the MGL provide for refunds. Refund includes refund of tax on goods and/or services exported out of India or on inputs or input services used in the goods and/or services which are exported out of India, or refund of tax on the supply of goods regarded as deemed exports, or refund of unutilized input tax credit.

A2.7 Job Work

Section 2(61) of the MGL provides that *job work* means undertaking any treatment or process by a person on goods belonging to another registered taxable person and the expression *job worker* shall be construed accordingly.

The principal has the option to send taxable goods without payment of GST to a job worker and bring it back, after processing, to any of his own place of business, for supplying such goods on payment of GST or export them. The principal also has the option to directly supply final products to end customers on payment of GST or export from the premises of job worker itself, subject to fulfilment of applicable conditions. GST credit is allowed in case of direct receipt of inputs or capital goods by the job worker, subject to receipt of goods back by the principal within specified period.

A2.8 Electronic Commerce

Section 2(41) of the MGL defines electronic commerce to mean the supply of goods and/or services including digital products over digital or electronic network. According to Section 2(42), electronic commerce operator means any person who owns, operates or manages digital or electronic facility or platform for electronic commerce. Every electronic commerce operator shall collect an amount calculated at the rate of 1 percent of the net value of taxable supplies made through him where the consideration with respect to such supplies is to be collected by him [Section 56(1) of MGL]. The amount so collected is called as tax collection at source (TCS). The operator would need to make payment of such tax collected at source to Government and file periodical returns for the same. This provision is not applicable when the electronic commerce operator is making supplies himself, and not just facilitating the supply by another person.

A2.9 Assessment and Audit

According to Section 57 of the MGL, every registered taxable person shall himself assess (self-assessment) the taxes payable by him and furnish a return for each tax period as specified under Section 34.

As per Section 63 of the MGL, any officer of CGST or SGST authorized by his Commissioner by a general or specific order may undertake audit of any taxable person for such period, at such frequency and in such manner as may be prescribed. The taxable person shall be informed at least 15 days prior to conduct of audit. The audit shall be completed within a period of 3 months from the date of commencement of audit. On conclusion of audit, the proper officer shall, within 30 days, inform the taxable person, whose records are audited, of the findings, the taxable person's rights and obligations and the reasons for the findings. Where the audit conducted results in detection of tax not paid or short paid or erroneously refunded, or input tax credit wrongly availed or utilized, the proper officer may initiate action under Section 66 or 67 of the MGL.

A2.10 Demands and Recovery

There are provisions in the MGL for the purpose of recovery of tax short paid or not paid or amount erroneously refunded or input tax credit wrongly availed or utilized.

Section 66 provides for the determination of tax not paid or short paid or erroneously refunded or input tax credit wrongly availed or utilized for any reason other than fraud or any wilful misstatement or suppression of facts.

Section 67 deals with the determination of tax not paid or short paid or erroneously refunded or input tax credit wrongly availed or utilized by reason of fraud or any wilful misstatement or suppression of facts.

Section 69 deals with cases where tax collected is not deposited with the Central or a State Government. A notice will be issued. Principles of natural justice will be followed and an order will be issued. It is to be noted that such order has to be invariably issued within 1 year of the date of issue of notice.

A2.11 Search, Inspection, Seizure and Arrest

Section 79 of the MGL deals with the search, inspection and seizure powers of tax authorities.

As per law dictionary and as noted in different judicial pronouncements, the term *search*, in simple language, denotes an action of a government machinery to go, look through or examine carefully a place, area, person, object etc. in order to find something concealed or for the purpose of discovering evidence of a crime. The search of a person or vehicle or premises etc. can only be done under proper and valid authority of law.

Inspection is a softer provision than search to enable officers to access any place of business of a taxable person and also any place of business of a person engaged in transporting goods or who is an owner or an operator of a warehouse or godown.

Inspection can be carried out by an officer of CGST/SGST only upon a written authorization given by an officer of the rank of Joint Commissioner or above. A Joint Commissioner or an officer higher in rank can give such authorization only if he has reasons to believe that the person concerned has done one of the following:

1. Suppressed any transaction of supply.
2. Suppressed stock of goods in hand.
3. Claimed excess input tax credit.
4. Contravened any provision of the CGST/SGST Act to evade tax.
5. A transporter or warehouse owner has kept goods which have escaped payment of tax or has kept his accounts or goods in a manner that is likely to cause evasion of tax.

An officer of the rank of joint commissioner or above can authorize an officer in writing to carry out search and seize goods, documents, books or things. Such authorization can be given only where the Joint Commissioner has reasons to believe that any goods liable to confiscation or any documents or books or things relevant for any proceedings are hidden in any place.

The term *seizure* has not been specifically defined in the MGL. In Law Lexicon Dictionary, *seizure* is defined as the act of taking possession of property by an officer under legal process. It generally implies taking possession forcibly contrary to the wishes of the owner of the property or who has the possession and who was unwilling to part with the possession.

The term *arrest* has not been defined in the MGL. However, as per judicial pronouncements, it denotes 'the taking into custody of a person under some lawful command or authority'. In other words, a person is said to be arrested when he is taken and restrained of his liberty by power or colour of lawful warrant.

Commissioner of CGST/SGST can authorize a CGST/SGST officer to arrest a person if he has reasons to believe that the person has committed an offence attracting a punishment prescribed under various provisions of the CGST/SGST Act (Section 81 of the MGL).

A2.12 Offences and Penalties

The MGL codifies the offences and penalties in Chapter XIX. It lists the following 21 offences in Section 85.

1. Making a supply without invoice or with false/incorrect invoice.
2. Issuing an invoice without making supply.
3. Not paying tax collected for a period exceeding three months.

4. Not paying tax collected in contravention of the MGL for a period exceeding 3 months.
5. Non-deduction or lower deduction of tax deducted at source or not depositing tax deducted at source under Section 46.
6. Non-collection or lower collection of or non-payment of tax collectible at source under Section 56.
7. Availing/utilizing input tax credit without actual receipt of goods and/or services.
8. Fraudulently obtaining any refund.
9. Availing/distributing input tax credit by an Input Service Distributor in violation of Section 21.
10. Furnishing false information or falsification of financial records or furnishing of fake accounts/documents with intent to evade payment of tax.
11. Failure to register despite being liable to pay tax.
12. Furnishing false information regarding mandatory fields for registration.
13. Obstructing or preventing any official in discharge of his duty.
14. Transporting goods without prescribed documents.
15. Suppressing turnover leading to tax evasion.
16. Failure to maintain accounts/documents in the manner specified in the Act or failure to retain accounts/documents for the period specified in the Act.
17. Failure to furnish information/documents required by an officer in terms of the Act/Rules or furnishing false information/documents during the course of any proceeding.
18. Supplying/transporting/storing any goods liable to confiscation.
19. Issuing invoice or document using the identification number of another person.
20. Tampering/destroying any material evidence.
21. Disposing of/tampering with goods detained/seized/attached under the Act.

The word *penalty* has not been defined in the MGL but judicial pronouncements and principles of jurisprudence have laid down the nature of a penalty as: (a) a temporary punishment or a sum of money imposed by statute, to be paid as punishment for the commission of a certain offence and (b) a punishment imposed by law or contract for doing or failing to do something that was the duty of a party to do.

A2.13 Prosecution and Compounding of Offences

Prosecution is the institution or commencement of legal proceeding, i.e. the process of exhibiting formal charges against the offender. Section 198 of the Criminal Procedure Code defines *prosecution* as the institution and carrying on of the legal proceedings against a person.

Section 92 of the MGL codifies the major offences under the Act which warrant institution of criminal proceedings and prosecution. 13 such major offences have been listed as follows:

1. Making a supply without issuing an invoice or upon issuance of a false/incorrect invoice.
2. Issuing an invoice without making supply.

3. Not paying tax collected for a period exceeding 3 months.
4. Not depositing any tax that has been collected in contravention of the Act for a period exceeding 3 months.
5. Availing or utilizing credit of input tax without actual receipt of goods and/or services.
6. Obtaining any fraudulent refund.
7. Furnishing false information or falsification of financial records or furnishing of fake accounts/documents with intent to evade payment of tax.
8. Obstructing or preventing any official in the discharge of his duty.
9. Dealing with goods liable to confiscation, i.e. receipt, supply, storage or transportation of goods liable to confiscation.
10. Receiving/dealing with supply of services in contravention of the Act.
11. Tempering with or destroying any material evidence or documents.
12. Failing to supply any information required of him under the Act/Rules or supplying false information.
13. Attempting to commit or abetting the commission of any of the above 11 offences.

The scheme of punishment provided in Section 92 is as follows:

Offence	Punishment (imprisonment extending to)
Tax evaded exceeding ₹ 250 lakh	5 years and fine
Tax evaded between ₹ 100 lakh and ₹ 250 lakh	3 years and fine
Tax evaded between ₹ 50 lakh and ₹ 100 lakh	1 year and fine

Section 320 of the Code of Criminal Procedure defines *compounding* as to forbear from prosecution for consideration or any private motive.

As per Section 97 of the MGL, certain offences out of the 13 listed above may, upon payment of the prescribed (compounding) amount, be compounded and such compounding is permissible either before or after the institution of prosecution.

Compounding is to be permitted only after payment of tax, interest and penalty and compounding shall not affect any proceeding already instituted under any other law.

A2.14 Appeals and Revisions

According to Section 98 of the MGL, any person aggrieved by any decision or order passed against him has the right to appeal. It must be an order or decision passed by an *adjudicating authority*.

The time limit to file appeal to First Appellate Authority is 3 months from the date of communication of order or decision. However, some decisions or orders (as provided for in Section 112 of MGL) are not appealable.

Commissioner may call for and examine any order passed by his subordinates and in case he considers the order of the lower authority to be erroneous in so far as it is prejudicial to revenue, he can revise the order after giving opportunity of being heard to the noticee.

A2.15 Advance Ruling

As per Section 113 of the MGL, *advance ruling* means a written decision provided by the authority to an applicant on specified matters or questions.

The matters enumerated in Section 116 for which advance ruling can be sought are as under:

1. Classification of any goods or services under the Act.
2. Applicability of a notification issued under provisions of the Act having a bearing on the rate of tax.
3. Principles to be adopted for the purposes of determination of value of the goods or services under the provisions of the Act.
4. Admissibility of input tax credit of tax paid or deemed to have been paid.
5. Determination of the liability to pay tax on any goods or services under the Act.
6. Whether applicant is required to be registered under the Act.
7. Whether any particular thing done by the applicant with respect to any goods or services amounts to or results in a supply of goods or services, within the meaning of that term.

The objectives of having a mechanism of advance ruling are the following:

1. To provide certainty in tax liability in advance in relation to an activity proposed to be undertaken by the applicant.
2. To attract foreign direct investment (FDI).
3. To reduce litigation.
4. To pronounce ruling expeditiously in transparent and inexpensive manner.

Appendix 3

GST Rates for Services

GST rates on various services were approved by GST Council in its Fourteenth meeting held on May 19, 2017 in Srinagar (Jammu and Kashmir). The Council broadly approved the GST rates for services at Nil, 5 percent, 12 percent, 18 percent and 28 percent. Subsequently, some changes were made in the rate structure in the Council's Seventeenth meeting held on June 18, 2017.

S. No.	Brief description of the service	GST rate (percent)	Input tax credit (ITC) status
1.	Transport of goods by rail	5	With ITC of input services
2.	Transport of passengers by rail (other than sleeper class)	5	With ITC of input services
3.	Services of goods transport agency (GTA) in relation to transportation of goods [other than used household goods for personal use]	5	No ITC
4.	Services of goods transport agency in relation to transportation of used household goods for personal use.	5	No ITC
5.	Transport of goods in a vessel	5	With ITC of input services
6.	Renting of motorcab	5	No ITC
7.	Transport of passengers by: (i) air-conditioned contract or stage carriage other than motorcab, (ii) a radio taxi.	5	No ITC
8.	Transport of passengers by air in economy class	5	With ITC of input services
9.	Transport of passengers, with or without accompanied belongings, by air, embarking from or terminating in a Regional Connectivity Scheme Airport.	5	With ITC of input services
10.	Supply of tour operators' services	5	No ITC
11.	Leasing of aircrafts	5	With ITC of input services
12.	Selling of space for advertisement in print media	5	With full ITC
13.	Services by way of job work in relation to printing of newspapers	5	With full ITC
14.	Transport of goods in containers by rail by any person other than Indian Railways	12	With full ITC
15.	Transport of passengers by air in other than economy class	12	With full ITC

Contd...

16.	Supply of food/drinks in restaurant not having facility of air-conditioning or central heating at any time during the year and not having licence to serve liquor	12	With full ITC
17.	Renting of hotels, inns, guest houses, clubs, campsites or other commercial places meant for residential or lodging purposes having room tariff ₹ 1,000 and above but less than ₹ 2,500 per room per day	12	With full ITC
18.	Services provided by foreman of chit fund in relation to chit	12	With ITC of input services
19.	Construction of a complex, building, civil structure or a part thereof, intended for sale to a buyer, wholly or partly.	12	With full ITC but no refund of overflow of ITC
20.	Temporary transfer or permitting the use or enjoyment of any intellectual property (IP) to attract the same rate as in respect of permanent transfer of IP	12	With full ITC
21.	Supply of food/drinks in restaurant having licence to serve liquor	18	With full ITC
22.	Supply of food/drinks in restaurant having facility of air-conditioning or central heating at any time during the year	18	With full ITC
23.	Supply of food/drinks in outdoor catering	18	With full ITC
24.	Renting of hotels, inns, guest houses, clubs, campsites or other commercial places meant for residential or lodging purposes where room tariff of ₹ 2,500 and above but less than ₹ 7,500 per room per day	18	With full ITC
25.	Bundled service by way of supply of food or any other article of human consumption	18	With full ITC
26.	Services by way of admission or access to circus, Indian classical dance including folk dance, theatrical performance, drama	18	With full ITC
27.	Composite supply of works contract	18	With full ITC
28.	Services by way of admission to entertainment events or access to amusement facilities	28	With full ITC
29.	Services provided by a race club by way of totalisator or a licensed bookmaker in such club	28	With full ITC
30.	Gambling	28	With full ITC
31.	Supply of food/drinks in air-conditioned restaurant in 5-star or above rated hotel	18	With full ITC
32.	Accommodation in hotels including 5 star and above rated hotels, inns, guest houses, clubs, campsites or other commercial places meant for residential or lodging purposes, where room rent is ₹ 7,500 and above per night per room	28	With full ITC

Contd...

33.	Transfer of the right to use any goods for any purpose (whether or not for a specified period) for cash, deferred payment or other valuable consideration (supply of service)	*	
34.	Any transfer of right in goods or of undivided share in goods without the transfer of title thereof (supply of services)	*	
35.	Supply consisting of transfer of title in goods under an agreement which stipulates that property in goods shall pass at a future date upon payment of full consideration as agreed (supply of goods)	*	
36.	All other services not specified elsewhere	18	With full ITC

*Same rate of GST and compensation cess as on supply of similar goods.

Source: Government of India, Central Board of Excise and Customs (website).

Appendix 4

Services Exempted from GST

(These services are the same as were exempted from the erstwhile service tax levied by the Central Government)

S. No.	Brief description of the service
1.	Services by government or a local authority
2.	Services by the Reserve Bank of India
3.	Services by a foreign diplomatic mission located in India
4.	Services relating to cultivation of plants and rearing of all life forms of animals
5.	Service by way of access to a road or a bridge on payment of toll charges
6.	Transmission or distribution of electricity by an electricity transmission or distribution utility
7.	Services by way of renting of residential dwelling for use as residence
8.	Services by way of extending deposits, loans or advances
9.	Services by way of transportation of goods: (i) by road except the services of (a) a goods transportation agency; or (b) a courier agency; (ii) by inland waterways.
10.	Services provided to the United Nations or a specified international organization
11.	Services provided by operators of the common bio-medical waste treatment facility to a clinical establishment by way of treatment or disposal of bio-medical waste or the processes incidental thereto
12.	Services by a veterinary clinic in relation to health care of animals or birds
13.	Services by an entity registered under Section 12AA of the Income Tax Act, 1961 by way of charitable activities
14.	Services by a specified organisation in respect of a religious pilgrimage facilitated by the Ministry of External Affairs of the Government of India, under bilateral arrangement
15.	Services provided by an arbitral tribunal
16.	Services provided by an educational institution to its students, faculty and staff
17.	Services provided by the Indian Institutes of Management (IIMs)
18.	Services provided to a recognized sports body
19.	Services by an artist by way of a performance in folk or classical art forms of music, dance, or theatre
20.	Services by way of collecting or providing news by an independent journalist, Press Trust of India or United News of India
21.	Services by way of giving on hire: (a) to a state transport undertaking, a motor vehicle meant to carry more than twelve passengers; or (b) to a goods transport agency, a means of transportation of goods
22.	Transport of passengers, with or without accompanied belongings, by air, embarking from or terminating in an airport located in specified states

Contd...

23.	Services of life insurance business provided by way of annuity under the National Pension System
24.	Services of life insurance business provided or agreed to be provided by the Army, Naval and Air Force Group Insurance Funds to members of the Army, Navy and Air Force
25.	Services provided by an incubate
26.	Service by an unincorporated body or a non-profit entity registered under any law for the time being in force, to its own members by way of reimbursement of charges or share of contribution
27.	Services by an organiser to any person in respect of a business exhibition held outside India
28.	Services by way of slaughtering of animals
29.	Services received from a provider of service located in a non-taxable territory
30.	Services of public libraries by way of lending of books, publications or any other knowledge-enhancing content or material
31.	Services by Employees' State Insurance Corporation to persons governed under the Employees' Insurance Act, 1948
32.	Services by way of transfer of a going concern, as a whole or an independent part thereof
33.	Services by way of public conveniences such as provision of facilities of bathroom, washrooms, lavatories, urinal or toilets
34.	Services by government, local authority or governmental authority by way of any activity in relation to any function entrusted to a municipality under Article 243W of the Constitution
35.	Services received by the Reserve Bank of India, from outside India in relation to management of foreign exchange reserves
36.	Services provided by a tour operator to a foreign tourist in relation to a tour conducted wholly outside India.
37.	Services by way of pre-conditioning, pre-cooling, ripening, waxing, retail packing, labelling of fruits and vegetables which do not change or alter the essential characteristics of the said fruits or vegetables
38.	Services by way of admission to a museum, national park, wildlife sanctuary, tiger reserve or zoo
39.	Services provided by Government or a local authority to a business entity with a turnover up to rupees twenty lakh (ten lakh rupees in a special category state) in the preceding financial year
40.	Services provided by Employees Provident Fund Organisation (EPFO) to persons governed under the Employees Provident Funds and Miscellaneous Provisions Act, 1952
41.	Services provided by Insurance Regulatory and Development Authority of India (IRDA)
42.	Services provided by Securities and Exchange Board of India (SEBI)
43.	Services provided by National Centre for Cold Chain Development
44.	Services by way of transportation of goods by an aircraft from a place outside India up to the customs station of clearance in India
45.	Services provided by Government or a local authority to another Government or local authority
46.	Services provided by Government or a local authority by way of issuance of passport, visa, driving licence, birth certificate or death certificate

Contd...

47.	Services provided by Government or a local authority by way of tolerating non-performance of a contract for which consideration in the form of fines or liquidated damages is payable to the Government or the local authority under such contract
48.	Services provided by Government or a local authority by way of: (a) registration required under any law for the time being in force, (b) testing, calibration, safety check or certification relating to protection or safety of workers, consumers or public at large, including fire license, required under any law for the time being in force
49.	Services provided by Government or a local authority by way of assignment of right to use natural resources to an individual farmer for cultivation of plants and rearing of all life forms of animals, except the rearing of horses, for food, fibre, fuel, raw material or other similar products
50.	Services by Government, a local authority or a governmental authority by way of any activity in relation to any function entrusted to a panchayat under Article 243G of the Constitution
51.	Services provided by Government or a local authority by way of assignment of right to use any natural resource where such right to use was assigned by the Government or the local authority before April 1, 2016
52.	Services provided by Government or a local authority by way of allowing a business entity to operate as a telecom service provider or use radiofrequency spectrum during the period prior to April 1, 2016, on payment of licence fee or spectrum user charges, as the case may be
53.	Services provided by Government by way of deputing officers after office hours or on holidays for inspection or container stuffing or such other duties in relation to import export cargo on payment of merchant overtime charges (MOT)
54.	Services by an acquiring bank, to any person in relation to settlement of an amount up to two thousand rupees in a single transaction transacted through credit card, debit card, charge card or other payment card service
55.	Services of leasing of assets (rolling stock assets including wagons, coaches, locos) by Indian Railways Finance Corporation to Indian Railways
56.	Services provided by any person for official use of a foreign diplomatic mission or consular post in India or for personal use or for the use of the family members of diplomatic agents or career consular officers posed therein.
57.	Taxable services, provided or to be provided, by a Technology Business Incubator (TBI) or a Science and Technology Entrepreneurship Park (STEP) recognized by the National Science and Technology Entrepreneurship Development Board (NSTEDB)
58.	Taxable service provided by State Government Industrial Development Corporations/Undertakings to industrial units by way of granting long term (thirty years, or more) lease of industrial plots from so much of tax leviable thereon, as is leviable on the one time upfront amount (called as premium, salami, cost, price, development charges or by any other name) payable for such lease
59.	Services provided to the government by way of transport of passengers with or without accompanied belongings, by air, embarking from or terminating at a regional connectivity scheme airport, against consideration in the form of viability gap funding (VGF)
60.	Services provided by cord blood banks by way of preservation of stem cells or any other service in relation to such preservation

Contd...

61.	Services by way of training or coaching in recreational activities relating to arts or culture
62.	Any services provided by National Skill Development Corporation and other such agencies
63.	Services of assessing bodies empanelled centrally by Directorate General of Training, Ministry of Skill Development and Entrepreneurship by way of assessments under Skill Development Initiative (SDI) Scheme
64.	Services provided by training providers (Project implementation agencies) under Deen Dayal Upadhyaya Grameen Kaushalya Yojana under the Ministry of Rural Development by way of offering skill or vocational training courses certified by National Council For Vocational Training.
65.	Services by way of sponsorship of sporting events
66.	Services provided by way of pure labour contracts of construction, erection, commissioning, installation, completion, fitting out, repair, maintenance, renovation, or alteration of a civil structure or any other original works pertaining to the beneficiary-led individual house construction/enhancement under the Housing for All (Urban) Mission/Pradhan Mantri Awas Yojana (PMAY)
67.	Services by way of pure labour contracts of construction, erection, commissioning, or installation of original works pertaining to a single residential unit otherwise than as a part of a residential complex
68.	Services of general insurance business provided under specified schemes
69.	Services of life insurance business provided under specified schemes
70.	Services by way of collection of contribution under Atal Pension Yojana (APY)
71.	Services by way of collection of contribution under any pension scheme of the State Governments
72.	Service of transportation of passengers, with or without accompanied belongings, by specified means
73.	Services by a person by way of: (a) conduct of any religious ceremony; and (b) renting of precincts of a religious place meant for general public, owned or managed by an entity registered as a charitable or religious trust
74.	Services by a hotel, inn, guest house, club or campsite, by whatever name called, for residential or lodging purposes, having declared tariff of a unit of accommodation less than one thousand rupees per day or equivalent
75.	Services by way of transportation by rail or a vessel from one place in India to another of specified goods
76.	Services provided by a goods transport agency, by way of transport in a goods carriage of agricultural produce etc.
77.	Services by the specified persons in respective capacities such as business facilitator or a business correspondent to a banking company with respect to accounts in its rural area branch
78.	Carrying out an intermediate production process as job work in relation to cultivation of plants and rearing of all life forms of animals
79.	Services by way of loading, unloading, packing, storage or warehousing of rice
80.	Services by way of right to admission to circus, dance, or theatrical performance etc.
81.	Services provided by Government or a local authority where the gross amount charged for such services does not exceed ₹ 5,000

Contd...

82.	Healthcare services by a clinical establishment, an authorised medical practitioner or paramedics
83.	**New Exemption:** Services provided by the Goods and Services Tax Network (GSTN) to the Central Government or State Governments/Union Territories for implementation of Goods and Services Tax (GST)

Source: Government of India, Central Board of Excise and Customs (website).

Select Bibliography

Select Bibliography

Ahmad, E. and N. Stern (1991), "Theory and Practice of Tax Reforms in Developing Countries", Cambridge University Press.

Ahmad, E. and N. Stern (1984), "The Theory of Tax Reform and Indian Indirect Taxes," *Journal of Public Economics*, 25, 259-298.

Aronson, Richard (1985), "Public Finance", New York: McGraw-Hill Book Company.

Bagchi, Amaresh et al. (1994), "Reform of Domestic Trade Taxes in India: Issues and Options", National Institute of Public Finance and Policy, New Delhi.

Barrand, Peter (1991), "The Treatment of Non-Profit Bodies and Government Entities under the New Zealand GST", *International VAT Monitor*, January.

Bird, Richard and Oliver Oldman (ed.) (1967), "Readings on Taxation in Developing Countries", The Johns Hopkins Press, Baltimore.

Bird, Richard (1970), "Taxation and Development", Harvard University Press.

Bird, Richard and P. Gendron (1998), "Dual VATs and Cross-border Trade, Two Problems and One Solution", *International Tax and Public Finance*, 5(3).

Canada Department of Finance (1987), "Federal Sales Tax Reform", Government of Canada.

Cutt, James (1969), "Taxation and Economic Development in India", New Delhi: Vikas Publications.

Empowered Committee of State Finance Ministers (2008), "A Model and Roadmap for Goods and Services Tax in India", New Delhi.

—*First Discussion Paper on Goods and Services Tax in India,* New Delhi, November 10, 2009.

Gobin, Roy T. (1980), "An Analysis of the System of Sales Taxation in Caribbean Market", *Public Finance*, Volume XXXV, No. 2, 272-273.

Government of India, *Report of the Taxation Enquiry Commission,* (Chairman: John Matthai), 1953-54, Volumes I, II and III.

—Report of the Central Excise Reorganisation Committee, (Chairman: A.K. Chanda), 1963.

—*Report of the Committee on Sales Tax,* (Chairman: R.G. Saraiya), 1964.

—*Final Report on Rationalisation and Simplification of Tax Structure,* (Chairman: S. Bhoothalingam), 1968.

—*Report of the Central Excise (Self-Removal Procedure) Review Committee,* (Chairman: B. Venkatappiah), 1973.

—*Report of the Indirect Taxation Enquiry Committee,* (Chairman: L.K. Jha), 1977, Part I.

—*Report of the Indirect Taxation Enquiry Committee,* (Chairman: L.K. Jha), Part II, January 1978.

—*Report of the Expert Committee on Tax Measures to Promote Employment,*

(Chairman: V.M. Dandekar), 1980.

——*Report of the Expert Committee on Replacement of Sales Tax by Additional Excise Duty,* (Chairman: Kamlapati Tripathi), January 1983.

——*Long Term Fiscal Policy,* December, 1985.

——*Report of the Technical Study Group on Central Excise Tariff,* (Chairman: J. Datta), Part I, 1985.

——*Report of the Commission on Centre-State Relations,* (Chairman: R.S. Sarkaria), 1988, Part I.

——*Interim Report of the Tax Reforms Committee,* (Chairman: Raja Chelliah), December 1991.

——*Final Report of the Tax Reforms Committee,* (Chairman: Raja Chelliah), Part I, 1992.

——*Report of the Task Force on Indirect Taxes,* (Chairman: Vijay Kelkar), December 2002.

——Ministry of Finance, Report on Implementation of the Fiscal Responsibility and Budget Management Act, 2003 (Chairman: Vijay Kelkar).

——*White Paper on State-Level Value Added Tax,* (Chairman: Asim Kumar Dasgupta), 2005.

——Ministry of Finance, *White Paper on Black Money*, May 2012.

——Ministry of Finance, *Report on the Revenue Neutral Rate and Structure of Rates for the Goods and Services Tax (GST)*, December 4, 2015 (Chairman: Arvind Subramanian).

——Ministry of Finance, *Budget Papers* (various years).

——Ministry of Finance, *Economic Survey* (various issues).

——*Reports of Finance Commissions.*

——Ministry of Finance, *Indian Public Finance Statistics,* (various issues).

——Ministry of Law and Justice, *Constitution of India.*

James, Simon and Christopher Nobes (1978), "The Economics of Taxation", Oxford: Philip Allan.

Keen, Michael, "Targeting and Indirect Tax Design," Inequality and Fiscal Policy, International Monetary Fund, 2015.

——"Targeting, Cascading, and Indirect Tax Design," International Monetary Fund, WP/13/57, 2013.

—— "The Anatomy of the VAT," International Monetary Fund, WP/13/111, 2013.

Kuo, C.Y., Tom McGirr and Saya Poddar (1988), "Measuring the Non-neutralities of Sales and Excise Taxes in Canada", *Canadian Tax Journal*, 38.

Mahler, Walter (1970), "Sales and Excise Taxation in India", New Delhi: Orient Longman Ltd.

McLure, Charles (2000), "Implementing Sub-national VATs on Internal Trade: The Compensating VAT (CVAT)", *International Trade and Public Finance*, Vol. 7.

Millar, Rebecca (2007), "Cross-border Services: A Survey of the Issues", in Krever, Richard and David White (eds.), 'GST in Retrospect and Prospect', Brookers Ltd.,

New Zealand.

Musgrave, Richard and Peggy Musgrave (1989), "Public Finance in Theory and Practice", New York: McGraw-Hill Book Company.

National Council for Applied Economic Research (2009), "Moving to Goods and Services Tax in India: Impact on India's Growth and International Trade".

OECD (2004), "Report on the Application of Consumption Taxes to the Trade in International Services and Intangibles", Centre for Tax Policy and Administration, OECD.

Peacock, Alan and Francesco Forte (eds.) (1981), "The Political Economy of Taxation", Basil Blackwell, Oxford.

Poddar, S. and M. English (1997), "Taxation of Financial Services under a Value-added Tax: Applying the Cash-flow Method", *National Tax Journal*, 89-111.

Poddar, Satya (1990), "Options for s VAT at the State Level", in M. Gillis, C.S. Shoup and G. Sicat (eds.), 'Value Added Taxation in Developing Countries', Washington, World Bank.

——"Consumption Taxes: The Role of the Value Added Tax", in Patrick Honohan (ed.) (2003), 'Taxation of Financial Intermediation: Theory and Practice in Emerging Economies', World Bank and the Oxford University Press.

——"VAT on Financial Services: Searching for a Workable Compromise", in Krever, Richard and David White (eds.) (2007), GST in Retrospect and Prospect', Brookers Ltd., New Zealand.

Poddar, Satya and Amaresh Bagchi (2007), "Revenue-neutral Rate for GST", *The Economic Times*, November 15.

Poddar, Satya and Nancy Harley (1989), "Problems in Moving from a Flawed to a Neutral and Broad-based Consumption Tax", *Australian Tax Forum*, Volume 6, Number 3.

Poddar, Satya, and Eric Hutton (2001), "Zero-Rating of Inter-State Sales under a Sub-national VAT: A New Approach", paper presented at the National Tax Association, 94th Annual Conference on Taxation, Baltimore, November 8-10.

Pomeranz, Dina (2013), "No Taxation without Information: Deterrence and Self-Enforcement in the Value Added Tax", Harvard University and NBER.

Prest, A.R. (1970), "Public Finance in Theory and Practice", London: Weidenfeld and Nicolson.

Rao, Kavita (2014), "Revenue Implications of GST and Estimation of Revenue Neutral Rate: Estimates for 2011-12", National Institute of Public Finance and Policy, New Delhi.

Rao, M. Govinda (2001), "Report of the Expert Group on Taxation of Services", Government of India, March.

Reserve Bank of India, *Report on Currency and Finance* (various years).

Sandford, C.T. et al. (1981), "Costs and Benefits of VAT", London: Heinemann Educational Books.

Shakdher, S.L. (1979), "The Budget and the Parliament", National Publishing House,

New Delhi.

Sury, M.M. (1996), "Sales Tax in India Since 1938", *Journal of the Indian School of Political Economy*, Volume 7, No. 1, January-March.

—(1994), "Excise Duties in India: 1894-1994", *Journal of the Indian School of Political Economy*, Volume 6, No. 1, January-March.

—(1988), "India: Structure and Reform of Indirect Taxes", *Bulletin for International Fiscal Documentation*, (Amsterdam), Volume 42, October.

—(1987), "Excise Concessions to Small Scale Industries in India: Some Issues", *Small Industry Bulletin for Asia and the Pacific*, United Nations, ESCAP, Bangkok, No. 22.

World Bank (2015), "Fiscal Policy for Equitable Growth", India Development Report.

Indexes

Subject Index

Name Index